THE THINGS IN HEAVEN AND EARTH

AMERICAN PHILOSOPHY

Douglas R. Anderson and Jude Jones, series editors

THE THINGS IN HEAVEN AND EARTH

An Essay in Pragmatic Naturalism

JOHN RYDER

FORDHAM UNIVERSITY PRESS NEW YORK 2013

Fordham University Press also publishes its books in a variety of electronic formats. Some content that appears in print may not be available in electronic books.

Library of Congress Cataloging-in-Publication Data

Ryder, John, 1951–
The things in heaven and earth : an essay in pragmatic naturalism / John Ryder. — 1st ed.
p. cm. — (American philosophy)
Includes bibliographical references and index.
ISBN 978-0-8232-4468-3 (cloth : alk. paper) — ISBN 978-0-8232-4469-0 (pbk. : alk. paper)
1. Naturalism. 2. Pragmatism. 3. Philosophy, American—20th century. 4. Buchler, Justus, 1914– 5. Dewey, John, 1859–1952. 6. Randall, John Herman, 1899–1980. I. Title.
B944.N3R93 2013
146—dc23

2012033437

Printed in the United States of America

15 14 13 5 4 3 2 1

First edition

for Lyuba
through whom the things in heaven and earth
shine so brightly

Contents

Acknowledgments

This study has been many years in the making, and there are therefore a great many debts to acknowledge. Because his influence permeates nearly every page, the most important such debt is to Justus Buchler, with whom I had the privilege to study as a graduate student. His brilliance and philosophical creativity have been a continual influence throughout my life and career, and his professional and personal grace have served as a model I can only hope to emulate, even if only in small measure.

Other teachers at Stony Brook University also contributed significantly to my own thinking in systematic metaphysical matters, most significantly David Dilworth and Robert Neville. The Department of Philosophy in those years was as rich an intellectual environment as a graduate student could imagine, and in the ensuing years I have been fortunate to have sustained profound philosophical and personal friendships with many of my fellow students who have been instrumental in my own thinking and in many of the ideas that fill these pages. I would thus like to take the opportunity to acknowledge and to thank James Campbell, Richard Hart, Armen Marsoobian, Paul Thompson, Kathleen Wallace, Lawrence Cahoone, and Marjorie Miller for their continuing critical inspiration.

Three professional organizations have provided extraordinarily fertile ground for philosophical impetus over the years, the first of which is the Society for the Advancement of American Philosophy (SAAP). A number of colleagues I have come to know through SAAP have served as informal mentors, especially John McDermott, John Lachs, Joseph Margolis, Beth Singer, and the late Peter Hare. Others have been friends and influential in my ongoing exploration of American philosophy and philosophical matters generally, among whom I would like in particular to mention Larry Hickman, Charlene Haddock Seigfried, Herman Saatkamp, Robert Corrington, Scott Pratt, Vincent Colapietro, Richard Shusterman, and the late Michael Eldridge.

The second organization of note has been the Central European Pragmatist Forum (CEPF), through which I have had the privilege of coming to know a number of people outside the United States who are doing significant work in pragmatism and in American philosophy generally. I would especially like to acknowledge Emil Višňovský, Krystyna Wilkoszewska, Carlos Mougan, Gert-Rüdiger Wegmarshaus, Miklós Nyírő, and Alex Kremer. Overlapping with CEPF, though not necessarily through it, I have been fortunate to count among my friends and philosophical colleagues Sami Pihlström, Igor Hanzel, Leszek Koczanowicz, Nina S. Yulina, Andrei Marga, Krzysztof Skowroński, and Nikita E. Pokrovsky. Through their inspiration and criticism my thinking, and this book, is richer than it would otherwise be.

The third organization to mention is the Alliance of Universities for Democracy (AUDEM), which through its concern with the role of universities in democratic development has provided an opportunity to discuss with people from many fields and many countries the application of ideas that for me have their roots in Deweyan democracy. Among the many friends and intellectual colleagues in AUDEM who, though they may not realize it, have influenced this work I would like to acknowledge László Komlósi, Martha Merrill, Julia Watkins, Vera I. Zabotkina, Ilie Rad, Irina Naumova, Mariana Cernicova-Buca, Jerry Wall, Dorothy McClellan, Russell Meyer, David Hake, David Payne, and Peter Cooper.

Others have been gracious in their time and attention, sometimes through reading and commenting on chapters of the manuscript and at times through philosophical conversation. I would like to thank Henry Steck and John Marciano, and acknowledge the late David Craven, in this regard, and especially Robert Howell. Bob's openness and insightful criticism of many aspects of this overall project have been far more valuable to me than he knows, for which I am most grateful. I am also grateful to the reviewers for Fordham University Press who made useful suggestions and who saved me from errors that had made their way into the manuscript. Any that remain are of course my responsibility alone. I would also like to thank Douglas Anderson, the general editor of the series in which this book appears, and Helen Tartar and Thomas Lay of Fordham University Press for their interest in and support for the book. I am also grateful to the many other people at Fordham University Press, especially the editorial, design, and marketing staff, who worked to see the project from manuscript to book.

Most important, this book would never have been written, certainly not in its current form, without the influence and support of Lyubov Bugaeva. She has been the most present muse and the most persistent critic. For these and other reasons, the book is dedicated to her.

INTRODUCTION

When Hamlet says, "There are more things in heaven and earth, Horatio, than are dreamt of in your philosophy," he is responding to Horatio's surprise at hearing the voice of the ghost of Hamlet's murdered father. Horatio's surprise is of course understandable. We organize our expectations based on the regularities of our experience, and our experience does not, for the most part, include ghosts. In our philosophies, in turn, we tend to systematize the regularities of our experience, and generally we do so with an admirable degree of rational sophistication. Here Hamlet suggests, based on the experience he just had, that Horatio's rational systematization of his own experience, which is to say Horatio's philosophy, fails to account for "the things in heaven and earth."

I should like to generalize Hamlet's remark and say that our philosophies have to a large extent failed to account adequately for the things in heaven and earth. We have been so busy for a couple thousand years trying to determine what does and what does not exist, and how we might know what does or does not exist, that we have constructed philosophies that manage to leave too much out, and frequently distort what they leave in. As a result, when we then attempt to understand our experience or to apply our general philosophical conceptions to our experience the consequence is a distorted understanding of ourselves, our world, and the many problems, personal and social, that we face.

At the risk of monumental hubris, this book is an attempt to do justice to the things in heaven and earth, whatever they may be, and to propose a way to understand and account for them, without exception or distortion. One driving assumption throughout is that there is no good philosophical reason for concerning ourselves with deciding whether this or that exists. That we have traditionally asked such questions as "do minds exist," or "does God exist," or "do universals exist" is understandable, but ultimately pointless. The motivation behind such questions is sensible enough: We wish to understand our experience as fully and as clearly as possible. We would do better, however, to ask different sorts of questions if understanding is what we seek. For example, in the attempt to understand what a human being is and what one can do, it is better to ask not whether minds exist but how we might understand the many and varied aspects of the human being. We have had reason to describe some aspects of human being and experience as mental, some as physical, some as emotional, some as spiritual. Instead of wondering whether or not there really are minds, bodies, emotions and spirits, or whether any one can be subsumed under the other, it is more valuable to consider how we might understand human being such that all of these traits hang together. In a similar vein, there is no point in wondering whether God really does or does not exist. God has figured in countless people's experience throughout human history, and it is more fruitful to consider how we might understand God and matters religious in such a way that they too hang together and answer well enough to our experience.

Others have made this point before, though the tendency has been to infer from the inadequacy of the traditional philosophical enterprise that there is no point in asking general questions about being and knowledge. This is the Wittgensteinian tradition, and it has been given new energy in recent decades by Richard Rorty. With this inference I do not agree, and thus there is a second driving assumption of the book: When we consider philosophical questions having to do with social and political issues, or with the ethical or aesthetic, or any other less general topic, we invariably have some more general conceptions of how things are that inform our specific analyses. Either we are explicit about those general conceptions or we smuggle them in. If we smuggle them in without explicit rationale then we run the risk of putting to use general concepts that may well not stand the test of examination, in which case our more detailed analyses may not be as reliable as we think they are. The alternative is to examine our general assumptions explicitly and explore their justification. To do so is to engage in the enterprise of general ontology and of epistemology.

Thus, unlike the Wittgensteinian or Rortyan rejection of metaphysics and epistemology, we here embrace them, though not in traditional ways. As I have said, the metaphysical—or better, ontological—question is not whether this or that exists, but rather how we might understand whatever it is that exists. And the epistemological question is not whether knowledge is to be understood as justified true belief, or how we might distinguish knowledge from opinion, but rather how we may understand knowledge given the fact that we come to know things in many ways, from experience and science through art and action. The consequence of asking ontological and epistemological questions in these, rather than traditional, ways is that we have a philosophical approach that in many ways is quite different from the dominant analytic and continental traditions.

The book, then, is a consideration of the things in heaven and earth, and as the subtitle indicates it does so through the lens of pragmatic naturalism. Just what that is taken to mean is described in the first part of the book, Chapters 1 and 2. The second part, Chapters 3 through 7, is an articulation, justification, and application of the ontological and epistemological dimensions of pragmatic naturalism. Part III, Chapters 8 through 11, considers some of the ramifications of pragmatic naturalism in the area of social and political philosophy.

In its explicit appropriation of pragmatism the current volume is of a piece with other recent books and, if it does not sound too grandiose, of a tenor of the times. It has become increasingly clear to a number of philosophers that the now traditional division of contemporary philosophical schools or styles into the analytic, continental, and pragmatic is pointless and indeed detrimental. Rorty of course made this point over thirty years ago, but his response was to abandon much of philosophy as traditionally understood and redefine it. Whatever the merits of his approach may be, the vast majority of philosophers around the world have not followed him. What has happened instead is that philosophers are coming to think that the future of the discipline lies in a rapprochement of some sort among the three.

More specifically, the rapprochement among the three tends to regard pragmatism as the tradition that can enable us to synthesize the best and most important of analytic and continental insights into a conceptual perspective that speaks fruitfully to current philosophical and general human issues. Three outstanding works that command our attention in this regard are Richard J. Bernstein's *The Pragmatic Turn*, Joseph Margolis's *Pragmatism's Advantage*, and Larry A. Hickman's *Pragmatism as Post-PostModernism*.[1] The sensitivity that these authors demonstrate to insights regardless of their philosophic sources is a model the rest of us would do well to emulate. Furthermore, their understanding of the conceptual resources and power of the pragmatist tradition is right on the mark. This volume is an attempt to develop further the basic idea that pragmatism helps us deal with pressing concerns and avoid the traps that much of analytic and continental philosophy has unwittingly fallen into.

This is, however, an essay not simply in pragmatism but in pragmatic naturalism. I will say more below, and throughout the book, about what that means here. At this point, though, it is worth noticing that even in such stellar examples of the contemporary trend to develop the insights of pragmatism as Bernstein, Margolis, and Hickman, there is little mention of naturalism, or at least the naturalism on which I draw in this volume. Each of these authors would, I think, agree that the pragmatism they endorse is a naturalistic philosophic perspective. In fact, all explicitly agree on the need to develop a nonreductive naturalism. It is interesting, though, that they make no explicit effort to claim, or reclaim, the naturalistic tradition that had already accomplished this, and in which pragmatism developed through the middle of the twentieth century. Hickman of course directly draws on Dewey, and to that extent is at work in the American naturalist tradition, but the reader would not know from what Hickman does that at Columbia University Dewey was swimming in an overtly naturalist stream that included, over the decades, a number of important philosophers from F. J. E. Woodbridge to John Herman Randall Jr. to Justus Buchler. Margolis comes the closest to an express treatment of naturalism in his chapter titled "Reclaiming Naturalism," though even there he makes no mention of the Columbia Naturalism that had already developed many of the insights that he, Bernstein, and Hickman, correctly call for.

The present volume is an effort to complement these authors by explicitly drawing on the resources and accomplishments of the Columbia Naturalism of the middle years of the last century, especially as it developed in the hands of Randall and Buchler. For whatever reasons, this tradition has been overlooked, and continues to be overlooked. It contains, however, a number of resources that when put to work help us to address the issues to which Bernstein, Margolis, and Hickman point, and to do so to useful effect, or so I will attempt to demonstrate. Among them are a specific conception of the kinds of philosophic questions it is worthwhile to ask, and a specific theory of relations that, as we will see, has far-reaching ramifications in both technical and applied respects. Thus, what is needed in contemporary philosophy is not pragmatism alone, but a pragmatic naturalism that draws on a fuller treasure of historical resources in the effort to address contemporary concerns.

There are a number of fundamental conceptions that appear and reappear throughout the book, and there is some value in introducing them at this point. The first is the conviction, also explored by Richard Bernstein more than twenty-five years ago, that contemporary philosophy has gone very wrong in the dualism of objectivism and constructivism. Bernstein addressed the problem in terms of a split between objectivism and relativism.[2] Unfortunately, the two positions have hardened in the intervening years, and we may now put the problem in terms of the divide between modernism and postmodernism. This is an issue that has as much to do with ontology as it has to do with epistemology, and I will consider it in both dimensions. To put the point briefly, the reason this conceptual struggle is unacceptable is that it forces a choice between two perspectives, both of which have some degree of justification. The important point to make is that the choice is unnecessary because it is possible, or so I will argue, to embrace in a single philosophic perspective the plausible insights of both sides of the divide. That perspective is pragmatic naturalism, and the fact that it can encompass critical aspects of both modernism and postmodernism is one of its virtues and an aspect of the general argument for its conceptual adequacy.

We may also point out that there is a certain Hegelian flavor to this approach to modernism and postmodernism. If they may be understood as thesis and antithesis, then pragmatic naturalism performs something of an *Aufhebung* in offering a way to synthesize them. As with other such Hegelian maneuvers, through their synthesis in pragmatic naturalism both modernism and postmodernism, or better objectivism and constructivism, are to a certain degree transformed. Each now accommodates the other, and to that extent is different from what it had been. That there is a Hegelian character to some of this ought not be surprising, particularly because Hegel serves as a background to much of the pragmatic naturalist point of view, especially through Dewey.

A second general theme that pervades the book is the desirability, indeed the necessity, of relationality. Pragmatic naturalism is a blend of two philosophic traditions—pragmatism and naturalism—that received their most thorough elaboration in an American context in the late nineteenth through the twentieth centuries. Both have been complex conceptual developments with a good bit of variety within them. For our purposes I draw, as I have said, on two specific strains of those traditions: the instrumentalism of John Dewey and the ordinal naturalism of Justus Buchler. For both of them relationality is a central concept in their respective approaches to any subject. It should be pointed out that there are differences between Dewey and Buchler, and in fact Buchler saw himself in some measure as improving on Dewey's achievements.[3] Whether or not he did so is not a concern of this study. What is a concern is to articulate, develop, and apply the specific theory of relationality that informed their understanding of things. Indeed, it is this ordinal, constitutive relationality that more than anything else gives pragmatic naturalism its character and, I will argue, its value.

This may be the occasion to point out that by explicitly drawing on Dewey and Buchler, the pragmatic naturalism that is developed and defended here is quite different from much of what passes for pragmatism or naturalism in contemporary philosophy. Much of contemporary pragmatism, or what is generally called neopragmatism, draws heavily from the tradition of Peirce, James, Dewey and Mead, though to a large extent it does so within an analytic context. This is true as much of Rorty, despite his rejection of much of the thrust of contemporary analytic philosophy, as it is of others who have not rejected it. Some of the more prominent neopragmatists, for example, Rorty and Hilary Putnam, have a good understanding of the earlier pragmatic tradition, while others, it seems, do not. In any case, they tend to develop the pragmatic side of their thought within the assumptions and problematics of the analytic and not the pragmatic tradition. This is the reason theirs is a "neopragmatism." Pragmatic naturalism as understood in this study is not neopragmatism. It turns not to Rorty or Putnam or Brandom but to Dewey and the earlier tradition. Unfortunately, one sometimes encounters the idea that this earlier, classical pragmatism is of historical interest only and has been superseded by more recent developments. As will become clear to the reader, that is not an assumption of this book. On the contrary, our assumption is that the basic points of view of classical pragmatism, especially the relationality of Dewey's instrumentalism, have not been sufficiently understood and appreciated, and that there is, in fact, a great deal of philosophic advantage to be had by once again taking them seriously.

There is a related problem with what has come to be understood as naturalism in contemporary analytic philosophy, especially epistemology. I will have occasion at more than one point in the chapters that follow to explore naturalism of this sort and to develop a criticism of and alternative to it. It may suffice at this juncture simply to point out that contemporary epistemological naturalism has its roots in the work of W. V. O. Quine, as is well known. Quine himself understood the naturalism that had developed through the twentieth century, to which he in some ways was an heir. Unfortunately, his many followers seem to be blissfully unaware of that tradition, and that, coupled with their numbers and power in contemporary philosophical life, have enabled them simply to ignore it. At this point very few people writing about naturalism seem even to be aware of the vibrant tradition of Columbia Naturalism that was at its strongest in the first half of the twentieth century, or of the related naturalism of George Santayana. This is an extraordinary and deplorable condition in that the work of Santayana and of the Columbia naturalists from Woodbridge and Dewey through Randall and Buchler has been evaded rather than engaged, to the detriment of contemporary philosophy. Pragmatic naturalism as understood throughout this volume turns explicitly to the Columbia Naturalist tradition, primarily in its expression in Dewey, Randall and Buchler. The point is not to praise the tradition, though there is good reason to do so. It is rather to engage it, develop it and apply it to issues of current theoretical and practical concern. If I succeed in doing that to some valuable extent, then no greater praise is necessary or even possible.

This suggests a third theme that runs throughout the book, and that concerns its pragmatic side, particularly with respect to argumentation and valuation. The point will be made more than once that it has been a mistake for the philosophical enterprise to model itself on mathematics, which it has done through its reliance on deductive argumentation as its most central method. No such approach is taken here. This is not to say that deductive and inductive logic are not valuable, or that argumentation of some kinds is inappropriate. The mistake is thinking that in doing philosophy we should set about to prove anything along the lines of a deductive proof in mathematics. Any reader looking for deductive certainty here will be disappointed, because there is none to be found. I readily assert that I am certain of none of this, and I have made no effort to achieve deductive certainty about any of it. The reason for that is simply that deductive certainty is unavailable and anyway unnecessary. The book can be taken, however, as a pragmatic argument. I wish to demonstrate two things only, which are the plausibility and usefulness of pragmatic naturalism, and thereby offer useful resolutions of a number of issues of current concern. If I have done so then the book is successful as far as it goes. I say "as far as it goes" because even if pragmatic naturalism as developed and applied here is both plausible and useful, it does not follow that no other set of ideas may not also be plausible and useful in some significant respects. Pragmatic naturalism is a pluralist philosophic point of view in the sense that it looks to further query, inquiry, and exploration, not to close them off. Nature is complex, and there is no good reason to insist that any one way at it has a monopoly on access, understanding, and truth. This is not to say that all philosophic approaches are equally useful. Some are dead ends. But not all are, and the fact that pragmatic naturalism embodies this pluralist, open understanding of philosophy is part of its justification, and thereby an aspect of its usefulness and, on pragmatic grounds, its value. This, I take it, is the point urged so strongly by Bernstein, Margolis, Hickman, and others.

A book that purports to include all the things in heaven and earth can easily be misunderstood as an attempt to discuss them all. That I do not attempt, and in any case it would be absurd to try. For one thing I do not know all of what constitutes heaven and earth, and even if that were possible and I did know, no one person is equipped to address them all. And in any case the point is not to talk about everything but to articulate a philosophic perspective through which it is possible to make sense of whatever experience and thought reveal or generate, however they reveal or generate it. In some respects the issues discussed in these chapters are chosen not because they are necessarily the most important but because they reflect my interests and, I should like to think, my competence. There are many other issues a book like this could discuss. I do not discuss them largely because other people have done and are doing so to far greater effect than I could. One might have included a discussion of theoretical ethics, for example, but the reader would be better served to turn to those who are writing in ethical theory, such as Jennifer Welchman, Paul Kurtz, Emil Višňovský, Kathleen Wallace, and Gregory Pappas[4]; and to the many profound writings on general moral matters by John McDermott and John Lachs[5]; and to works on applied ethics by Andrew Light and Paul Thompson on environmental issues, or Erin McKenna on animal rights, or Beth Singer on human rights, or Thomas Hilde on social policy, or Armen Marsoobian on genocide, or Shannon Sullivan on race.[6] There are other important applied issues as well—for example, in the general area of technology—but no one handles such matters as well as Larry Hickman.[7] One might well deal with feminism and its related concerns, but writers such as Charlene Haddock-Seigfried and Marilyn Fischer are doing so far better than I could.[8] And though I will have occasion to talk about education, especially in Chapter 9, there is a good deal of interesting work on education in general being done by Jim Garrison and others, and on civic education in particular by Carlos Mougan and Gert-Rüdiger Wegmarshaus.[9] And then there is the large body of work that has kept the light on the pragmatic naturalist tradition and its antecedents for many years. A reader may profitably turn to any of the studies by James Campbell, Michael Eldridge, Thomas Alexander, Vincent Colapietro, Hans Joas, Douglas Anderson, Sami Pihlström, Scott Pratt, and many others.[10] There is no shortage of philosophical writing that goes as far or farther than this book in making the case for the value of pragmatic naturalism.

Finally, a word is in order about the structure of the book. The reader will find that at many points the text doubles back to discuss again a point that had been raised previously. There are reasons for this. First, the earliest chapters are in a sense an overview of the entire analysis, so that what follows returns to the themes of the first two chapters and develops them in more detail. Second, some issues have such centrality to the overall project that they bear repeating in more than one context. For example, I have mentioned that ordinal, constitutive relationality is a central concept of pragmatic naturalism. To understand nature relationally, however, is to break in fundamental ways from the more common assumptions of philosophy in both the past and the present. Specifically, it is to break from ways of thinking that have dominated at least Western philosophy since the early modern period. As a result, the concepts and metaphors of that period, or what I will frequently refer to as the Newtonian or Baroque view of things, are an important contrast to a relational ontology and its application to social and political matters. In light of that fact, the Baroque concepts and metaphors are relevant when discussing relational particulars as well as in the analysis of international relations and foreign policy. Indeed, because of the importance of relationality, the concepts and metaphors of the Baroque serve as a background foil for our approach to being and knowledge as well as to democracy, international affairs and contemporary political culture generally. Thus, the reader will find the point made at several turns and in varying contexts. If the reader would like a single image in terms of which to approach the book, one may think of it rather like a spiral. It will double back here and there to issues previously discussed, but each time from a slightly different angle, the differences made possible by the fact that we will have passed that way before.

The book, to make the point once again, is an attempt to describe a pragmatic naturalism, to develop some of its ramifications, and to make the case in application to contemporary theoretical and practical problems that it is a useful and therefore valuable philosophic approach for us to take. The reader will, of course, be the judge of how successful the enterprise is, and in the end of the value and wisdom of pragmatic naturalism in general.

PART ONE

CONTEMPORARY PRAGMATIC NATURALISM

The significant question is, not whether anything is "real" or not, but how and in what sense it is real, and how it is related to and functions among other reals.

—John Herman Randall Jr., *Nature and Historical Experience*

ONE

RECONCILING PRAGMATISM AND NATURALISM

Philosophy, Descartes's noteworthy effort notwithstanding, does not have the luxury to begin at the beginning.[1] Like most other forms of inquiry and query, it has no choice but to engage a topic in light of its own history. Our study of pragmatic naturalism and its many virtues is no exception. We stand on the shoulders of the many prominent thinkers who have passed this way before, and the many who are doing so today. Nevertheless, beginnings there must be, even if only relative, so we will start with definitions. Our ultimate goal in this chapter is to describe pragmatism and naturalism, to demonstrate how they fuse into a single coherent whole, and some of the conceptual ramifications of the philosophic frame of mind that we call pragmatic naturalism.

In addition to definitions, there are, in fact, two topics with which this study begins. The first concerns the reconciliation of pragmatism and naturalism, and the second deals with the broader context of the relation between what I will call, for a lack of better terms, modernism and postmodernism. There is a relation between these two themes. It will be developed more below, but it can be expressed briefly by saying that pragmatism is a species of postmodernism, while naturalism is a species of modernism. If postmodernism can be meaningfully reconciled with modernism then it would become possible to talk about a way to reconcile aspects of naturalism with aspects of pragmatism. The reconciliation of pragmatism and naturalism is advantageous for those of us with an interest in these philosophic traditions, and a rapprochement between modernist and postmodernist points of view, while possibly unsettling to those who have put all their eggs in one basket or the other, would allow the rest of us to pursue philosophical issues consistently while drawing on both traditions. This is a theme that several chapters will address, prominently here and in Chapter 5, where the emphasis will be on "world making" and the relation between objectivity and constructivism.

It may sound strange to many even to talk about the reconciliation of pragmatism and naturalism. One reason might be that many people use the term "pragmatic naturalism" to refer to a cluster of ideas in American philosophy in the twentieth century. There is indeed a place for the term, and we here adopt it unapologetically, but one has to be careful in its use, if only because pragmatism and naturalism are not the same thing. There are, for example, pragmatists who can plausibly be considered not to be naturalists. Charles S. Peirce comes to mind, certainly Josiah Royce, by extension C. I. Lewis, and probably William James as well. There are also naturalists who are not pragmatists. George Santayana was overtly critical of pragmatism; Frederick J. E. Woodbridge came at naturalism from an entirely other, Aristotelian angle; Roy Wood Sellars sounded more like a dialectical materialist than a pragmatist; and Justus Buchler, with his systematic approach to metaphysical generalization, thought that pragmatism missed the boat in a number of respects. If there are pragmatists who are not naturalists, and naturalists who are not pragmatists, then obviously it cannot be the case that pragmatism and naturalism are basically the same philosophic perspective.

The clearest example of an important philosopher who was both a pragmatist and a naturalist was John Dewey. He would have been content, I imagine, to have himself described in either or both ways, though he would probably have wanted to make sure that he had the last word in defining both terms. That would not have been unreasonable on his part, since in this case as in many others definitions matter. We will look more closely at the meaning of the terms "pragmatism" and "naturalism" in a moment. There are clearly standard meanings, though, in which it is proper to say of Dewey that his philosophical inclinations tended in both directions. That being the case, it is therefore possible, assuming some significant degree of consistency on Dewey's part, for there to be something that can be called pragmatic naturalism. However, those who use the expression would not want, I do not think, to have it refer only to Dewey or to the overtly Deweyan way of thinking. We would like its meaning to be broader and for it to encompass more philosophical possibilities. It is therefore sensible to take a close look at the definitions of, and the relation between, the two.

Definitions

We turn now to definitions, and begin with pragmatism. First, when I use the term "pragmatism" I do not refer to the work of Richard Rorty, though Rorty was certainly entitled to consider his work to be pragmatist. Rorty has been enormously influential, and his appropriation of the term has given it new currency. It is increasingly common in recent years for philosophers in the Anglo-American tradition to refer to themselves as pragmatists or to some aspect of their work as pragmatic. Rorty's influence has been even stronger abroad. It is not uncommon in many places in Europe, for example, to find the term "pragmatism" virtually equated with his work. In the United States it is more common for Rorty and those whose work is influenced by his to be referred to as "neopragmatists," but the distinction seems to have been nearly obliterated elsewhere in the world.

Let me say clearly that I do not have any deep antipathy toward Rorty's work, as many others do. I have my misgivings and disagreements, most deeply with what I think is his profoundly mistaken and destructive ethnocentrism, but there is nothing unique or unusual about that. In the end I do not think that he has made significant philosophical contributions that had not been made already by others, in many cases more profoundly. On the other hand, Rorty made important contributions as a public intellectual. He has given a range of philosophical ideas a place in American intellectual culture and abroad that they have not had previously, or have not had for several decades. He also brought reasoned philosophical judgments to bear in important contemporary social and cultural issues with an impact only dreamed of by most of the rest of us. That is all to his credit, and his detractors unfairly fail to recognize the importance of such contributions.

Nevertheless, his pragmatism is philosophically anemic when it is compared with the older pragmatist tradition in America. The thinness of his version of pragmatism—or neopragmatism, if it is necessary to make the distinction—is that he has no interest in many of the central questions that have interested philosophers, including pragmatists and naturalists, for centuries. Rorty made his mark by arguing against the value of considering traditional questions concerning the traits of nature and knowledge. By so doing he abandoned far too much of our intellectual tradition. He treated our long-standing inclination to consider metaphysical and epistemological issues as analogous to medieval theological hairsplitting, and also believed that the one is no more valuable than the other. Time will tell, of course, but for now it seems to me that we give up far too much by refusing to consider, for example, whether it is more reasonable to regard nature as finite or infinite, as atomistic or relational, as accessible only by science or by other means as well. Similarly, we give up too much if we refuse to wonder about the character of knowledge in relation to belief, opinion, experience, reason, science, and art. Certainly, many of the specific ways we have approached these questions have turned out to be dead ends, but it weakens one's intellectual powers to reject the enterprise altogether. In one sense this entire volume is an extended attempt to demonstrate the importance, theoretically and practically, of continuing to take up some of the traditional technical questions of philosophy within a pragmatic naturalist framework.

Rorty's central objection to traditional metaphysics and epistemology is that they have assumed the wrong metaphor; that is, the philosophers who have engaged in those enterprises have presumed that it was their task to "reflect" reality accurately, that mind serves as a mirror of reality. There is an important insight here, though again Rorty was not the first to notice it, as he himself makes plain. His own work was based on Wittgenstein, Heidegger, Dewey, and many others. He may not have been aware initially, though, that even in the American traditions other than Dewey's the point was made in almost the same language. Santayana in *Scepticism and Animal Faith* similarly rejected the metaphor of mind as "mirror."[2] In any case, Rorty does not seem to have noticed, or else he simply ignored, the possibility that the broadly pragmatist rejection of "correspondence" conceptions of knowledge does not compel one to abandon attempts to understand the world. One can continue to raise and pursue questions of the general character of nature or knowledge within a generally pragmatist framework. In such a case the pragmatist dimension of the enterprise is relevant in determining the adequacy of one's answer to metaphysical or epistemological questions. For example, whether we regard nature to be finite or infinite may not be a matter of accurately reflecting reality, but more a question of determining which point of view does the most work for us, which one gets us to where we need to be. If our conception of things hangs together better by treating nature as infinite, if doing so helps to settle more questions than it creates, and does so in a way that helps push our inquiries further, then the value of that perspective resides precisely in its fruitfulness. In more overtly pragmatist language, it works better for us, and that, if not a definition of truth, is at least a critical criterion. We will have more to say about the importance of pragmatic argument and criterion of adequacy of this kind in a later chapter. Let it suffice here to point out that the pragmatist turn does not require, as Rorty wanted it to, a rejection of the more traditional philosophical enterprise of making sense of nature and knowledge. Again, this entire book is in a sense a sustained argument, a pragmatic one at that, for the reasonableness of this proposition.

It is to the credit of earlier pragmatists that they understood the continuing significance of traditional epistemological and metaphysical issues. Each in his own way, Peirce, James, Royce, Dewey, Lewis, and others have by their respective examinations of nature and knowledge shed light on many important aspects of human being and our surroundings. No one who has a glimmer of Dewey's account of experience, for example, can fail to appreciate its insights, even if one disagrees with aspects of it. The same is true for James on truth, or Peirce on meaning. For reasons like these it is the more traditional, more robust pragmatism of Peirce, James, Mead, and Dewey through such contemporaries as McDermott, Campbell, Hickman, and many others that I have in mind when considering a reconciliation of pragmatism and naturalism. The more detailed characteristics of pragmatism of this sort will emerge as we proceed.

There is a similar complexity in defining "naturalism." In recent decades, stemming from the work of W. V. O. Quine more than from anywhere else, the term "naturalism" has assumed a meaning it had not had before. Quine argued in "Epistemology Naturalized" that questions having to do with knowledge are best left to the empirical sciences, specifically in this case to psychology. The move from traditional epistemology and metaphysics to an exclusive reliance on the natural sciences is a generalization of Quine's recommendation, but it is precisely this that has in many contemporary philosophical circles come to be called naturalism. There is a school of thought today that calls itself naturalist, and it holds that only the natural and empirical sciences are capable of providing genuine knowledge of the world. Furthermore, so-called naturalism of this sort tends to be treated as a sort of materialism, usually a reductive materialism, in which it is taken as a given that nature consists of the objects and properties that are amenable to natural scientific inquiry and nothing else. In fact, in Anglo-American philosophical circles this has come to be the dominant meaning of the term "naturalism," and criticisms of naturalism most frequently take the form of objections to this sense of the term.[3] For the sake of clarity and at the risk of belaboring the obvious, let me state as forcefully as possible that when I discuss pragmatic naturalism throughout this book, I do *not* mean the term in this sense. If a reader is familiar with naturalism only in the Quinean, Anglo-American sense, then I ask him or her to be patient and follow this presentation of, and pragmatic argument for, naturalism in a different, and older, sense.

In the Wittgensteinian spirit of allowing use to determine meaning there would be little point in objecting to the term having assumed the meaning that it has. Nonetheless, it is important to recognize that the term "naturalism" has been in use for a much longer time than the view it currently designates, something Quine, if not most of his followers and detractors, fully recognized. There are many philosophers in the American tradition who would have referred to themselves as naturalists but who would never have accepted the primacy, never mind the exclusivity, of the natural sciences as a source of knowledge, or the description of nature as consisting only of that to which the natural sciences have access. That sort of scientistic view of things is far too narrow, and it has little in common with the American naturalism of George Santayana, Frederick J. E. Woodbridge, John Herman Randall Jr., Ernest Nagel, or Justus Buchler, to mention only a few.

American naturalism of this more traditional vintage has a broader, more tolerant conception of things, and it is willing, even eager, to allow for multiple ways of getting at them. This is, in fact, one of the intellectual virtues of American naturalism. Far too often scholars want to minimize or eliminate the significance of one or more aspects of our experience in the interest of promoting others. The motivation for this may be understandable in that scholars are, presumably, trying to understand things. But even given a defensible spirit, the result is that we eliminate, for example, the power of poetry or music to convey understanding, and relegate it to the "merely" expressive rather than the cognitive. But I can think of no good reason to follow anyone in this direction. In any given case it is quite possible that we can have more to learn from the poet than from the natural scientist, so that any conception that rules the poet out of court has missed the boat already. Similarly, there is no good reason to insist that only material objects and processes exist, and that anything else in our experience—for example, such phenomena as consciousness—must be explained in terms of material objects and their processes. The American naturalists, despite their other differences, have tended to insist on these points, and their philosophy is the richer for it. It is this broader, more tolerant naturalism that I speak of when I raise the possibility of the reconciliation of pragmatism and naturalism. And as with pragmatism, the details and ramifications of this American naturalist tradition will emerge throughout the present volume.[4]

The Tension Between Pragmatism and Naturalism

Here is the tension between pragmatism and naturalism. For pragmatism, the central category is experience. It is most important to keep in mind that this is not the experience of the empiricists, the passive reception of sense data, nor is it subjective, but something broader and more inclusive. For Peirce, for example, experience is a function of need, and knowledge is what satisfies need. For James, even the distinction between subject and object is secondary to "pure experience." Dewey, as we have seen, understands experience, or what he also calls "culture," as the interaction of human beings with their environments. The environment, in other words, has its traits by virtue of that interaction. Experience in Dewey's hands is active, indeed constitutive of that with which it interacts. For the sort of pragmatism represented by James and Dewey at least, nature is understood in terms of experience. This is fairly strongly stated in James, and it is clear in Dewey as well. Neither of them would have said simply that we "make the world up" in any simplistic sense, and in fact they both made some effort to insist on a degree of "objectivity"—that is, independence in certain senses from interaction with people, on the part of the "things" of the world. Nevertheless, the thrust for Dewey, as for James and other pragmatists, is that experience is the constitutive context in which nature takes its shape.

Naturalism goes at this quite the other way around. For the naturalist (remembering that this is the *American* naturalist tradition and not the scientistic tradition), the central category is nature, and experience is an aspect of it. Consider the view of someone like Santayana. As central as experience was for him—for example, "animal faith"—it is to be understood within the context of broader categories, in his case the realms of being, or essence, matter, truth, and spirit. Justus Buchler provides another interesting example. Experience was a significant interpretive category for him. In fact, it is crucial, as he develops it in his theory of judgment, for an understanding of human being. Even given its importance, however, experience for Buchler resides in a broader theory of nature, in this case his ordinal, relational ontology. Experience for the naturalist can only be understood if examined within a broader framework that includes, and in some cases is based on, a specific understanding of nature.

In a nutshell, for pragmatism nature is understood in terms of experience, and for naturalism experience is understood in terms of nature. These appear to be contradictory philosophical perspectives, or at least widely different approaches, so that pragmatic naturalism may seem to be an oxymoron.

This problem can be solved in a way that allows for pragmatic naturalism, and in the process can help us to see more clearly: (1) the detailed traits of the pragmatic naturalist perspective, (2) its virtues and applicability as they will be developed throughout this book, and (3) some of the other issues of moment in contemporary philosophy. First, though, another point about Rorty is in order, since he too confronts the problem. He deals with it, though, by abandoning the naturalist, objectivist, or modernist side altogether, at least as a philosophic issue. He argues, as we have seen, that it really does not make any sense to try to figure the world out in any naturalist or objectivist sense. For him, the pragmatist or constructivist side is all that is left. The apparent inconsistency between pragmatism and naturalism may well be the reason Rorty embraced one and abandoned the other. If so, he jumped the gun, and I daresay misunderstood pragmatism in the process.

This move is both unnecessary and unwise. It is unwise because there is fairly obviously a world independent of us. It is worthwhile to understand how the world works and what in general it is like, or so we will try to demonstrate. And it is unnecessary because in the end it is possible to retain consistently the critical aspects of naturalism and the central insights of pragmatism, as we will go on to argue. This is one of the reasons it is important to understand that in talking about pragmatism we do not mean to refer to Rorty. Rorty's neopragmatism makes naturalism irrelevant, and there is no point at all in talking about a reconciliation. Traditional pragmatism, by contrast, is mindful of the naturalist angle, and in a figure like Dewey one can almost sense the desire for, or even assumption of, a reconciliation.

I have begun to refer to naturalism as a kind of objectivism or realism, and I mean this in the sense that by relying on nature as the central category of analysis, naturalism will inevitably take the view that there are aspects of nature that are real and significantly independent of us. In other words, there are aspects of nature that possess their traits objectively. To this extent naturalism is a species of modernism. I also refer to pragmatism as a form of constructivism in the sense that for the pragmatists—the James and Dewey versions especially—pragmatism involves the idea that the process of experience, in the broad sense of interaction, is constitutive of what is experienced. This is the interaction of the experiencer and the experienced to which we alluded earlier. To this extent, pragmatism is a species of postmodernism.

The reconciliation of pragmatism and naturalism will inevitably, then, take us through aspects of the modernist-postmodernist debate. After making our way through it we can return to pragmatism and naturalism directly.

The Reconciliation: Modernism and Postmodernism

There are, no doubt, those who would object even to the use of the terms "modernism" and "postmodernism" on the grounds, presumably, that in each case the term is too broad and therefore obscures too many important differences among a variety of related positions. There is something to be said for this concern, but there is no need to allow it to prevent us from moving forward. There are indeed many important differences between traditional empiricism and rationalism, or between Platonism and Aristotelianism, or between deconstruction and Wittgensteinianism. And there may not be one single strain of ideas that runs through all the traditions that might fall under the umbrella of either modernism or postmodernism. But it is still the case that there are at least family resemblances among them, which means that there may be some sense in clarifying what those resemblances are. In the end there are pragmatic reasons for doing so, largely that it helps us to see certain aspects of the problem that are otherwise obscured.

In fact, clarifying the relationship between modernism and postmodernism is one of the more important technical issues facing contemporary philosophy. Unfortunately, many philosophers have either ignored or quickly dismissed those who do not hold their views. Those working in the modernist tradition, especially in forms of analytic philosophy, have been dismissive of many of the insights of literary and philosophical postmodernism. Similarly, many who might be described as postmodernists have been too quick to abandon important and defensible aspects of modernism, including analytic methods and traditions.

These extremes are mistakes because there is good reason to maintain aspects of both the modernist and postmodernist perspectives.[5] The issue can be considered in terms of four key propositions that map out the family resemblances of many of the philosophical traditions that have prevailed during the past several centuries. The first two express a modernist point of view, while the second two embody a postmodernist angle of vision:

1. Natural phenomena have objectively determinate traits.
2. The traits of natural phenomena are knowable.
3. The process of inquiry is necessarily conditioned and perspectival.
4. Human interaction with the rest of nature, cognitive or otherwise, is active and creative.[6]

The first two propositions are modernist in the sense that they assert an independently existing reality and our ability to learn about it. The third and fourth propositions are postmodernist in the sense that they assert that we do not just encounter a world waiting for us, but rather that the processes we employ in investigating our world—in fact, the process of experience itself—condition what we find and are therefore constructive of what we find. And it is useful to point out here, so as not to lose the thread of the discussion, that naturalism shares the view expressed by propositions 1 and 2, while pragmatism shares the view embodied in propositions 3 and 4.

In an effort to defend the virtues of dispassionate inquiry many philosophers and scientists have supported propositions 1 and 2 by rejecting 3 and 4. Similarly, many philosophers, literary theorists, and others—in an effort to debunk the myth of simple and pure objectivity, either ontological or epistemological—have rejected 1 and 2 in support of 3 and 4.

In the end, though, it is possible and desirable to endorse all four propositions simultaneously. It is desirable because there is certainly a world independent of us, and certainly components of that world have traits that are independent of our experience of them and independent of any purposes of ours. And certainly, aspects of that world and some of its traits are knowable to us. Engineering would be impossible otherwise. But it is equally certain that inquiry is conditioned and perspectival, if only in the sense that we inquire and think within a context, within a tradition and a history, and as Peirce, James, Dewey, and many others have made abundantly clear, for reasons and with purposes. And it is equally true that our experience conditions the world in which we are related, more or less significantly depending on the circumstances, so that nature is altered as a consequence of its complex relations with us.

I confess that this all seems so abundantly clear to me that I am tempted, having made the point, to move on. I also realize, however, that it is not so obvious to many other people, so it is better to dwell here a bit longer. Propositions 1 and 2 assert the existence and knowability of traits of natural entities independent of our experience; and there is little doubt, I assume, that material objects at least possess independent and cognitively available traits. We may describe a room any way we please, but we will only be able to enter or leave it through the doors or windows, and our description of the room does not alter their location. The obviousness of this point is the reason, I suspect, that natural scientists have so much trouble taking contemporary humanities professors seriously, in that they suspect that all the talk about constructing our experience means to deny it. If it does mean to deny it, then postmodernism understood in this way is in fact absurd. We examine, study, and learn about the material world, and of course we affect it, but we do not create it. We do not create planets and mountains; we do create buildings and roads and doors and windows, but we do not as a rule create the materials out of which they are made; when we do create the materials out of which they are made, we do not create the elements out of which the materials are made. Even when we affect or alter the material world, we do so through objects and natural entities that ultimately are not our creation, and to that extent their traits are determined objectively.

Things are less clear when we talk about the nonmaterial aspects of nature, which may be the reason some philosophers and others have been inclined to claim that matter is all that exists. I will discuss this point again in later chapters, but for now allow me to stipulate, with a few quick illustrations, that it cannot be true that matter is all that exists. Fictional characters, for example, exist in their own right, and they have certain specific and identifiable traits. Don Quixote in his own romantic way rails against the injustices of the world. That Don Quixote is not a spatial entity, and is in fact a human creation, in no way suggests that he does not "exist." He exists as a fictional character, with all the general characteristics possessed by fictional characters and all the specific characteristics possessed by his own in particular. This point requires much more elaboration, including the articulation of an ontological apparatus to give it sufficient coherence, all of which will be developed as we proceed. But just on the face of it we can say with some confidence that even with respect to at least some nonmaterial entities there is every reason to posit independently possessed traits, about which we can know something.

The situation is more difficult when we consider other types of nonmaterial entities—for example, moral and aesthetic values, or laws of nature, or principles of logic. Leave aside the question of whether they exist or not, though we will return to it. For now the question is whether, if they do exist, it is reasonable to say of them that they exist independently of our experience, or at least that they have some traits independent of our experience. The answer seems to be that they would possess at least some traits that could plausibly be described as objective—that is, independent of what we might say about them. If certain propositions are related to one another in certain ways—for example, the way a conclusion is related to the premises of a standard sort of syllogism—then we cannot simply describe them differently and think that we have therefore reconstructed them. In fact, we can discover new traits of logical principles, or natural laws, or of mathematical entities. And we do, in fact, discover them; we do not simply invent them. The solution of Fermat's Theorem was in part a discovery, or a set of discoveries, notwithstanding the fact that new mathematics was invented to accomplish it.

It is at the very least plausible, then, to hold that natural entities possess traits independently of us and that we can know something about them. But what about propositions 3 and 4, which postulate that the process of inquiry is perspectival and conditioned, and that human interaction with the rest of nature is active and creative? To many philosophers who regard themselves as clear-thinking realists, it seems obvious that when one experiences a tree outside his window there is nothing in any significant sense constructive or creative about it. One perceives the tree simply enough, and therein lies the experience. While this may seem to some an illustration of experience plain and simple, there is in fact nothing plain or simple about it. The complexity derives from the fact that there are several assumptions built into the question, assumptions that if overlooked account for the apparent simplicity. For example, the "clear-thinking realist" assumes that the object, in this case a tree, is a discrete individual entity that has no particularly complex relations with its environment. In fact, it assumes a traditional physics whereby a discrete object is impinged upon by light, which is then reflected into the sensory mechanism of the perceiver, whose own neurobiological apparatus then transforms the sense data into an image. Without bothering with the details, it is easy enough to point out that this model of perception is simplistic at best. For one thing, the image we see in the end has as much to do with the characteristics of the specific sensory mechanism and neurophysiological processes as it does with the sense data it receives. If our optical mechanism and the processes by which it functions were differently constructed, there is every reason to believe that the image we see would be quite different. For that reason alone, the clear-thinking realist is missing something important when he gives the example of the perception of the tree outside his window as an illustration of a passive, inactive experience.

But there is another question we also need to ask: whether we should take a relatively simple sense perception to be the paradigmatic case of experience. On the face of it there is no reason to do so, since there are clearly many different kinds of experiences. When we say that someone is experienced, for example, we do not mean that she has received a large amount of sensory data. For one thing, experience in this sense is cumulative in a way that simply receiving sense data is not. Furthermore, a person who is experienced has not merely undergone something, even if cumulatively. Such a person has interacted with his environment in ways that resulted in knowledge, growth, and maturity. Social experience has the same general characteristics. The experience of being an American, for example, is not about receiving sense data, nor is it simply about receiving anything at all. It describes in a word an indefinitely broad range of interactions with one's social environment, with political distinctions and products of human activity. It denotes membership in a culture, perhaps more than one, to the nature of which one contributes in his experience. Cultures are not merely received; they are produced and reproduced, and surely to be a member of and participant in a culture is part of what it means to have experience.

Many other senses of experience are similarly interactive and creative. Having an aesthetic or religious experience, while it certainly includes a sense of undergoing, is not only an undergoing. If nothing else, the meaning of an aesthetic or religious experience is an important constituent of the experience, and meaning is not simply undergone or received; it is constructed. It is not constructed out of nothing, to be sure; on the contrary, it is constructed within a web of intersecting and interactive constituents that provide one having such an experience the raw material out of which meaning is generated. But the web of intersecting and interacting constituents is itself the product of countless people in ongoing interaction with their material, social, and historical environments. There is nothing remotely passive about an aesthetic or religious experience. The continuous interaction with one's environment, in some sense undergone and in others undertaken, is the broad context in which experience, in even the simplest sense, occurs. That experience is contextual; the fact that in various ways and in different situations it weaves together material, social, and historical factors, is the reason Dewey said that he might prefer to use the word "culture" to denote it. It is also the reason that it has been a shocking mistake on the part of traditional empiricism and its contemporary advocates to treat experience in general on the model of sensory impressions. Even if the reception of sense data were a simple passive matter, which in any case it is not, such experience would hardly be the paradigmatic case.

I will assume that at least a plausible case has been made for proposition 4, that an individual's interaction with the rest of nature, with his environment broadly understood, is active and creative. Proposition 3 is a logical implication of this point. If experience, individual and communal, is located so to speak in a relational network of social, historical, and material factors, then the idea of abstract inquiry—inquiry undertaken outside of any context or from no perspective—is impossible. There are always, and necessarily, reasons we ask the questions that we do, and in the ways that we ask them. This is not a condition we should bemoan, as if we have lost something precious in the recognition of the meaninglessness of abstract inquiry. It simply describes the situation we are in. Realizing this, though, is extremely important for the legitimacy of the inquiry we do conduct. If our perspectives and purposes in asking questions condition the process of inquiry itself, then an as-clear-as-possible understanding of the nature of our perspectives and purposes is critical if we are to avoid overloading the results of our inquiry. It is also critically important if we are to understand one another as fully as possible. The full meaning of the perspectival and contextual nature of inquiry is an extremely rich and complicated matter. Perhaps the most important contribution of a good deal of postmodern writing has been the consideration of just this question. It is a thorny issue that traditional epistemology tried simply to argue away, but at that enterprise it cannot succeed.

So at the very least we have plausible reasons for accepting the claim that all four propositions are true. This means that two fundamental characteristics of both the modernist and postmodernist points of view are simultaneously plausible. They are all plausible enough, in fact, that we have every good reason to accept them. One implication of this is that those who would reject wholesale the modernist or the postmodernist perspectives are mistaken. At least at the level of these four fundamental characteristics, the two broad contemporary approaches to nature and knowledge are compatible.

That is not the end of the story, however, because we are now led to ask what are basically transcendental questions in the Kantian sense: What is nature like such that the four propositions are true simultaneously? What are the traits of nature that make such a situation possible?

The Possibility of Reconciliation

We have seen that we have reason to accept the truth of the four propositions, and we now turn to the question of how that can be. The possibility of the truth of all four propositions—that is, the possibility of the reconciliation of modernism and postmodernism, and by extension pragmatism and naturalism—rests first on the distinction between the objective and the absolute. This is a critically important point because a great deal of philosophic mischief has been done by failing to make this distinction. There is a widespread assumption that if inquiry (our access to the rest of the world or nature) is always perspectival and conditioned, then it no longer makes sense to talk of objective inquiry, and, therefore, of knowable objective traits or characteristics of things. But this is a non sequitur. If our relation to the world around us is necessarily perspectival and conditioned, what follows is that neither we nor the rest of the world to which we are related possess absolute traits, and that knowledge is never absolute. This is so because whenever terms are in relation, the relation influences the terms. That is to say that all particulars are relational, a point I will explore and defend in a later chapter. To say that there is a knowledge relation between a knower and a known is automatically to say that both the knower and the known are conditioned by each other, more or less relevantly depending on the case, as a result of that particular relation. But to say that there are no absolute traits is not the same as to say that there are no objective traits. In other words, conditionality and objectivity are not incompatible conditions.

The key to appreciating this point is to realize that objectivity in this sense does not mean "unconditioned." That is to say that for traits to be determined objectively is not equivalent to traits being determined unconditionally. Objectivity in this sense means, simply, not determined by the purposes or interests of the inquirer. An example may help to illustrate the point. Some years ago an interesting phenomenon occurred on the horse farms in Kentucky. Pregnant mares were mysteriously having spontaneous abortions at an alarming rate, worrying those whose livelihood depended on the birth of healthy foals. Analysis of the stillborn fetuses indicated that there was a high level of cyanide in their systems, and there was a correspondingly high level of cyanide in the mares' blood. It was clear that the poison was responsible for the deaths of the fetuses, but the question remained where the poison had come from. One possibility that was explored was that the poison had come from the tent caterpillars eaten inadvertently by the mares, though at that point other possible sources had not been ruled out. Entomologists, chemists, botanists, and veterinarians hastened to try to solve the problem.

Here is a case where fairly sophisticated biological and chemical inquiry is called into play, and the interests and motivations of the inquirers and those connected to the horse farms is fairly clear. There was a strong financial interest in locating the source of the poison and eliminating it from the mares' diet. There were motivations and purposes in the inquiry that were far removed from pure, unconditioned inquiry. The process of inquiry, in other words, was conditioned and perspectival in easily identifiable respects. Nevertheless, whatever was to be discovered through such conditioned and perspectival inquiry would be objectively the case. Whatever caused the poisoning of the mares' diet would be discovered, not invented or created, despite the conditionality of the process of inquiry. It would be a finding, not an invention, assuming of course that it was all done honestly. The point is that the chemical nature of the food source and its effects on the mares and their fetuses is objectively determined, despite the conditional and perspectival character of the process of inquiry undertaken to detect it. Those traits are not absolute, however. If it were to turn out to be the caterpillars, for example, it is the relation between the caterpillars and the foliage eaten by the mares, as well as the relation between the chemistry of the mares' and their fetuses' blood systems, that would determine the overall consequence. The traits of the constituent elements of the situation are relational, not absolute, but they are no less objectively determined.

The reason the distinction between the absolute and the objective is important is that it allows us to remove any mystery from the compatibility of conditioned inquiry and the objectivity of traits. This is of course an epistemological point, but the ontological also needs to be underscored. We have so far made an argument for allowing that perspectival and conditioned inquiry can yield objective results. The possibility of knowledge in some traditional sense is thereby assured, but the character of *what* we learn about—that is, the nature of the aspects of the world into which we inquire—is also important. As we have seen in the example of the Kentucky horses, the various factors of the mares' feeding habits, the food they are inclined to eat, and the possible effect of tent caterpillars on the food, describe a web of interrelated entities. The factors themselves, the various traits they posses and the effects of those traits on other constituents of the situation, are determined not by our wishes or our contexts, but by the relations themselves. There is what we can call, following Justus Buchler, a *natural definition* of the traits possessed by the constituents of the situation. That is to say that the characteristics of each of the constituents are defined not by us but by nature, by the relations in which they stand to one another regardless of us. Once we enter the picture, and new relations are established, now with us, the traits of the constituents of the situation alter to some extent. Their meanings are altered—in this case significantly for those involved in raising horses—and we may to some degree alter the way nonhuman constituents are related to one another. This means that as human beings enter the situation we become another of its constituents, and we influence the natural definition of the constituents in any number of ways.

The picture is not appreciably different with respect to nonmaterial entities. Mathematical entities have the properties they do by virtue of natural definition, as do dreams, hopes, and fictional characters. Human beings may or may not interact with such entities in any given case; but if and when we do, we become, as in the case of the Kentucky horses, a factor in the natural definition, a contributing constituent in the objective determination of the traits of all the constituents.

The key to all of this is relationality, a point we will make much of in the chapters that follow. If we begin to think about natural entities, by which I mean anything at all, material or not, actual or possible, general or particular, as relational rather than atomistically absolute, it becomes possible to see how things, and again that means anything and everything, are at the same time conditioned and in possession of objectively determined traits. And this is true both of entities that are related to people and those that are not.

It turns out that thinking about things relationally is not so easy, primarily, I suppose, because in the bulk of our intellectual tradition we are inclined to regard individuals as essentially or inherently unrelated to one another. The traditional philosophical concept of substance describes something with its traits, at least its primary traits, possessed entirely independently of anything else. Though the term "substance" in its technical philosophical meaning is not much in use anymore, the basic concept is very much alive and influential. For example, the traditional concept of the atom was understood in this way. In fact, the entire edifice of modern natural science, mathematics, and social science was constructed on this assumption, and in many respects the assumption continues to prevail. The Newtonian model of the physical world, and the mathematics that were developed to make it work, describe discrete individuals, each with its own traits independent of all the others, interacting with one another according to determinable and describable regularity. The success of this model of reality was so great that it permeated even the social sciences that were developing in the eighteenth century. Societies came to be understood as collections of discrete, essentially unrelated individuals, each in possession of certain traits, natural rights among the most important of them. Modern political theory was built on this assumption, in that from Locke through most of the eighteenth century, political theorists argued that the primary purpose of government was to protect the natural rights of individuals. Communities were either artificial constructs from inherently unrelated individuals or they were mere collections of human "atoms" held together by natural principles of one sort or another. In economic theory, for example, the basic principles of the marketplace came to be described in terms of discrete individuals, each with its own inherent and independently determined economic interest, each acting independently to pursue its own interest. What one might expect to be a chaotic result is not so partly because, like the ultimate elements of the physical world, the whole is held together by natural law, in the case of economic theory expressed metaphorically by Adam Smith's "invisible hand." A similar point can be made about the understanding of international relations, as we will see in a later chapter.

If modern science, philosophy, mathematics, and social, political, international relations, and economic theory have been rooted in the assumption of discrete and inherently unrelated individuals then it is little wonder that it might prove difficult to conceive of things differently. Nonetheless, there is reason to do precisely that. Consider another example that lends itself easily to the point: an ecosystem—for example, a pond that for the moment has no relation to people. The constituents of the pond all exist in a web of relations such that each conditions the others. In some cases of an ecosystem like this the relations between two or more specific constituents may be so great that some are a condition of the very existence of others. If the chemical nature of the water is altered, it may become impossible for certain plants and other organisms to survive. In a scenario like this it is impossible to conceive of the constituents as possessing entirely independent traits, even what used to be called "primary attributes." Size, shape, weight, and color, not to mention behavioral characteristics, are each conditioned by the relational web that constitutes the system. No constituent of the pond has its traits "absolutely." The constituents all exist and have the traits that they do by virtue of the specific relations among them.

If we introduce people into the system, either simply as constituent members or as inquirers, the general point does not change. The human constituents are related to other components of the ecosystem and their traits are therefore conditioned in the same way. If the humans are inquirers or investigators, then the relation qualifies the inquiry in the sense that it provides a condition or perspective in which the inquiry is carried out.

A relational conception of nature invites us to abandon the Newtonian, atomistic conception of things in favor of a model expressed by an ecosystem. To do so of course raises many questions: Are all relations of the same sort? Are all relations equally constitutive? Is the web of relations infinitely complex, or is there a limit? What is the role of stability and change? If individuals are constituted relationally then how are they individuated—that is, how is identity determined? These and questions like them are the substance of philosophical inquiry. I am suggesting that a philosophical naturalism, particularly one that has a pragmatic, constructivist dimension, needs a relational view of nature. In that case it becomes the task of the pragmatic naturalist to take up the general question raised by the shift to a relational perspective. Some such work has been done already, most extensively by the Columbia University and Stony Brook University philosopher Justus Buchler in his ordinal naturalism.[7] It is the task of this book to extend that work by speaking to the nature, rationale, plausibility, and many-sided implications of an ordinal, pragmatic naturalism.

The Reconciliation: The Possibility of Pragmatic Naturalism

One of the advantages of the example of an ecosystem, other than the fact that it is rather obviously relational, is that it is the kind of model Dewey himself used as a cornerstone of his pragmatic naturalism. This is the significance of the claim often made that unlike most philosophers of the modern age, who have worked from a conceptual model drawn from traditional Newtonian physics, Dewey's conceptual model was drawn from biology, specifically Darwinian biology. For Dewey it is precisely the biological model that emphasizes relationality. When Dewey used the concept of a situation, or more specifically a problematic situation, this is the sort of thing he had in mind. It is not surprising, then, that he could develop a pragmatic naturalism, in that he was working with the idea of relational, mutually constitutive elements of a situation. Dewey, the primary example of a pragmatic naturalist, was able to develop a coherent philosophical perspective because he was working with a relational conceptual model that made it possible.

We have shown that our experience indicates the desirability of the constructivism inherent in pragmatism as well as the objectivity that is characteristic of naturalism. We have also shown that through a relational understanding of nature it is possible for the two to coexist in a single, coherent philosophic position, a relational perspective that itself has been developed most fully within the American naturalist tradition. In the end the philosophical adequacy of a pragmatic naturalism, and the relational view of nature implicit in it, will itself be determined pragmatically. There are no empirical tests we can conduct to determine whether nature is constituted by simples or complexes, whether entities possess their traits absolutely or relationally, whether experience is passive or interactional, and whether inquiry is perspectival and constructivist or pure and merely reflective of reality. There are also no deductively rigorous arguments we can use to demonstrate one or the other general perspective. The adequacy of a pragmatic naturalism, the sort that has been shown here to be both possible and desirable, will in the end be determined by the conceptual work it can do. In the chapters that follow, I will endeavor to clarify in greater detail the character of pragmatic naturalism, its rational and experiential implications, and its pragmatic justification through an exploration of some of the work it does.

TWO

THE VALUE OF PRAGMATIC NATURALISM

Once pragmatism and naturalism have been reconciled, which I assume has been successfully done in the preceding chapter, it is necessary to specify in greater detail what pragmatic naturalism is and what its virtues are.[1]

The Traits of Pragmatic Naturalism

The first of its traits, which it shares in general outline with other forms of naturalism, is that nature is broadly and richly enough conceived that there is no philosophical need to posit anything outside nature. The usual candidate for the designation "nonnatural" is the "supernatural," so we are in effect saying here that philosophical inquiry can and should be undertaken without having recourse to the supernatural. We need to be clear about what this does *not* mean. First, it does not mean that naturalism necessarily does without a concept of the divine. Personally I do not see, and never have seen, the point of a naturalist theology, but others do see the point, and there is nothing about the naturalist conception of nature that necessarily precludes a meaningful theology. Of course, the effort of Santayana to liberate the aesthetic and other traits of traditional spirituality from the supernatural is well known, as is Dewey's attempt to free the language and ethical aspirations of traditional religion from their supernatural home.[2] But others have attempted something that looks more like theology, though in a consciously naturalistic philosophical context. John Herman Randall Jr. is one of the more outstanding contributors in this respect, and more recently Robert Corrington has attempted his own version of a naturalist theology, in his case relying on a more or less Buchlerian, ordinal ontology.[3] I will focus on the question of a pragmatic naturalist theology, and a discussion of God and faith, in Chapter 6.

This point suggests two additional observations about what treating nature as the comprehensive category does *not* mean—first, that nature is equivalent to the material world, and second, that scientific inquiry is the only method that can produce knowledge of nature.[4] With respect to matter, I would if pressed want to argue for a form of materialism, but like Santayana I would also say that it seems patently false to say at the same time that nature is all there is and that nature is equivalent to the sum total of matter, i.e., that only matter exists. The experience of all of us is replete with the nonmaterial, from the products of imagination to meanings to emotions. The sort of materialism I want to defend involves the claim that matter is the ontological sine qua non of everything else, but matter is not for that reason any "more real" than other existences, and certainly not exclusively real. Pragmatic naturalism is not reductively materialistic.[5]

Nor is pragmatic naturalism friendly to the claim that all knowledge derives from the methods of the natural sciences. On the one hand, none of us seriously doubt the epistemological value of the sciences, regardless of how we might describe the scientific method. If we did seriously doubt it we would not get into a car, drive across a bridge, or for that matter even get up in the morning. As I pointed out in the previous chapter, our lives from moment to moment rely on the principles of engineering, and the principles of engineering are impossible without the results of basic science. But that is not to say that every activity we undertake or everything we think we know is the direct or even indirect result of the natural sciences and the engineering it enables.

Some have urged that naturalism go beyond its interest in the natural sciences and begin to take more seriously the social sciences.[6] I would endorse this call, but go further and say that naturalism, if it is to take seriously the breadth of experience and of nature itself, also needs to look much more closely at the humanities and the arts. This point will be developed at greater length in Chapter 7, but it needs to be made at this point as I describe the general contour of pragmatic naturalism. Literature, music, poetry, the visual arts, theater, even philosophy, can reveal to us knowledge and understanding of no less significance than that derived from the natural and social sciences. I am convinced that a careful reading of Dostoyevsky can provide us with as much understanding of human motivations as any systematic psychological study. In any case, Dostoyevsky's insights are at least part of the story of human behavior, to such an extent, in fact, that they offer us something scientific studies do not and cannot reveal. Something similar can be said about other great works of literature, music, art, or philosophy. I have not the slightest doubt, for example, that my understanding of myself, or life, or the world, is enhanced by listening to nearly anything Franz Schubert wrote. Schubert does not do that for everyone, but then neither does Einstein or Quine, which says nothing about the epistemological value of their work. Science, to use a pragmatist metaphor, is one tool in the pursuit of knowledge. It is a critically important tool, but it is not the only one, nor is it in all respects and situations the most important, valuable, or useful one. Not all aspects of nature are amenable to the methods of science. Some require the poet, the composer, the painter, or the philosopher.

Part of the problem traditionally is that we are too quick to assume that anything of cognitive significance must come to us in the form of bits of data or information. But we do not simply assimilate the world; we manipulate it as well. Sometimes our manipulations assert something, sometimes they display or exhibit something, and sometimes they consist of action. None of these three ways of interacting with the world, or three ways of judging it, to use that word in a certain technical sense that will be developed as we proceed, has a monopoly on cognitive significance. Thus, the exhibitive manipulation that constitutes a painting, to choose one example from the many possible, selects aspects of nature and combines them in ways that, ideally, we have not seen before. In doing so it brings into focus traits or characteristics of nature that reveal something new to us. This is why the visual arts, music, literature, and poetry can be and often are cognitive. We do in fact learn something from novel and insightful ways of manipulating form and color, or sounds, or words, no less than we do by the manipulation in the natural sciences of objects and processes. An adequate pragmatic naturalism understands this.[7]

We have to this point somewhat circled around the concept of nature and our access to the complexes that constitute it. One might ask, however, for a more positive and direct definition of nature on the grounds that without it we are begging critical questions. I will say more below about whether pragmatic naturalism is foundationalist in the sense that it rests on firm logical or definitional foundations, but for now let us assume that it is not foundationalist in this sense. Still, one may wonder whether a definition of nature is in order, particularly because the term can be and is used in so many different ways. We can contrast nature, in one sense, with the artificial, or in another we can contrast it with the statistically infrequent, unusual, or abnormal, and in our sense we have contrasted it with the supernatural. So the question can reasonably be asked, given its range of possible meanings, just how we are to define it.

There are a couple relevant points that need to be made in response to a request for a definition. First, we may acknowledge that the term "nature" is used in ordinary language and in common philosophical parlance in a variety of different ways, with different meanings, without generating any philosophical problems. There is no need to insist that this or any other word have only one meaning. Second, we have offered a definition of a kind, i.e., that nature is "whatever there is," presuming that further elaboration of the philosophical issues raised by or within pragmatic naturalism will gradually give the idea more flesh. But is this good enough?

I would like to say that it *is* good enough, and the fact that it is says something important about the way the concept functions for a pragmatic naturalist. To give a more ramified definition at this point—for example, that nature is whatever reveals itself to the senses, or whatever we encounter in experience, or whatever can be posited without contradiction, or whatever is the case, or whatever is actual, or whatever is possible—would be too limiting, and in any case would simply raise more questions. To say that nature is "whatever there is" is purposefully to leave open the full range of actualities and possibilities, realities and imaginings. This does not mean that no imaginable concept is excluded. We have already said that our understanding of nature excludes the supernatural, which is to say that there is no supernatural, at least not in the standard orders of experience or articulation in which the term is usually intended to apply. This in turn suggests that whatever there may be, it is continuous with something else, i.e., that there is nothing that is entirely other.

All this suggests that for the pragmatic naturalist nature does not serve as a category in any normal sense. It is not simply one among a number of concepts that taken together constitute a philosophical system. Rather it suggests a general perspective or frame of mind. The pragmatic naturalist philosopher is predisposed to give whatever there is, or whatever there may be, the benefit of the ontological doubt, at least as a point of departure. He or she is prepared to try to understand whatever is encountered or invented as being among the complexes of nature, even, as we have seen, the divine. This is why Buchler in his examination of the idea of nature ended up describing nature as simply "providingness."[8] Nature is not simply this or that, but rather it is "whatever there is." No other definition is possible, and no other would in any case capture the role the concept plays for pragmatic naturalism.

So the category of nature is sufficient to our purposes, nature itself is wider than the physical world, and the natural sciences are not the only source of knowledge. Furthermore, pragmatic naturalism takes a relational view of nature. I have made this point in the previous chapter, but it has such centrality for an adequate pragmatic naturalism that we will repeat it a number of times, and develop its rationale in various contexts. The basic ontological idea is that all "things," i.e., anything whatsoever, are constituted by constituents and their relations, and that no constituent, no matter how deeply or broadly one looks, or how thoroughly one analyzes, is atomic. Or to put the point positively, every thing, entity, or complex is constituted by its constituents and their relations, including the constituents themselves. Furthermore, constituents are not identical to parts in any normal sense. The history of a complex may be among its relevant constituents, for example, as might its social or physical context. All complexes are relationally constituted, whatever the detailed relations may be for any given entity.[9]

It is also important to understand that this ordinal conception of relations is not a theory of "internal" relations. Relations understood ordinally or internally might easily be confused with one another because both describe relations as constitutive. The ordinal theory of relations, however, discards both internal and external relations. Relations are not external to the terms related because they are constitutive. And they are not internal to the terms related because, first, there are no external relations with which to contrast them, and secondly, and more importantly, ordinal relations do not constitute a final, overarching system or whole. We will return to this point later, but for now suffice it to say that nature understood ordinally is not a "whole," if only because relations ordinally understood function in contexts. A whole would have no context, and therefore no ordinal location, and therefore no identity. Neither external nor internal relations, as traditionally understood, have a place in an ordinal theory of relations.

The reason relationality of this kind is crucial to pragmatic naturalism is, as we have seen, that it is what allows the reconciliation of the differing philosophical approaches of pragmatism and naturalism. Neither Dewey nor Buchler put it quite this way, though Randall did: One of the critical differences between the two is that pragmatism privileges experience while naturalism privileges nature. Even granting the point that experience as meant here is the interactive experience of Dewey, i.e., culture, and not the passive reception of sense data of the empiricists, this disconnect would be fatal to any effort to reconcile them unless it were possible to show that experience and the rest of nature are related to one another in such a way that the world can be understood as the interconnection of experience and the rest of nature without reducing either to the other. A relational ontology allows us to do precisely this by making it possible to say that complexes of nature are constitutive of experience, and that experience is constitutive of the complexes of nature to which it is related. Thus, the two are integrated without experience being defined away and without nature being inappropriately read through the prism of the human interaction within it.

The final definitional point is that for pragmatic naturalism philosophical ideas are justified by their success. This of course is not a novel point with respect to pragmatism, but it is less commonly applied in naturalist circles. Nonetheless, even the more technical philosophical aspects of pragmatic naturalism, by which I mean its naturalist side, cannot be justified by reason alone. Let us take the claim that "nature is to be understood relationally" as an example. There is no amount of deductive argument or analysis that will force or even enable us to say that this claim is true and that its alternatives—for example, that "nature is to be understood atomistically"—are false. The best that argument can do is to demonstrate that it is logically possible, or reasonable, or maybe even desirable, to hold that nature is to be understood relationally. Even if I were the cleverest philosopher since Aristotle, and even if I were able to demonstrate rationally to the satisfaction of every reader the appropriateness of the proposition that nature is to be understood relationally, sooner or later some less clever philosopher would have a counter-argument, or an objection, or a rational alternative. One may want to point out that this is in fact what has happened and continues to happen to every philosophical proposition made, and one would be right to do so, but that observation simply makes the point. I would go so far as to say that philosophers have misconstrued our enterprise by understanding it through an analogy with mathematics, wherein propositions can be proven. But even if one does not want to go as far as that, it is nonetheless appropriate for us to regard pragmatic naturalism as subject to pragmatic valuation. It is appropriate, for example, for us to accept and put to work the proposition that nature is to be understood relationally if we can render the proposition consistent and meaningful, and if by putting it to work we are able to do things we are not able to do otherwise, and create relatively few new problems along the way. The same principle of valuation should be taken to apply to other aspects of pragmatic naturalism as well, and of course to the many issues and problems that philosophy can appropriately address.

So to sum up the definitional side of pragmatic naturalism: It is a relational philosophy; it is a philosophy for which nature is a category sufficient for all things; it holds that nature consists of more than material objects; it proceeds as if natural science is one of several sources of knowledge; and it is a philosophical perspective that expects to be evaluated by its usefulness and value in philosophical and other contexts. We may now consider the question of what value it does in fact have. Each of the specific virtues of pragmatic naturalism highlighted is related to one or another of the defining characteristics just described.

The Virtues of Pragmatic Naturalism

First, pragmatic naturalism avoids the many artificial dualisms that have driven philosophy into too many dead ends. Whenever he had the opportunity, Dewey bemoaned the many bifurcations that have characterized Western philosophy over the centuries, and he quite rightly thought that we would do well to get past them. Despite his efforts, and those of many others, philosophy seems to have accommodated itself to, and even continues to thrive on, those same dualisms: mind and body; belief and knowledge; self and world; individual and society; etc. One might reasonably wonder why these dichotomies have the strength and longevity that they do, and the answer is simple. They continue to attract our attention and often to drive our thinking because in each case both sides of the dichotomy have a compelling claim on our attention. No matter our reasonable philosophical and scientific efforts, and even contortions, to explain human being in material terms, there remain aspects of our experience that continue to drive us to appeal to mind of some kind and in some sense. And though the Berkeleyan idealist and the Buddhist may insist on the insignificance and even illusory character of body, the rest of us cannot live without it. One could go on to make similar observations about the terms of the other dualisms mentioned above. In each case the terms taken alone are plausible enough, but when juxtaposed to one another as mutually exclusive alternatives they make trouble. But why is that? Why does the juxtaposition of mind and body become a technical "problem" around the discussion of which philosophers have made entire careers? The answer, and this applies to all the dualisms mentioned and no doubt to others as well, is that we have continuously misunderstood what they are. Mind and body are a problem for each other only if we insist that each is in some technical or nontechnical sense a "substance" or atomic entity, and that the two are substances or "atoms" of radically different kinds, or that there is no way to understand how they interact. Such misunderstandings force us to define one or the other away, or to reach for inappropriate metaphors, such as the contemporary inclination to understand mind as either a computer or as a piece of software, that are dubious at best and at worst detrimental.[10]

There is no need within a pragmatic naturalist framework to distinguish mind and body, or belief and knowledge, or self and world, or individual and society, in such a way that each becomes a problem for the other. For one thing, a relational ontology allows us to make the distinctions that mind and body suggest without assuming that in essence each is entirely different from the other. On the contrary, if approached relationally we are driven to say that mind, or in any case mental complexes, are in any number of ways constitutive of bodies, and bodies constitutive of mind and mental events. There is nothing stranger in saying this than there is in saying that eating ice cream makes me happy. Furthermore, if we are prepared to say that the value of ideas is in the work they do, then we never need to ask the questions that constitute the "mind/body problem" in the first place. Or if we find that we do, then the terms, the concepts, and whatever relations we posit for them will stand or fall on the adequacy of what they accomplish for us. This is not to say that there is nothing potentially interesting going on in philosophical inquiries into mind, or that philosophers should not undertake such inquiries. Philosophers should undertake any studies that interest them. If something of significance emerges from philosophical studies of mind and consciousness then so much the better.[11] It is simply to say that mind, body, and their interaction, though they pose important neurophysiological and neurochemical questions, do not generate any serious philosophical conundrums. That we have thought they do pose such puzzles is an illustration of the fact that we have been misconceiving them all along. Philosophy, in what we can call the Humpty-Dumpty Fallacy, has unnecessarily and artificially shattered a fairly coherent world into many pieces, and cannot seem to get it back together without creating monsters. One value of pragmatic naturalism is that it does not compel us to push Humpty-Dumpty off the wall in the first place.

A second virtue of pragmatic naturalism, closely related to the first, is that it allows us to avoid the reductionism common to much of contemporary philosophy. As we pointed to above, philosophers have too routinely allowed nature to be carved up into competing categories—i.e., mind and body, self and society, individual and complex, etc.—even while knowing that the dichotomies thus created are themselves problems that must be addressed. One of the ways philosophers have traditionally tried to deal with the inadequacy of their many dualisms and dichotomies is to reduce one side to the other: mind being dissolved into body, the biological into the physical and chemical, the social into the individual. The problem with such reductionism, besides the technical difficulties of trying, for example, to describe all mental events in purely physical or neurochemical terms, is that the conception of nature and of our experience that results is no more plausible than the dichotomies the reductions are intended to mend. A memory may be delightful, but a neurochemical process cannot be delightful, except perhaps to a neurochemist. So even if neurochemical processes of certain kinds are necessary conditions of a memory, the two are not identical. A philosophical analysis that attempts to make one of them disappear into the other is no more acceptable than the philosophical analysis that initially turned them into absolutely distinct categories or kinds of entities.

It was suggested that one of the virtues of pragmatic naturalism is that it does not compel us to push Humpty-Dumpty off the wall, i.e., we are not compelled to slice nature into irreconcilable pieces. The same characteristics of pragmatic naturalism that make this possible also allow us to accept the multiplicity of nature without any need to dissolve some of it into the rest. Each complex of nature possesses the traits that define it as the complex it is and not another. Precisely how it is related to other complexes is critical to understanding its traits. If a specific memory can only arise in certain neurochemical conditions, then that memory's relations to those specific neurochemical processes are among its traits and defining characteristics. Such a relational understanding of memory and neurochemistry makes it possible for us to recognize and acknowledge the diversity in nature while at the same time accounting for the close, and in many cases necessary, relations among them. In this respect pragmatic naturalism follows in the footsteps of some of its intellectual ancestors. Spinoza, for example, though without the relational dimension, also painted a picture of nature with, as he put it, infinite attributes. There is a rich tradition in the history of philosophy, of which Spinoza is only one example, of careful attempts to avoid reductionism. Pragmatic naturalism is the contemporary expression of that tradition.

A third virtue of pragmatic naturalism, also pointed out in the previous chapter, is that it allows us to accept the reality of our experience, contra many postmodernisms. Among the tragedies of philosophy in recent decades is that many philosophers (whom I will here call, perhaps inappropriately, postmodernists) who emphasize experience or language or the human subject tend to fear objectivity because they suspect that it ignores the human perspective. The result of the all too frequent fear of or hostility to objectivity has been a denial of its very possibility. The tragedy of this is that philosophers, scientists, and others who continue to insist that there are traits of nature that do not depend on us tend to ignore the postmodernists, and vice versa. In some sense this is not necessarily a problem because the two sets of scholars are often working on different issues and questions. But in many ways each could benefit from the insights of the other, and they too often fail to do so.

This, however, is a problem we can avoid. As we saw in the previous chapter, there are two factors that contribute to the difficulty: (1) The more or less constructivist view that knowledge and inquiry are always perspectival, and (2) the mistaken though common assumption that if *x* is not absolute then *x* is not objective. The pragmatist side of pragmatic naturalism would endorse the claim that knowledge and inquiry are always perspectival because they are accomplished from some angle or point of view and they are always undertaken for a reason, i.e., to do something; knowledge therefore is never absolute. Similarly, the naturalist side of pragmatic naturalism is likely to acknowledge that whatever place human beings and our experience has in nature, there remain aspects or traits of nature that are what they are, entirely independent of human interaction with them. This is to say that in at least some respects human perspective is irrelevant to the traits of nature, which means there are traits of nature that are objective.

I have addressed this point in the previous chapter, but it is sufficiently important that we should go over the ground again. This complication can be dealt with if we carefully sort out how perspective, objectivity, and absoluteness are connected with one another. The good news is that the relational ontology of pragmatic naturalism allows us to do precisely that, and in such a way that we can understand that the absence of absolute knowledge does not preclude objectivity, either epistemological or ontological. When I see our now familiar door at the side of the room I see it from a point of view, from a perspective, but the door is no less objectively there and not somewhere else. Traditionally this commonsensical observation has lead to the bifurcation between the world as it is in itself, i.e., the door with its objective traits, and the world as it is experienced, i.e., the door from my particular angle of vision.

Though Kant contributed tremendously to the development of European intellectual life, this particular Kantian move has been pernicious, and it continues to seep into our way of thinking about this problem: If our epistemology is perspectival but our ontology is objectivist, there must be a gap between them. But this is a non sequitur. Perspective is inconsistent with absoluteness, such that if our perception of the door is perspectival it cannot be absolute. This is, in the end, the reason knowledge is always contextual. This is a problem for objectivity only if to be objective is to be absolute. If, however, we are willing to separate the two, then there is nothing puzzling about the fact that the traits of the door—i.e., its location, size, etc.—really are the traits of the door, and that we encounter the door from some angle and in some context. We can see that there is no problem here once we realize that given a relational ontology, the objective traits of the door are themselves relationally constituted regardless of the door's relation to us as perceivers. Every aspect of the natural complex that is the door—its location, size, shape, weight, material properties, functions, color, and so forth—is itself in a complex set of relations with the other constituents of the door and with the broader relational contexts in which the door finds itself. There is, in other words, nothing absolute about the door in the first place. It, like every other complex of nature, is thoroughly relational, and its relation to us as perceivers is one more relation that contributes to its traits. The entire relational web of door and its perception is decidedly not absolute, but it is nonetheless objective in that the relations are what they are and not something else, including our perspectival perception and knowledge of the door. This being the case, we can see that the relational ontology of pragmatic naturalism enables us to retain the realism of ordinary experience even while appreciating the many insights of recent constructivist philosophy. I will return to the issue of constructivism in Chapter 5.

The fact that we are able to approach our experience relationally, and without recourse to reductionism, allows us to suggest a fourth virtue of pragmatic naturalism, which is that it permits us to acknowledge the multiple facets not only of nature in general but also of our experience and creativity, specifically art, music, poetry, literature, theater, etc. Several of the points that have so far been made speak to the advantages of naturalism over other philosophical approaches. This point speaks to the value of pragmatic naturalism over other varieties of naturalism that focus, sometimes exclusively, on the natural sciences. By insisting on the monopoly of science in the production of knowledge, too many naturalists are forced to deny, overlook, or suppress the experience any reasonably sophisticated person has when attending a concert, viewing an exhibition, reading a novel, or watching a play.

The point was made earlier that there is something cognitively significant about the arts, something well understood by those who work in the arts. The Adagio of Schubert's C Major Quintet helps us understand the human condition more deeply; Monet reveals various dimensions of the Parliament Building on the Thames and its relation to different kinds of light; Picasso's *Guernica* speaks volumes about war and its effects on civilian populations; and throughout his vast production Shakespeare brings into focus human strengths and frailties. These are not simply nice sounds, pretty pictures, and clever words, though they sometimes are all those. They are judgments rendered, with the greatest skill and insight in the manipulation of sound, rhythm, form, color, and language, on aspects of nature and our experience. They bring into focus dimensions of nature, traits of our world, that are otherwise either unavailable to us or available less dramatically. None of these insights is produced by science, though in many ways once made by great composers, painters, and writers, science can augment them. But if we insist on science as the sole source of knowledge and understanding we will miss these insights and thereby do violence to our experience. By encouraging a philosophical approach that fully and enthusiastically incorporates the creative arts and humanities as cognitively significant activities, pragmatic naturalism gives us naturalism together with the full riches of our experience. To say that the arts are or can be cognitive raises a host of questions and demands more careful consideration. I shall deal with this issue more thoroughly in Chapter 7.

A fifth virtue of pragmatic naturalism is that it avoids the logical pretensions of much of historical and contemporary philosophy. Despite our reliance on deduction, the fact is that philosophers have *proven* very little to one another, and virtually nothing that lasts very long. If the goal of philosophy is to arrive at deductively demonstrated proofs, then our discipline is a dreadful failure. But that is not the goal of philosophy, or anyway it need not be. The importance of deduction and inference is not to enable us to prove anything, but to provide tools that are useful in arriving at consistent positions that have some acceptable degree of plausibility. Such positions will then stand or fall to the extent that they do the work we want them to do. And they will last only until they cease to do that work, or until the work is no longer needed, or until another position is developed that does it better. Something like what Thomas Kuhn said about developments in the natural sciences is applicable to philosophy: Philosophy changes over time, and from place to place, not because we progressively build on the results of prior proofs, but because new approaches are introduced with enough plausibility that they capture our imaginations, or because old problems about which we once argued are no longer of moment, or because new problems emerge for which older methods are ill adapted.

This does not mean that argument is inappropriate in philosophy. It would be rather self-defeating to argue against argument. The point rather is that there are several different sorts of argumentation, and that it is unnecessary, indeed unwise, to insist that deductive argument is the only or most proper form of reasoning in which philosophers should engage. For one thing, as we all know, there are inductive and abductive argument as well, and for another there is, alongside deductive, inductive, and abductive reasoning, pragmatic reasoning. One can argue, as I do throughout this book, for the plausibility, reasonableness, or even desirability of a particular idea or intellectual commitment. Plausibility, reasonableness, and desirability are of course not the end of the story.

Proposition p may be plausible or reasonable yet turn out on the strength of other evidence to be false; and proposition q may be desirable in some ways but not others, or to a greater or lesser extent in different contexts. So plausibility, reasonableness, and desirability are not simple and clear-cut principles of valuation of an idea or proposition. They are, nonetheless, plausible, reasonable and desirable.

Is this reasoning circular? Well, yes, but so much the worse for deductive validity in this case. Pragmatic naturalism does not pretend to approach the world from an unshakable foundation. Pragmatic reasoning begins wherever it is, assumes whatever the situation compels it to assume, and goes from there. Philosophy does not have the luxury to begin at the beginning, a point we have already made. If intellectual bootstrapping of this sort is circular, then so be it. Dealing with the philosophical dimensions of our experience, and of nature, is not mathematics, and philosophers do our own enterprise a disservice by pretending that it is. The upshot of this attempt to expand philosophical methodology beyond deductive argument is to make the point that one of the values or virtues of pragmatic naturalism is that it is a way of understanding philosophical inquiry such that it retains its rigor and significance without pretending to be something it is not, will never be, and need not even desire to be.[12]

The last of the virtues of pragmatic naturalism to which I would like to point has to do with social—in fact, political—life: Pragmatic naturalism enables us to avoid ideology. As something of a prelude to a much fuller discussion in Chapters 10 and 11, let us consider as an example international relations and foreign affairs. In this area nothing is more dangerous than ideology, by which I mean a tenacious commitment to one's concepts, perspectives, and ideas regardless of evidence and experience. Ideologies, both religious and political, have been responsible for more suffering and evil than can be noted here. Recent experience with the ideologies of fundamentalist Christianity, Judaism, and Islam, as well as that of neoconservative imperial aspirations, offer only the most current examples of the destructiveness of ideology no matter the end to which it is put.

Pragmatic naturalism, by virtue of its experimentalism and fallibilism, is a corrective to ideology, and its intellectual tradition is sufficiently sophisticated and broad in application as to provide a rich mine from which we can draw. In 1916, in *Democracy and Education*, Dewey gave an initial definition of "democracy" that included the necessity of cultivating common interests with members of one's own community and with those across borders. This characteristic of a democratic society gives us a way to reconceive international relations and foreign policy. If a democratic nation should be expected to pursue and cultivate interests with those abroad, then its foreign policy cannot be based solely, as foreign policy traditionally has been, on "national interest," at least not as long as national interest is determined without a serious consideration of the interests of other nations.

The implications of this shift would be enormous, especially by contrast with traditional realist and liberal approaches to international relations, not to mention the recently influential neoconservative variety. For one thing it implies the sacrifice of some degree of national sovereignty. For another, traditional approaches to foreign policy and international relations assume some set of commitments—for example, democracy, free trade, revolution, human rights, power, or religion—in the interests of which a national government would then conduct its policy. One of the shortcomings of all of the traditional approaches is that they are conducive to the development of an ideological commitment to whichever values they endorse. It becomes politically difficult or impossible to compromise, and one's overall values become not virtuous ends but weapons with which to bludgeon other nations. It may be appropriate in other spheres of life for our values to dominate our decisions and actions, but not in foreign policy. The reason is that in foreign policy one is by definition dealing with other nations. If the other nations also hold tenaciously to their fundamental values, foreign policy becomes not diplomacy but simply war by other means.

A pragmatic naturalist foreign policy, by contrast, must by definition derive the interests of its government and nation in collaboration with the nations with which it interacts. In that case it is much less likely that an overarching ideological commitment can short circuit the pursuit of the democratic ends of the cultivation of shared interests. Conditions may or may not be right at any given time for the expansion of the values of democracy, or human rights, or whatever other set of social values one holds most dear, but even if they are not, a foreign policy based on the pursuit of shared interests will encourage rather than impede communication, and that is surely a virtue in both secure and dangerous times.

It is worth pointing out that the relationality of pragmatic naturalism also supports this approach, by contrast especially with the assumptions of traditional realism. The discipline of international relations dates to the creation of the modern nation state, specifically to the Treaty of Westphalia in 1648. Like so much else that was born in the seventeenth century and matured in the eighteenth, conceptions of the modern nation state assumed the atomism that was common to Baroque era physics, mathematics, psychology, economics, epistemology, metaphysics, and music. Nation states were understood as discrete entities, each of which possessed its characteristics and defining traits independently of the others, and which interacted with one another more or less like balls on a billiard table. In such an environment, one that informed Hobbes's "war of all against all" as well as the more tempered versions of such liberals as Locke, the role of diplomacy and foreign policy was to manage the interactions of the balls as they rolled around the table. At worst, one wanted to minimize the damage created by the occasional collision of balls, and at best, one might manage the course around the other balls in such a way as to benefit oneself. At bottom, this is still how contemporary realism sees the world of international relations, and these are the results it hopes for in foreign policy.

If, however, the international world is not Baroque in this sense—that is, if we understand nation states not as "atoms in a void" but as having their characteristics and defining traits constituted by their relations with one another, then the foreign policy picture changes accordingly. It no longer seems natural for nations to interact based on self-defined national interests. If the very traits and nature of nations are formed in their relations with one another, then it only makes sense to conceive of interests as developing within that same relational network. In other words, in an international environment relationally understood, the pursuit of common interests becomes the more obvious course for any nation's foreign policy to take. Pragmatic naturalism, then, has the added value of encouraging, and providing the resources for, a revised approach to international relations and foreign policy that could well contribute to the solution of many of the more difficult problems facing all nations.

In the chapters that follow, many of these points will be explored in greater detail. I begin with a more detailed look at the characteristics of and rationale for a relational, ordinal ontology.

PART TWO

BEING AND KNOWING

Whatever is, in whatever way, is a natural complex.

—Justus Bucher, *Metaphysics of Natural Complexes*

THREE

AN ONTOLOGY OF CONSTITUTIVE RELATIONS

I have made the claim that a central characteristic of pragmatic naturalism is its relational, ordinal ontology, and I have offered the beginnings of a case for its plausibility.[1] It is necessary now to describe in greater detail what an ordinal ontology is and how it can be taken seriously as a general ontological framework.[2]

The General Ontology

The history of philosophy is dominated by the idea that although in experience there is ample evidence of relations among entities, behind or underneath those relations is something nonrelational. For Platonic idealism it is eternal forms, for the many forms of Aristotelianism it is substance, and for modern rationalism and empiricism it is also substance in one or another of its versions. For Berkeley it is mind, and for Descartes it is material or mental substance. With few exceptions, those who were inclined to reject the existence or knowledge of a nonrelational substratum were driven to a more or less serious skepticism. Hume comes to mind as an example of one form of such skepticism. By the twentieth century in British philosophy—for example, in Russell—talk of substance gave way to an assumption of some variety of atomism. And in another strain of thought (I have the later Wittgenstein in mind), the attempt to describe the general character of entities was abandoned altogether, as it has subsequently been in much of contemporary philosophy. Rarely, however, has the possibility been entertained that what exists—that is, anything at all—can be usefully understood as relational in its nature, and without dissolving the identity of individual and distinct complexes into a single whole of internally related entities. On the contrary, it has usually been taken for granted that if there are relations in reality, then there must be absolute or nonrelational entities of some kind that stand in relation. As the early Wittgenstein put it in an implied but striking non sequitur, the simple is implied by the complex, so that the existence of the simple object is a logical necessity. In this he was following Leibniz, who put it rather starkly: If there are complexes there must be simples.[3]

By contrast with this dominant trend in the history of European philosophy, we want to propose that whatever is, in any sense or way at all, is in its nature complex, and complex in such a way that its nature is constituted by the relations among its traits, and that its traits, whatever they are, are themselves relationally constituted complexes. This is a complicated proposition, which we will now unpack. I should point out, as we will see in more detail in the next chapter, that there are indeed precedents for a relational ontology, especially in nineteenth-century German and British idealism. Hegel, Green, and Bradley all argued for a relational understanding of things, but they did so with a conception of internal relations and in a way that drove them to either objective or subjective idealism. A relational ontology, however, need not be idealistic in either of these senses. It is possible, in fact, to argue for a materialist ordinal ontology, though it is admittedly a minority position.[4] In any case, a relational ontology of the pragmatic naturalist variety, the ontology of constitutive relations developed here, is not committed to the relationalism of the idealist sort.

Nor is there any commitment, stated or implied, that relations are either internal or external. That distinction is a common one in the history of philosophy, and the reader who is inclined to think that relations must be either internal or external is being asked to suspend that assumption. We are here presenting an ontology in which relations are to be understood as not internal or external but constitutive. They are not external because they are not extrinsic to the nature, character, or identity, of the complex they constitute. And they are not internal because the complex they constitute is not a closed system of any kind. To distinguish between internal and external relations is to assume that some relations are relevant to an entity's identity and others are not. But the suggestion here is that all relations are relevant, more or less strongly, for the identity of the complex they constitute. This does not render them internal relations, however, because all relations, or in any case relations for the most part, are constitutive of multiple complexes, which is to say that they are located in multiple orders of relations. They are neither internal in any spatial sense, nor are they necessarily parts of a complex. And again, though all relations are relevant in some way to the identity of a complex, they do not thereby create a system. Complexes, we may say, open out to the rest of nature. The distinction between internal and external relations is in fact irrelevant for an ordinal, relational ontology. Such a distinction has its home in a much different ontological picture than is being developed here.

The idea, again, is that everything, by which we mean material objects, ideal entities, histories, ideas, dreams, fictional characters, logical principles, actualities, possibilities, God, human being, and anything else one can mention, point to, or create, whether a human product or not, is constituted by its traits and the relations among them. The details of an ontology of constitutive relations, as we will call this general idea, can be described both positively and negatively, i.e., both by what it means and what it does not mean. We will begin with the negative description.

Any entity of any kind whatsoever, let me use "complex" as the term with the widest possible scope, is constituted by the relations among its traits. It is important to understand that a trait is not to be understood as contained in a complex, nor is a complex to be understood as a container of traits. As we have said, the traditional distinction between internal and external traits is misleading. Traits are neither internal nor external, neither "contained in" a complex nor outside of it. Rather, they are more or less strongly relevant to the nature of the complex. Some traits of a complex are parts of the complex, but not all are. The root system of a plant, for example, is a part of the plant and a constitutive trait. But the chemical characteristics of the plant's physical environment are not parts, yet they are constitutive traits of the plant in that they are directly relevant to the plant's health and its activities. The metaphors of a complex as a container or as a collection of parts must be given up if we are to understand an ontology of constitutive relations.

The tendency to understand a complex as a container or as a bundle of traits has given rise to another common idea that must be rejected. It is often asserted, or at least implicitly accepted, that everything that exists constitutes a whole of some kind, and therefore we can speak of creation as a whole, or the "whole of nature." Sense can be given to such expressions if one is careful. It is possible to speak of the whole of nature, for example, if by that expression one means simply everything that "is" in a distributive sense. But it is senseless to speak of "nature as a whole" if one means a whole system of nature. A relational ontology neither assumes nor implies an overarching, integrated system of complexes, or a sense of nature or reality in which everything is related to everything else. There are complexes, innumerable ones at that, and each is constituted by its relations, but there is no reason to think that each is constitutively related to all the others. There is not, in other words, a whole of nature in the sense of one big complex.[5]

It has also been common in the history of philosophy to regard some things as "more real" than other things: parts more real than a whole, or a whole more real than its parts; traits more real than a complex, or a complex more real than its constituent traits; causes more real than effects, or effects more real than their causes; the physical more real than the ideal, or the ideal more real than the physical; the actual more real than the possible, or the possible more real than the actual; the fictional more or less real than the nonfictional. An ontology of constitutive relations accepts no claim to ontological priority, i.e., that something is more real than something else. On the contrary, a relational ontology assumes an ontological parity among all complexes of every kind. To say that a complex is more or less real than its constituents would in fact be self-contradictory, since all constituent traits are themselves complexes, and all complexes are themselves constituent traits, a point that will be elaborated shortly. All complexes of any kind have whatever traits they have; all complexes have their own set of actualities and possibilities; each is efficacious in some respect or other. There is nothing more to the question of reality than that, and there is no meaning to degrees of reality at all. Complexes can be said to have degrees in other respects—for example, a complex can be more or less relevant or important in some specified way—but it cannot be said to be more or less real. Ontological parity is a fundamental principle of an ontology of constitutive relations.[6] In this respect, an ontology of constitutive relations is metaphysics in a different sense than frequently understood. For many philosophers, to do metaphysics is to determine what is or is not real. Systematic metaphysics as exemplified by a relational ontology is not an attempt to develop a "reality list." It is, rather, an effort to articulate basic concepts and categories in terms of which we understand what exists, whatever that might include. That is the sense of saying, as we have, that "whatever is" is complex and relationally constituted.

This shift in the conception of the proper role of metaphysics allows us to avoid many traditional problems. We do not have to burden ourselves with the question of whether nature is "really" physical or "really spiritual," or "really" both. We do not need to decide whether the products of imagination—for example, fictional characters—"really" exist. We do not need to wonder whether possibilities exist, or whether we should talk not about possibilities but possible worlds. We do not need to concern ourselves over the ontological status of universals, or make a choice between the existence of universals or particulars. There is no need to worry ourselves over the question of whether there are "really" mathematical entities, or logical rules, or natural laws, or moral laws. We face all of these traditional metaphysical alternatives and say simply that they all exist!

This will no doubt bother those who, like Quine, have a taste for a reality less liberally populated. One may of course have whatever aesthetic preferences one wants, but there is also a philosophical responsibility not to allow one's preferences to distort one's understanding of nature and experience. The centuries of agonizing over the questions mentioned in the previous paragraph have left us with countless philosophical proposals that in one way or another fail to do justice to our experience and to the variety and richness of the complexes we encounter in nature. We encounter not only particulars but relations as well; we live enmeshed in both particulars and universals; we have little doubt in ordinary experience whether the products of our imagination are real or not—consider the child's fear of the closet in the dark or an attentive reader's reaction to the trials of an attractive character. The student of mathematics might struggle mightily with irrational numbers, and it is pointless to say that he need not because they are not real. His struggle to understand them is sufficient evidence of their reality.

To say that we simply need not worry about what is or is not real allows us to avoid some traditional philosophical problems, but not all. One of the questions raised by such a tolerant ontology that bothered Quine concerns the problem of individuation. If we allow the reality of the imaginary bald man in the doorway, then where does it end? How many imaginary bald men are there in the doorway, and how could we tell one from the other? This sounds like a thorny problem, but appearances can be deceptive. First, for the most part, doorways do not have any imaginary bald men in them, so for practical purposes it is rarely a problem. It becomes a problem when the philosopher poses it as one. In that case the answer is that there are as many imaginary bald men in the doorway as the philosopher posits, just as there are as many characters in a novel as the writer creates. We do not worry about how they will all fit into that little book, nor do we need to worry about how the imaginary men will fit into the doorway. And we may individuate them as we please. The philosopher who posits them is free to determine what counts as a single imaginary man, and what distinguishes one from the other. The order of relations in which those imaginary men exist, in which they prevail, has whatever traits it has, and in this case because it is a product of the philosopher's imagination he or she is free to determine those traits. This is not to say that an ordinal ontology does not need to describe categories in terms of which identity may be understood, and I will do so below.

I also need to clarify a number of other characteristics of a relational ontology so that it may do justice to the complexity of nature and our experience when we attempt to appeal to it in order to understand something. At this point it is important to see that there is no effort to rule anything out of existence. Thus, the point of Randall's remark is that we need to understand not *whether* something exists but *how* it exists. The plausibility of a general, relational ontology may be judged not by whether it is tolerant, or whether it suits this or that aesthetic taste in its understanding of reality, but whether it helps us to come to more satisfactory terms with nature and our experience.

For a relational ontology, then, we will understand the phrase "whatever is is complex" as descriptive of every possible complex of every possible kind, we will avoid thinking of a complex as a container of traits, we will not assume that there is an overarching complex or system of reality, and we will reject the idea that some complexes are more real than others. These points now allow us to develop our definition of a relational ontology more positively. To do so we will introduce the concept of an "order," by which we mean a sphere of relatedness.

First, it is important to realize that every complex is an order of traits, which means that every complex *is* the specific web of relations of its constitutive traits. Every complex has innumerable traits, some more relevant to its character, some less. It is therefore difficult, perhaps even impossible, to provide an exhaustive list of a complex's traits. But even a short, representative list can help to illustrate the sense in which a complex is an order of traits. A specific tree, to use the same example as earlier, possesses physical traits at the subatomic, atomic, chemical, and biological levels. Among its traits are its physical parts, but also among its traits are its chemical interactions with its environment. Also among its traits is its place in its broader physical context—for example, whether it stands alone in a field, is part of a stand of trees, or is part of a forest. Its phylogenetic characterization is among its traits, as are the uses to which it might be put, whether by insects, birds, animals, or human beings. All of these traits, and many others, converge or intersect to form the complex that is this specific tree. The tree is an order of traits, the sphere of relatedness of its many and varied constitutive traits. The same can be said of any other complex and any other kind of complex, whether it be a logical principle, a fictional character, a piece of technology, or a human being.

If a complex is an order of traits, it is also always itself a trait of some more comprehensive complex, which is to say that a complex is always located in some more comprehensive order or orders. A tree is a constitutive trait of the soil in which it grows, for example. Insofar as it influences the chemical makeup of the air in its environment, it is a trait of its atmosphere. Perhaps it is a part of a forest, in which case it is a constitutive trait of the forest. Or perhaps it is an object of veneration, in which case it enters into relations with human beings in a certain way and becomes a constitutive trait of a community's religious practices. It is an individual member of some class of tree, and therefore a constitutive trait of that class, though any given tree is likely to be a minimally relevant trait of the class as a whole. In the case of the tree, it is a complex located in the orders of its atmosphere, a forest, a religious practice, and a species, and this short list is merely a representative but small sampling of the numerous ordinal locations of the complex.

The example of the tree is meant to be generalizable to any and all complexes. Every complex, then, is an order of traits, and is itself an ordinally located trait. It is obvious enough how a complex is an order of traits, but it may be less obvious why a complex must be located in at least one order. The reason is that the ordinal locations of a complex are among the traits that provide its character, its nature. Without ordinal location a complex has no contour, no overall character, which is to say that it is not a complex at all. This is an extremely important point. First, it indicates why, as we said earlier, there can be no such thing as an overarching complex that is reality or nature. Such a complex would not be ordinally located, and therefore would not be a complex. An unlocated complex is a contradiction in terms. This point is relevant for our general concept and understanding of nature, and it will be particularly relevant for our understanding of God in an ordinal context, as we will see in a later chapter. It also indicates the critical point that this is not a theory of internal relations. Second, the ordinal locations of a complex, what we can call its integrities, are what provide the complex's identity as just the complex that it is. One of the persistent myths in philosophy of this kind, in systematic metaphysics, is that identity requires an absolute entity of some kind. The suspicion seems to be that if we allow an entity to be understood as the interrelations of its traits then it becomes difficult or impossible to ascribe an identity to it. But this suspicion is unwarranted. A complex must be located in orders of relations, and each ordinal location provides an integrity of the complex. The totality of a complex's ordinal locations is its contour. Such an understanding allows us to posit the complex's identity in the relation between its contour and any of its integrities. To put it in a less technical way, the identity of any complex is the relation that prevails, for the most part through time, between the totality of its ordinal locations and any one or subset of them. The continuity of a complex through time is thereby expressed, and in such a way that allows the recognition of an ongoing identity through modifications in a complex's ordinal locations. A complex can alter its traits while maintaining its identity, which answers pretty well to our intuitions about identity through time.

Two other points require our consideration as we develop the idea of a relational ontology. The first concerns the meaning of the concept of existence and the second has to do with stability and change. Existence has always been a tricky business, and it is trickier still for an ordinal, relational ontology. Attempts to define existence seem to raise more problems than they solve. We might say that "to exist" means to be real, but that does not help much because we then have to define what it means to be real. Do we mean real as opposed to imaginary or fictional? What then to do about the "reality" of the imaginary or the fictional? When a child imagines a monster in the closet we can safely say that there is no real monster in the closet, but the *imaginary* monster is still real enough to be the cause of the child's fear and inability to sleep. It is not a material complex in the material closet, but it is a complex in the imagination and is located in the closet as imagined. We are in a similar situation with respect to the fictional. We may want to say that Hamlet does not exist in the sense that in medieval Denmark there was no such prince, but the fictional Hamlet surely exists insofar as it drives theatrical productions and makes or breaks careers. If the imaginary and the fictional exist in some plausible sense, then existence does not simply mean real, if real is to be contrasted with the imaginary or the fictional.

We might then try something else: for example, that to exist is to be actual, as opposed to merely possible. If this means, as it seems to, that actualities exist but possibilities do not, then we have a similar problem as we do when we define "existence" in terms of "reality." What do we make of the obvious efficacy that possibilities have? As I write I am creating an actual manuscript, for which there is a possibility that it will be published. However, it is not the actual manuscript that drives me to spend this particular Sunday afternoon in front of the computer; rather, it is the possible book, i.e., the possibility that the manuscript will be published and thereby transformed into a book. The possibility is the cause of my action, or at least one of its causes, and therefore exists surely enough, unless of course I am delusional about the intellectual value of the manuscript, in which case the delusion exists and is a real cause. Either way, we define existence in terms merely of actuality only at the expense of the obviously real possibilities, and that will not do.

These difficulties are important because they have everything to do with the extent to which philosophical discussions of existence intersect with the meaning we intend our existential propositions to have. It is perfectly reasonable to assert right now that there is a possibility that this manuscript will be published, however strong or remote that possibility may be. Any definition of existence that precludes the existence of this possibility flies in the face of our experience and perfectly normal assertions. Things become somewhat more puzzling with respect to negative existential propositions. It is surely sensible for parents to say that there is no monster in the closet, and they may even open the door and point to the monsterless closet as evidence. Nonetheless, there is a monster: In fact, there is the very monster alleged to be in the closet. To deny it, as we have said, is to ignore the child's experience. But this is not as puzzling as it may appear to be. The reason is that existence is a matter of ordinal location. The monster exists, or more precisely it prevails, in the order of imaginary entities, and in that and other possible orders it may have any number of describable and definable properties. What is not true of the monster is that it prevails in the order of materially delineated spaces in the room, i.e., it is not in the closet. To exist is to prevail in an order or orders, whatever they may be.

This becomes particularly important in some areas of philosophical analysis—for example, philosophical theology. A pragmatic naturalist, or this one at any rate, will claim that the God of monotheism does not exist. In a later chapter we will see how this particular negative existential proposition is handled ordinally, and what ramifications it may have for a naturalist understanding of religion. But to understand existence in terms of ordinal location at the same time means that God in some relevant sense does exist, a point we will also explore later. At a more trivial, though nonetheless instructive, level, it also means that Santa Claus exists, in case anyone was concerned about this. This is not to say that a jolly old fat man in a red suit who lives at the geographic North Pole prevails in the order of space/time, but it is to say that the very same jolly old fat man in the red suit who lives at the geographic North Pole prevails in other orders. I invite you to watch again *The Miracle on 34th Street* with this point in mind. Santa Claus prevails, as the film demonstrates, not only in the order of figures in the Macy's Parade, but also in romantic, legal, and political orders. The film is in fact a remarkably clever piece of philosophy when looked at in this way. In any case, the point is that both positive and negative existential statements are only meaningful, or we should say they are only fully meaningful, when understood ordinally, which is to say when existence itself is understood ordinally.

Prevalence, then, is a crucial category for a relational ontology. The correlative category is alescence, and it is in terms of the concept of alescence that we can make sense of change. For some ontological points of view—for example, process metaphysics—change is a fundamental category. For a relational, ordinal ontology it is not. Change, rather, is often an instance of alescence, though even that is not necessarily the case. We may define prevalence as the maintenance of traits with respect to a specific ordinal location, which as we have said is what it means to exist. Alescence, by contrast, may be defined as the alteration of traits with respect to a specific ordinal location. Thus, alescence, though the correlative category to prevalence, does not mean nonexistence; it means simply that there is an alteration of traits. But why is this not merely another way of saying change? The reason is that stability and change are not sufficiently general. Consider a complex in which change is more or less constant: an ocean and the persistently moving water that constitutes it. Change, at least with respect to the position of the water molecules, is a ubiquitous trait of an ocean. To that extent change is a prevailing characteristic of the complex that is an ocean. If that trait were to alter—for example, if the tides were to stop—then the alteration of traits, the alescence, would be from change to stability. Stability would be the alescent trait of the complex. Alescence is a concept of greater generality and scope than change, and it is introduced precisely to allow us to make categorial sense of just this sort of phenomenon. One of the implications of this point is that metaphysical systems that maintain change as a fundamental category—such as Whitehead's or even Dewey's—are ontologically inadequate in that they fail to achieve a categorial articulation of sufficient generality. An ordinal ontology, an ontology of constitutive relations, is not a process ontology or an ontology of change. The critical, more fundamental concept is not process or change, but relationality, or ordinal complexity, which itself is characterized by prevalence and alescence.

These concepts and categories taken together help us to avoid a good deal of unnecessary mystification concerning complexes. The identity and character of a complex is a function of its constitutive traits, including its ordinal locations. There is no mysterious ground of being required to understand this, nor is any source of being outside nature necessary. Complexes are what they are, they have the nature they have, by virtue of the relations among their many constituent traits, which are their ordinal locations. With respect to any complex, some of those traits and ordinal locations may involve human beings, but they also may not. In either case, the character of any complex is a matter of what we have called natural definition. A complex is what it is by virtue of the relations among the traits that constitute it. To better understand what a relational ontology looks like, it is worthwhile to consider a single illustration in more detail. We will look more closely at what it means to understand a human being relationally.

Relational Human Being

In Anglo-American philosophy, discussions of human being have dealt more than anything with the so-called "mind-body problem." This is a constellation of questions: Is a person a body and a mind? Are a mind and a body related? If so, how? Can a person be understood solely as a body? Can mental characteristics be reduced to physical characteristics? Is a person "essentially" a body or "essentially" a mind? How can a mind influence a body, or a body influence a mind? If a person is merely a complex body, how is intentionality possible? What is the relation between the processes of the brain and neurological system on the one hand and mental processes on the other? How can mind be studied? How does consciousness arise from neurophysiologic processes? Can a person be genuinely creative, or is a person's behavior simply a complex response to physical causes or behavioral programming? Are minds to be understood by analogy with computers? Some of these are questions that have vexed philosophers for a long time, but in their standard formulation they are misguided and unnecessary.

First, it is critical to realize that there is no philosophical necessity to rule out any of these traits of human being, and certainly not as a point of departure. The question for a metaphysics of human being is not whether persons are "really" this or that, minds or bodies, hardware, software, or "wetware." The question is rather, given what we have experiential or rational reason to ascribe to human beings—for example, material, mental, spiritual, and social properties—how do we best understand them and the relations among them? To take this ontologically tolerant view does not in itself imply anything about how we are to understand them. For example, we can certainly acknowledge that human beings historically and in individual experience have a spiritual dimension. Nothing, however, follows automatically from that observation about the content or meaning of the spiritual dimension. It does not necessarily follow that there is a creator God of the sort that the monotheistic religions posit, at least not with all the traits or ordinal locations that are typically ascribed to it. The character and meaning of the spiritual dimension awaits philosophical analysis, which will be taken up in a later chapter. The point now is simply that we can and should recognize as constitutive traits of human being whatever we encounter, which is to say, whatever traits prevail. Precisely how those traits prevail, and what they imply, are questions that naturally follow such recognition.

Second, from the perspective of a relational ontology there is no need to begin by assuming that there is an essential set of traits that *is* a person. There is no need to assume that a person *really* is a body, or *really* is a mind, for example. A person is the complex set of traits that constitute it, and of course the specific relations among those traits. One could offer at least a partial list of those traits, though that in itself would not be philosophically illuminating. Certainly, a person has physical and mental traits. Our bodies have physical characteristics and react to physical stimuli. We think, speculate, decide, and perform a range of other mental activities. We also have emotional traits and social traits. We have spiritual traits, religious aspirations, and erotic impulses. We are to some extent political animals, as Aristotle had it, and we have economic motivations. We have ethical as well as aesthetic dimensions. A person is all of these things, to some degree or other.

The traditional approaches to understanding human nature, especially through the philosophical mind-body problem, have tended to try to assert some priority among these and other human traits. The assumption seems to have been that there must be something, some essential trait or subset of traits, that makes something a person, and that it is the philosopher's task to determine what that is. However, once we give up this assumption, and instead say that a person, like any other complex of nature, is constituted by the relations among its traits, many of the problems and questions of traditional philosophies of human nature, and certainly of the mind-body problem, become moot.

Among the most damaging, indeed perverse, aspects of traditional Anglo-American philosophy of mind and philosophy of human being has been its tendency toward reductionism. Philosophers have relentlessly attempted to show that what seem to be rather obvious characteristics of human being are in fact illusory. Along these lines it has been argued that what appear to be mental characteristics can in fact be understood in purely physical terms, or that what appear to be volitions are in fact merely effects of physical or mental causes, or that what appear to be ethical judgments or commitments are in fact nothing other than the results of fairly complex behavioral conditioning. The tendency to reductionism, however, is a correlate of the inclination at the level of systematic metaphysics to insist on ontological priority. But a relational ontology suggests that there is no good reason—in fact, it is meaningless—to hold that some complexes or kinds of complexes are more real than others. Similarly, there is no good reason to assert or insist that some identifiable traits of human being are "really" something else: The mental really is the physical, or the ethical really the behavioral, or the behavioral really the neurochemical. A relational ontology is a tolerant ontology, thus differing radically from Quine's "taste for desert landscapes," and it is no less tolerant with respect to human nature. The reductionist tendencies of mind-body philosophers are unnecessary and unfounded. We are fully justified in accepting as relevant any and all traits of a person that can be observed, described, or articulated. In fact, we are able to appreciate more fully the range of traits that constitute a person, and by implication the complexity and richness of human life, when we avoid reductionism and accept at more or less face value the fact that a person, like any other complex, is constituted by numerous traits of various kinds in a range of relations with one another. An ontology of constitutive relations provides the conceptual categories through which such a view of human being is plausible, intelligible, and fruitful.

One of the reasons philosophers have wanted to locate some kind of essential character or trait of human beings, whether it be mental, physical, or spiritual, is the prevalent assumption that identity requires an absolute, i.e., nonrelational, ground, or to use older metaphysical language, a substance of some kind. Without some sort of unique, even atomistic, entity—for example, mind or spirit—many philosophers have thought there would be no way to ascribe identity, no way to individuate a particular person. Materialists, at least of the reductionist variety, have been content to ascribe identity to a complex physical entity, a body that despite its changes over time can nonetheless serve to individuate persons. This materialist approach to identity is interesting, in part because it entertains, though in too narrow a way, an important point: Identity does not require an absolute entity. The materialist's mistake has been to combine this insight with its reductionism, whereby he insists that rather obvious human characteristics such as mental activity must really be something physical. When shorn of this unjustified and stultifying approach, however, a more sensible understanding of identity emerges. Just as a complex human body can be individuated despite constant change over time, and given the relational nature of material traits, it is equally possible to ascribe identity to human individuals when their more varied traits are introduced. In other words, personal identity in all its richness can be posited in the ongoing relation between the ordinal locations of its traits, i.e., its integrities, and its gross integrity or contour. The many traits of an individual, indeed an individual's life as a whole, prevail in numerous orders of relations. Like any other complex, the specific sets of relations of a given human individual are its identity, and allow for its individuation. No absolute entity is necessary, nor is it useful or necessary to analyze away its complexity.

So far, we have suggested the plausibility of understanding a person in terms of the categories of a general relational ontology. But how, we may ask, does this help us to understand what is distinctive about human beings? What, at the most general level, is uniquely characteristic of human complexes as opposed to other kinds? Much can be said about this, and much has already been said.[7] For example, all temporal complexes prevail through some period of time, but individual human lives do not merely persist through time; rather, they have a trajectory. Persons do not simply act and react, nor do they simply undergo; humans experience and they judge. Complexes that merely act and react, or merely undergo, accumulate events, all of which are more or less relevant to their overall character or identity. For persons, by contrast, experience is cumulative; it confers on a person's life a direction, a trajectory. The trajectory of a person's life is not necessarily unidirectional, nor, presumably, is it preordained, or even conscious. It is rather the cumulative experience of that which a person undergoes and that which a person does.

Furthermore, persons act in ways that are, as far as we can tell, different from the ways in which most other advanced animals act. Specifically, they judge, which is to say, they select. There are, it would appear, other very advanced animals that also select, but persons do so in far more sophisticated ways. Human judgment, whether it be assertive, exhibitive, or active, manipulates other complexes of the world, other elements of experience, for reasons and to achieve specific ends. I will explore this conception of "judgment" in much more detail in Chapter 7 in connection with the issue of the cognitive character of art. It is enough at this point to say that in many cases the ends of judgments, and the means of judgment through which those ends are achieved, are unique to persons. Persons can manipulate complexes in order to solve mundane problems, but then so too can many other animals. Some can even learn fairly complex forms of problem solving and communication. Other animals, however, do not render judgments in order, for example, to understand or to express. And other animals do not assert in the sophisticated ways humans can—for example, in science and philosophy—nor do they exhibit the depth that persons do through literature, painting, dance, or music. Experience and judgment are distinctive, cumulative, and constitutive traits of the person.[8] And persons understood relationally are in full possession of all the traits they exhibit or exercise. Nothing needs to be explained away.

Ordinality Across the Board

The discussion of human being relationally understood is meant to illustrate both the possibility and the advantages of approaching any aspect of nature relationally. For our purposes it is merely an example, though if we were involved in a study of, for example, philosophical anthropology it would be a critical point. Ordinality is not restricted to an understanding of human being, but applies to any and all of the indefinitely numerous and varied complexes of nature. Because "whatever is" is a relationally constituted complex, the categories of an ordinal ontology are applicable to the philosophical study of any aspect of nature that warrants philosophical inquiry. Whether it be logic, poetry, politics, education, religion, history, biology, or any other dimension of nature or of our experience, a relational ontology provides the intellectual categories in terms of which it can be understood profitably. And in the process we can avoid many of the conundrums and implausibilities that have characterized the more traditional attempts to understand nature nonrelationally.

For example, Margaret Thatcher once famously said that there is no such thing as society.[9] In so doing she may have been politically clever, but she was ontologically mistaken. Only on the prerelational assumption that complexes are reducible to discrete elements can it be possible to say something as obviously absurd as that there is no such thing as society. Physicists, operating with the same prerelational assumption, have been known to say similarly absurd things about material objects—for example, that there are no solid objects, that a table is nothing but tiny particles moving at great speeds in what is primarily empty space or fields. A table is obviously many other things than that: It is the object that holds up our dinner plates; it is the object around which the family sits and talks, or not; it is an aesthetic object; in repressive political circumstances it is the object that provides people the only opportunity they may have to express themselves openly with their friends, family, colleagues, and so on. None of these are any less real traits of the table in that they are among its ordinal locations, or any less real traits than the subatomic characteristics of the materials that constitute it.

Much the same can be said about the society that Mrs. Thatcher had such trouble recognizing. This area is particularly important because so much of public policy turns on it. I will give much more detailed illustrations of this point in later chapters when we consider democracy, international relations, and other issues of social import. When Prime Minister Thatcher made her notable remark, she was saying something that should have been familiar to anyone who was aware of the traditional ontology that underlay her point: The only things that "really" exist, so this tradition goes, are ultimately discrete particulars. Whether they are atoms in the void, or individual economic actors, or individual nation states, or individual citizens, they are the realities, and anything they constitute by their proximity to or relations with one another are either of secondary importance, or "less real," or nonexistent. We have suggested, and will see again later in more detail, the distortions such a concept has wrought in our understanding of democracy and international relations.

Mrs. Thatcher was concerned in her remarks with pressing issues of public policy, and she meant to make the point that one ought not to undertake policy with an eye on "social needs" because the only thing that matters is individuals. It is individuals who strive, or not, socially and economically; who fail or succeed; who possess this or that right; who invest or not. "Society" is at most, she might have said, the cumulative result of these behaviors of individuals, and therefore individuals and not society are the proper objects of public policy. The good of society is not the issue because society does not exist as far as policy is concerned. Individuals exist, and good policy is directed at them. This is a case of the assumptions of neoclassical economics applied to policy, and neoclassical economics was itself the result of the assumptions of classical physics applied to the economic realm. Discrete individuals are the realities; their relations and the complexes those relations generate are of little to no value. Society does not exist.

I would not want to claim that one is necessarily pushed this far simply by accepting traditional, nonrelational ontology, but the tendency is there because the ontological priority and reductionism of traditional ontology point this way when applied to social issues. This is a problem to which a relational ontology is a corrective. There is a sense in which we are well aware of the fact that the inferences drawn from traditional, atomistic ontology, like Mrs. Thatcher's, are ridiculous. That is the reason her claim was remarkable. We knew what she meant, and we knew that it was silly, but without an alternative set of basic conceptual categories we had little alternative but to stamp our feet and point to the social realities all around us. But if the claim is that those realities are in some sense illusory, which is what saying that there is no such thing as society comes down to, then no amount of pointing is sufficient to carry the day. We need, rather, conceptual categories that allow us to demonstrate that complexes are no less real than their constituents, and constituents no less real than the complexes they constitute. This is the reason that an ontology of constitutive relations is a corrective, not only for technical metaphysical analysis but also for the full range of issues that are susceptible to philosophic inquiry.

Examples like this can be multiplied many times. In fact, the several issues that we will examine throughout this volume are themselves illustrations of the ways a relational ontology can help us come to terms with important dimensions of nature and experience, and do so without needing to explain things away or distort them. We will look at God and religious faith, at art and its cognitive dimension, at democracy, education, international relations and foreign policy, and at certain larger questions that we can call "moral" considerations, specifically cosmopolitanism and humanism. We will see that with a relational understanding of nature we are able to make sense of these dimensions of experience in ways that enable both comprehension and fruitful implications and consequences. That is not to say that every aspect of nature or experience can be understood in precisely the way people generally understand them. That would be impossible if for no other reason than people understand them differently. And in what is perhaps the most difficult issue of all for a pragmatic naturalist—God and religious faith—we run up against a case where the traditional understanding of a concept is inconsistent with the assumptions of a naturalist understanding of nature. What we are able to do is make sense of the phenomena in question, including God and religious faith, in meaningful ways without being forced to explain them away. One suspects that the reason this is possible, and the reason it is possible in so many cases, is that nature may, after all, be relational.

There no doubt remain obstacles to the acceptance of a relational ontology, at least for many philosophers. Perhaps it is simply a matter of unfamiliarity, but there may be more serious reasons as well. After all, there are reasons that the traditional understanding of the nature of things has had such a powerful and long lasting hold on our philosophical imagination. One of the reasons has been its success, and on our own pragmatic grounds that is not a reason we can take lightly. The proper response to the historical success of the nonrelational, atomistic understanding of nature is that such success has indeed been a very good reason to continue to employ it, but it is no longer successful, as I trust several of the following chapters will help to illustrate. But beyond the question of success, there are other technical points that need to be explored further. We have said that among the virtues of pragmatic naturalism is that it allows us to maintain both a defensible sense of objectivity in our understanding of nature and a satisfactory understanding of the constructivist dimension of experience and inquiry. We have also said that particulars are to be understood relationally. The following two chapters explore these dimensions in more detail. I turn first to one of the more central concerns of a relational ontology, i.e., whether there is sufficient reason to understand particulars to be relational.

FOUR

PARTICULARS AND RELATIONS

It is widely accepted that for the most part particulars do indeed enter into genuine relations, but that the particulars themselves are not relational.[1] I will call this the standard view, and it is one of the critical assumptions, perhaps the most critical, that underlies traditional, nonrelational ontology. This is a long-standing point of view, one that by now has the appearance of the commonsensical for many philosophers. One can find oneself, and I speak from more than one experience, the subject of barely polite derision when one suggests otherwise. As is the way with things of common sense, we so take them for granted that we rarely bother to reflect on them, or to wonder if after all they are so sensible. Common sense notwithstanding, I propose here to reflect on the standard view of particulars, and to demonstrate that (1) it is not necessary to treat particulars as nonrelational, and (2) that we would do better to replace the standard view with a relational account of the sort that we have been developing to this point. In doing this we will need to examine the two closely related issues of the nature of particulars and the nature of relations. We might best begin by considering some of the relevant history.

Historical Background

The standard view is not only widely accepted now, but it also has a long and well-connected history. It appears in Aristotle's *ousia*, as that which can be the subject of predication. It is part and parcel of the substance ontology of modernism in most of its forms: rationalist, empiricist, monadistic, or materialist. In twentieth-century English-speaking philosophy it found its ground in some of the early writings of Russell, and more recently it appears clearly and forcefully in D. M. Armstrong. By accepting the standard, what I will call "atomistic," view of particulars, Armstrong and Russell before him maintain a certain continuity with an earlier tradition represented in part by Hume, Locke, and others. Of course, as I have already suggested, nearly everyone else for one hundred years before and after Locke and Hume, with the exception of Hegel and his followers, took a similar approach to the nature of particulars, but the empiricists are especially important for twentieth-century philosophy in this respect because in Russell's day, for example, to defend the standard view of particulars was to take one's stand against idealism. In the later nineteenth century the sharpest critics of Hume and of the empiricist tradition were the British idealists, in particular F. H. Bradley and before him T. H. Green. One way to answer the idealists was to defend the sort of traditional empiricism against which they were arguing.

Green and Bradley had both argued that particulars are not the independent substances that empiricism, and even seventeenth- and eighteenth-century rationalism, took them to be. They argued, by contrast, that particulars are inherently relational, which is to say that relations cannot be avoided in any coherent account of what it is to be a particular. In this respect they were continuing a line of thought that had its modern origins in Hegel. While the most distinctive trait of Hegel's dialectical understanding of reality may be his category of contradiction, to understand phenomena as essentially contradictory requires the prior rejection of ontological simples and substance. Hegel substitutes for these categories an understanding of phenomena as in essential relation to one another. In the early chapters of the *Logic*, in which Hegel assesses prior philosophical systems and approaches, the view that phenomena are constitutively related is already apparent. In the "First Attitude of Thought to Objectivity," Hegel criticizes traditional metaphysics for positing a rigid contrast between possible characteristics such as finite and infinite, or simple and complex. He says of metaphysics that it "turned into Dogmatism," which "consists in the tenacity which draws a hard and fast line between certain terms and others opposite to them."[2]

In the central chapters of the *Logic* Hegel is more explicit. In "The Doctrine of Being," a determinate being is defined by its limit, and its limit is another determinate being: "The limit, as the negation of something, is not an abstract nothing, but a nothing which *is*—what we call an 'other.' Given something, up starts an other to us: We know that there is not something only, but an other as well." Hegel criticizes the traditional view for not understanding this essential connection among things. "To materialized conception," he says, "existence stands in the character of something solely positive, and quietly abiding within its own limits."[3] In all these remarks Hegel is rejecting the atomistic ontology of modernism in favor of the view that a thing is "essentially relative to another." He is even more clear about it in "The Doctrine of Essence." In a discussion of identity and difference, he cautions against too abstract a concept of identity, suggesting that identity contains "essentially the characteristic of Difference." Of identity and difference, he says, "the one is made visible in the other, and is only insofar as that other is."[4] Of existence in general Hegel says that "the existent therefore includes relativity, and has on its own part its multiple interconnections with other existents."[5] And, finally, Hegel is careful to point out that this complexity does not mean simply a collection or aggregate of absolutely distinct elements: "The external and mechanical relation of whole and parts is not sufficient for us."[6] The relation of whole and parts, presumably, is in fact not mechanical but relational and constitutive.

With Hegel in the background it is no surprise that Green and then Bradley would press the case against the standard view and in favor of a relational approach to particulars. Green's analysis is in his long Introduction to the 1886 edition of Hume's *Treatise*, which he edited with T. H. Grose. There Green, appealing explicitly to Berkeley, systematically develops a sustained criticism of Locke's treatment of particulars as essentially independent and of the role that view plays in Hume. Speaking of Locke, for example, Green says that "a consistent sensationalism must be speechless" because to judge at all is to bring an object into relation. The "'really existent' . . . ceases to be what in its mere singleness it is, and thus loses its reality, overlaid by the 'invention of the understanding.'"[7] Later in the essay Green makes it clear that objects cannot be consistently regarded as essentially independent or atomistic, since "The 'finding of resemblances and differences among objects that often occur to us' implies that each object is distinguished as one and abiding from manifold occurrences, in the way of related feelings, in which it is presented to us, and that these accordingly are regarded as representing permanent relations or qualities of the object."[8] For Green, the objects of sensation are constituted by their relations to consciousness, to judging minds, so that his rejection of the standard view is tied inherently to a Berkeleyan idealism.

Bradley's approach is different. Like Green and Hegel, he argued that it is impossible consistently to regard objects, or particulars, to be absolutely independent. "Related terms, if made absolute," he says, "are forthwith destroyed."[9] Contrary to Locke, Hume, and others who held the standard view, Bradley argued that relations must genuinely influence the nature of that which is related. The traditional Lockean account tried to interpret relations as properties of the objects or terms in relation. These properties, however, were understood as distinct properties of each term, so that if *a* and *b* are related by resemblance, for example, each possesses a distinct property. On this view, if *a* were to be eliminated, that change would not alter the character of *b*. This is the standard view rejected by Bradley and the others. They all held that a genuine relation must affect the terms of the relation. If *a* and *b* are related, then each has the property of being related *to the other*, so that if one were to be eliminated, the other is necessarily affected. Bradley develops this view by arguing that a relation is made possible because the related terms constitute a whole or unity. If a relation "is to be real," he says, "it must be so at the expense of the terms, or, at least, must be something which appears in them or to which they belong. A relation between *A* and *B* implies really a substantial foundation within them. This foundation . . . is the identity *X* which holds these differences together . . . —everywhere there must be a whole embracing what is related, or there would be no differences and no relation."[10] Bradley makes all particulars relational, then, but he does so only by dissolving them into a greater, and ultimately Absolute, unity. While Green's relational particulars imply a subjective idealism, Bradley's inference is to an objective idealism. Bradley's especially is a theory of internal relations, wherein entities constituted by their relations are ultimately subsumed into an all-embracing whole.

A dissatisfaction with both forms of idealism was partly responsible for the attempt to rescue the standard view, or something like it, from the relational perspectives of Bradley and Green. Before continuing that line of development, which will bring us to Russell's account of both particulars and relations, we should mention that pragmatic naturalism in twentieth-century American philosophy, which as is clear by now we take to be the preferable alternative to both idealism and empiricism, has generally gone unnoticed and therefore unappreciated in these discussions. The relational analyses of Royce, Dewey, Whitehead, and most recently Justus Buchler—but especially Dewey's—also have remote Hegelian backgrounds, up to a point anyway, but as we have been pointing out, they differ considerably from the idealists. By making the notion of an indeterminate situation central to both his ontology and epistemology, Dewey reflects the Hegelian idea of the essential interrelatedness of things, but he is able to do so without appeal either to the overt subjective idealism of Green or the absolutism of Bradley, or to the doctrine of internal relations and the corresponding view that reality is one big system or whole. Whitehead too, in his account of actual entities, identifies them as necessarily relational by the nature of the process that generates them, not by connection to consciousness or subsumption into an Absolute. Whitehead, like his idealist forebears, could not do without some sort of absolute entities, and he found them in eternal objects, the universal traits eternally available for ingression. We may say something similar about Royce. Like the Hegel of the *Phenomenology*, Royce was interested in the relation of individuals with one another, and like Hegel he gives a relational account of individuals. But also like Hegel, Whitehead, and the other idealists, Royce ultimately subsumes relational particulars in an absolute, in his case more along the lines of Bradley and Hegel than Whitehead or Green. It was Buchler, building on Randall and to some extent Dewey, who developed a more consistent relational ontology without recourse to any absolute, subjective or objective, or to the "block universe" characteristic of the theory of internal relations. We are thus able to develop the ontology of constitutive relations in the pragmatic naturalist tradition as the alternative to the idealists' treatment of relations and to the empiricists' rejection of relational particulars.

The Contemporary Problem

What I have been calling the standard view emerges in the twentieth century in large part from Russell. His response to the idealists was in one respect a return to the empiricist tradition of Locke in that he too asserted the independent, nonrelational, essentially atomistic nature of particulars. He did not, however, accept the traditional account of relations, since he accepted the idealist point that relations cannot be understood simply as distinct properties of the terms related. Part of the strength of Russell's approach, that is to say part of its appeal, derives from something of a consensus that the idealists cannot be right about the Self as the source of relations (Green), or the Absolute as the context of all relations (Bradley). If Russell or anyone else can offer a workable alternative, then something significant is thereby accomplished. Russell did so by rejecting a relational account of particulars, but a fundamental question for us is whether a relational ontology necessarily assumes or implies the undesired idealist conceptions. Or, can there be a compelling relational ontology that avoids Green's transcendent Self and Bradley's Absolute, as well as Russell's atomism?

This is the contemporary problem with respect to the possibility of a relational ontology. But is it really a problem? Why ask the question in the first place, one might wonder? The answer is that Russell's treatment of relations and his atomistic account of particulars is not an adequate alternative to Green and Bradley. Neither is the more contemporary version of a nonrelational ontology developed by D. M. Armstrong. The reasons neither are adequate will suggest the value of a nonidealist, relational conception of particulars in which relations are directly constitutive of particulars and without creating the problems associated with the idealist account of internal relations. I will proceed by first considering some aspects of Russell's analysis, then Armstrong's. At that point we will be in a position to point to a solution to the problem in the form of an ordinal ontology and some of its implications and ramifications.

One of the places Russell's early account of relations appears is in the *Principles of Mathematics*. The ontology of relations, which Russell articulates there, has been described as having "become the commonplace," such that "it does not therefore require much exposition."[11] Of course whether it is sufficiently adequate to be generally acceptable is part of what is at issue here, but a brief exposition is in any case in order.

Russell's analysis in the *Principles of Mathematics* is that the monadistic view, which he identifies explicitly with Leibniz, cannot be right because by treating relations as distinct properties of each of the related terms, the relation itself is overlooked. The relation "*A* is greater than *B*" cannot be read as "*A*(is greater than)" and "*B*(is greater than)," because that does not express the relation. Thus, if we read "*A* is greater than *B*" as in some way a predicate of *A*, it would have to be something like "*A*(is greater than *B*)." In that case, however, the predicate necessarily contains some relation to *B*, so *A* and *B* cannot be monadistically separated.[12] The monistic view—which is to say, Bradley's—cannot account for asymmetrical relations either, since it reads "*A* is greater than *B*" such that a predicate, in this case "greater than," holds of a whole or unity "*AB*." Russell argues that this would also be true of the relation "*B* is greater than *A*," so that the monistic view cannot distinguish the two.[13]

His alternative, and this is what has been described as commonplace, is that a relation between *A* and *B* is to be understood as a relation of *A* to some property and a relation of *B* to the same property.[14] A more precise formulation of this is needed, but Russell here seems to be allowing for an understanding of relations in terms of universals, in the sense that to say of two particulars that they stand in a certain relation is to say that they both possess some third term, a property, or universal. We should point out here, too, that this analysis is consistent with remarks Russell makes in *The Problems of Philosophy*. There, also in the context of rejecting both monadism and monism, Russell basically defines relations as "the sort of universals generally represented by verbs and prepositions."[15] Particulars themselves are not relational, since relations are by definition universals, and they account for the possession by a particular of a universal trait. The sharp distinction between universals and particulars is important here because it is part of what underlies the atomistic view of particulars. In his "Relations of Universals and Particulars," Russell makes the case for the sharp distinction between the two: "Thus the fact that it is logically possible for precisely similar things to coexist in two different places, but that things in different places at the same time cannot be numerically identical, forces us to admit that it is particulars, i.e., *instances* of universals, that exist in places, and not universals themselves."[16] The argument that seems possible on the basis of this kind of distinction is that since particulars are not universals, and since relations are universals, particulars are not relational. By identifying relations with universals in this way, Russell makes it seem exceedingly odd to talk about particulars as relational.

The same commentator who described Russell's view as commonplace also suggested that it was the end of the story, but is it? There is reason to think not, since Russell's analysis does not give a theory of relations as much as it explains one kind of relation, i.e., between particulars, in terms of another, i.e., between particulars and universal traits. This suggests that to handle the question of relations carefully we need to consider how to understand particulars and universals. Russell thought so too, presumably, because he continually revisited the question, and eventually changed his mind. Let us look again at "Relations of Universals and Particulars." In this essay, written around the time of *The Problems of Philosophy* and nearly a decade after the first edition of the *Principles of Mathematics*, Russell argues, as we have seen, for the distinction between universals and particulars, basically on the grounds that some things cannot occupy two distinct spaces simultaneously (for example, white patches) while other entities seem capable of doing so (for example, whiteness). One point to note about Russell's treatment of this is the way he defines "particulars"—i.e., as substances, distinguished by definition from relations and universals. A substance, or particular, is that which can only be the subject of a predication or term of a relation. Particulars are nonrelational and ultimately simple, which is to say divisible into simple constituents.

In "Relations of Universals and Particulars," then, Russell expresses the standard view. We should note, though, that Russell later rejected the standard view. He rejected atomism, of course, but he also rejected the argument of the 1911 paper, and by appeal to parsimony, the view that there must be substances that possess predicates and that stand in relation. He replaced the standard view by talking, interestingly enough, about "complexes" and "compresence." In its earlier definition a particular is unknowable because entirely inaccessible. It is, he says, simply a "peg on which to hang predicates."[17] As such, he goes on, it is "repugnant." In *Human Knowledge: Its Scope and Limits* the simple particular, the inaccessible peg, is replaced by a "complex of compresence," where "compresence" means all qualities that occur simultaneously or contemporaneously. Russell first illustrates this approach through describing one individual's experience, then applies it to the order of his experience, then to other people's experience, and finally to the physical world in general. Here, and again in *My Philosophical Development*, particulars have become complexes of compresence, or bundles of qualities. Such a complex is not simply a class of events, Russell says, since "it is something which exists not merely because its constituents exist but because, in virtue of being compresent, they constitute a single structure."[18] A complex or particular, in other words, obtains insofar as its constituents stand in a certain relation to one another. He actually uses the expression "complete complex of compresence," which is a complex in which all the constituents are compresent and nothing else is compresent with all the constituents.[19] It is this sort of complex that in Russell's view replaces the substantivist, atomistic particular of his earlier work and much of contemporary philosophy.

Russell's complexes have been criticized by Armstrong, who refers to the view as the Bundle theory of particulars. We need to make several points about Armstrong's treatment of Russell and about his criticisms of a relational view of particulars. First, it is not clear that Armstrong is careful enough with Russell. For example, he defines a complex of compresence as a "class," when Russell took care to distinguish it from a class. But maybe this is not important, since a class and a complex may be susceptible to the same objections. The second point to make, then, is that Armstrong does raise four arguments against the bundle view, all of which turn on an alleged problem with identity and individuation. As Armstrong puts it, a bundle theory requires the Principle of the Identity of Indiscernibles, in either a strong or weak form. The strong form, which says that particulars must differ in at least some nonrelational properties, may well not be true, and so not useful to the bundle theory. The weak form, which holds that the difference between particulars may involve relational properties, may not be true either, he says, but more seriously it involves the theory in circularity. In the end, he suggests, the weak form of the principle must give way to the strong form, which he has already argued may not be true, and certainly is not necessarily true.[20]

Whether there is anything circular in Russell I do not know. I do not at any rate see how Armstrong has shown that there is. I do think, though, and this is a third general point to make, that it is Armstrong who in a significant sense begs the critical question here, since in arguing against Russell's complexes he appeals to points that are true only if particulars are *not* complexes. Concerning the weak principle, for example, he simply asserts that "Relational properties cannot be used to differentiate particulars." But isn't this the issue? It will be true in the end that a relational ontology will have to provide some principle of identity and individuation, and that is not a simple matter, as we have already seen. But surely it is inappropriate simply to assert that it cannot be done, especially since, as we have also seen, it has been done. This points, fourthly, to one of our crucial concerns. An atomistic (i.e., the standard) conception of particulars is so ingrained, it seems, that it is simply assumed when, in fact, it needs to be defended or justified in some way. For example, Armstrong notices that a complex may have parts, and that such parts may themselves be particulars, in which case they too would be bundles of properties. It is logically possible for this process to go on ad infinitum. But without any ultimate parts, he says, "it is impossible to carry out the resolution of particulars into bundles of properties." But this is simply to assume that to make sense of particulars they must be simple.[21] A bit further on, in the process of defining particulars, Armstrong distinguishes between a "thick" and a "thin" conception of particulars. A "thin" conception is one in which a particular is abstracted from all its properties. Again, the standard view is simply a given. Finally, Armstrong says that "It seems natural to demand that whatever entities we identify as those of which the world is composed should be 'substances' in Hume's sense. That is, they should be logically capable of independent existence." It may or may not be "natural," but it is hardly self-justifying.[22]

There is one other aspect of Armstrong's analysis that warrants our attention before moving on. He has argued that there is something he calls the Relational Regress that is relevant to our concerns. He first raises this, along with a second "object regress," against the four forms of nominalism, which he is concerned to refute. His point is that any attempt to avoid talking about types or properties in describing particulars will covertly appeal to types, and thus involve itself in a vicious regress. But beyond the concern with nominalism, Armstrong argues that the relational regress applies to "all *Relational* analyses of what it is for a particular to have a property or for two or more particulars to be related in a certain sort of way."[23] To talk justifiably about relational particulars, as we are attempting to do, the relational regress must be answered.

Armstrong seems to hold that to give a relational analysis of an object having a property is necessarily to give an analysis in terms of an object being related to a type. Say, for example, that a box being white is taken to mean that a box is related to "white" or "whiteness." But since there are many instances of such a relation, there must then be a second order relation, i.e., between instances of whiteness and "whiteness." Either the relation of the box to "whiteness" is different from the relation of instances of whiteness to "whiteness" or it is the same. If it is different, then we are on our way to an infinite regress of relations explaining relations. If it is the same, then the original relation is being explained by appealing to itself, which of course is circular.[24]

Now if this argument works at all, it works only against a relational analysis in which the relations are understood exclusively as relations between particulars and universals. Armstrong approaches it this way, evidently, because he thinks that properties *must* be universals. He says further on, for example, in a discussion of internal and external relations, that *a is the father of b* cannot be taken as *a* having a relation *to b*, because that would treat a relational property as a relation between particulars, where a "genuine relational *property*" is a universal. The relation must be rather that there is a property of *a* that is *being a father of a child*.[25] This view of relations is certainly questionable, and Armstrong's own example suggests the point. There seems to be prima facie reason to hold that a father's relation to a child is exactly that, i.e., a relation of one *individual* to another, and an analysis that precludes my having a property that is a relation to another individual seems to miss the point of the relation. This is another example of how the traditional view forces us to deny the obvious—in fact, to ignore or even reject what we are actually trying to say—in order to maintain philosophical assumptions. The relational regress, then, is turned against an approach to particulars and universals in which, like Locke, particulars are substrata. Since, as Armstrong has argued in great detail, the many versions of nominalism have been shown to be wanting, a substrata analysis of particulars would have to involve a relation between substratum and universals, and off we go on the relational regress. But suppose now that we can articulate an ontology that is not nominalist, and so falls victim to none of the object or relational regresses from which the four types of nominalism suffer. Also suppose that this ontology does not treat relations in terms of substrata related to universals as Forms, and so is not subject to the other relational regress. Then we will have a relational analysis not subject to Armstrong's objections. Note here that Armstrong is right that a relational analysis is a regress. It is not, however, a vicious one. It would be vicious only if one thought that in the analysis one should eventually arrive at something that is not relational. But let us give that up, and regard *whatever there is* to be constituted relationally.

The Solution

At the risk of repetition, I would like now to describe again the view, which in some ways is related to Russell's later idea but without the emphasis on "compresence," that offers an alternative, relational understanding of particulars and is not subject to the objections of Armstrong. An ordinal ontology of constitutive relations has a more elaborate categorial apparatus, as we have seen, that allows it to handle the problems that drive the earlier Russell and then Armstrong to reject out of hand the possibility that particulars are relational. The idea is that all particulars are relational in the following sense: All particulars, let us now call them complexes (though "complex" is a more generic term than "particular" in that its scope includes not just particulars but whatever there is), are relational in the sense that no particular has its traits, its nature, independently of all other particulars. Another way to say this is that all particulars are constituted by their traits, and all traits are relational.

We need to make one more point before looking at more of the detail of this, and that point is methodological. As in the previous chapters, I do not intend to argue that the relational ontology proposed is a *necessary* truth, or that its traditional alternative, i.e., the standard view, is *necessarily* false. I will not, then, offer a priori arguments of the sort a philosopher might be used to. My approach is more pragmatic in a technical sense of that term. The entire project is an attempt to articulate a position, spell out some of its ramifications, see what work it does, and then judge it on the basis of those traits.

Our proposal, then, is for an ordinal ontology of constitutive relations. There are several things to notice about this:

1. It does not mean, as we have said, that all complexes are "internally" related to all other complexes. For one thing, to regard relations as constitutive of particulars, specifically through the necessity of location in one or more orders, is to deny the usefulness of the distinction between internal and external relations. Relations are constitutive, and more or less relevantly so, and no distinction between internal and external adds anything useful to that. So to say that all particulars are constituted relationally means simply that for any given complex, it is related necessarily to some other or others. The difference between this and positing a system of internally related particulars is significant because it allows us to avoid Hegel's and Bradley's results wherein all particulars are subsumed into the Absolute, and allows us to maintain a conception of nature that is open and, in James's phrase, "in the making."

2. Though all complexes are constituted by or through their relations with other complexes, nothing at this level of the general ontology specifies what those complexes must be. In other words, nothing in the general ontology requires that complexes be related, for example, to mind. This point is important because it allows us to avoid Green's, and Berkeley's, result wherein mind or consciousness is ultimately the source of identity, indeed of reality. Complexes are not constituted by their relations with mind, but by their relations with other complexes, which in any particular case may be minds, but certainly need not be. Complexes,

as we have said, receive *natural definition*.[26] Not only does this allow us to avoid the overt subjective idealism of Green or Berkeley, but it also indicates the proper response to the excesses of contemporary postmodernism. As we have already pointed out, the process of inquiry, and the perspective of the inquirer, of course condition the product of inquiry, but as Justus Buchler has put it, "A judgment about the world is a finding . . . but what is found is not the finding."[27] What is found in inquiry, and in query, or more generally interaction, of any kind, is a complex that is defined naturally by its multiple relations to a variety of other complexes, including sometimes inquirers, the process of inquiry, judgment, and interaction. We are thus able to have it both ways, so to speak. We can acknowledge the perspectivalist insights of postmodern criticism while retaining an appropriate sense of the "objectivity" of the complexes of nature.

3. Armstrong's concern about an unfolding of traits of complexes continuing ad infinitum is answered by ordinality. Once we understand complexes as necessarily located in orders of relations, and as themselves orders of relations that locate other complexes, it becomes possible to understand how constituents of complexes are themselves complexes without exception, and that there is nothing either logically or practically distressing about it. Thus there are no "ultimate parts." Our response to Armstrong's regress arguments renders this at least plausible. Every particular, including every trait or property of every particular, is relationally constituted. This conception has a number of virtues, especially methodological ones. It helps us to take seriously the complexity of objects of inquiry, and to take seriously the role their relations have in their natures. This in turn helps us to avoid a tendency toward reductionism, a method damaging not only in philosophy but also and perhaps more importantly in the natural and social sciences.

4. A corresponding implication is that just as there are no "ultimate" parts or simple constituents, so there is no ultimate whole. To say that complexes are relational is to say that they are constituted by the relations in which they stand to other complexes. Do not think of a complex as a container made up of its "internal" parts and contents. A complex is constituted as much by its "environment," or the orders of complexes of which it is a constituent. Among my traits, to add an example to the tree we

considered earlier, is not only my skin, which is in a set of relations to other traits of my body and to my physical environment, but also my being a philosopher, i.e., my relations with other individuals, organizations, professional activities, and so forth. I am, in other words, necessarily "located," to speak in terms appropriate to our ordinal categories, in some orders of complexes. The identity of a complex, as we have seen, is a function of those ordinal locations, from which it follows that no complex can be unlocated. If no complex can be unlocated, then there can be no "whole" of reality, no single "World."[28]

5. Finally, at least for current purposes, if all particulars are complexes and relational, which means that all traits and properties are relational, then we are committed to the view that universals are also relational. We accept the view, held by Russell and Armstrong, that there is very good reason to endorse a distinction between particulars and universals. There is an obvious difference between an object that is white and the whiteness that is among its traits. "Whiteness" and a "white object" have different traits, and different kinds of propositions will be true of them. It is true of a white object that it has certain spatial dimensions, which is not true of "whiteness." It is true of "whiteness" that it stands in a certain relation to the spectrum of light, but that relation does not hold of a white object except as a trait of its being white. So we accept the particular/universal distinction, but this is not an ontologically primary distinction. To treat it as such creates a whole range of problems. In *The Problems of Philosophy*, for example, Russell is forced to make some bizarre distinctions in order to accommodate the difference between particulars and universals when they are regarded as primary or primitive distinctions: "We shall find it convenient only to speak of things as *existing* when they are in time. . . . But universals do not exist in this sense; we shall say that they *subsist* or *have being*, where 'being' is opposed to 'existence' as being timeless."[29] I can find no sense to the distinction between 'being' and 'existence' other than one produced by sheer stipulation, the need for which is generated by nothing but an ontology that, because it cannot accommodate our experience, forces us to define our experience perversely. It is far better to regard both particulars and universals as complexes and as relationally determined. Both, for example, prevail in orders of relations - a white object, say a pen, in the order, among others,

of writing instruments, and whiteness in the order of color. This point distinguishes the relational ontology presented here from the realism of Plato's forms and Whitehead's eternal objects. A nonrelational entity of any kind, as Russell suggests, is inaccessible and to that extent is "repugnant."

Our attempt has been, and will continue to be throughout the rest of this part of the book, to add cumulatively to an understanding of a relational ontology. There is some risk of repetition in this strategy, but that may not be undesirable. To understand nature relationally is a novel enough approach, in the contemporary philosophical world at any rate, that repetition may help to make the point. But one hopes that the gradual unfolding of the general ontological idea is not merely repetitive, in that by returning again and again to the exposition of aspects of a relational ontology we gradually add to the detail of the conception, and thereby enrich both its understanding and an appreciation of its import.

This discussion of particulars and the possibility of understanding them relationally enable us to posit pragmatic naturalism and its ontology of constitutive relations as an alternative and corrective to the atomism of twentieth-century empiricism and the idealism of nineteenth-century theories of internal relations.[30] I should not like to claim that I have *proven* that particulars are to be understood relationally, but we have demonstrated the reasonableness of the more modest claim that it is plausible for particulars to be understood relationally. Moreover, by doing so we avoid many of the conceptual gymnastics that other philosophers have felt compelled to undertake, whereby they must deny that a father has a relation to a child, as Armstrong has said, or that we are forced to posit something called subsistence in addition to existence, as Russell proposes. These are cases, brought to us by the Humpty-Dumpty Fallacy of traditional metaphysics described in an earlier chapter, in which because of their admirable desire for conceptual coherence philosophers are driven either to deny what is obviously true or to say things that complicate our understanding well beyond necessity.

I have focused in this chapter on a specific issue, i.e., the nature of particulars, which bears on the objectivist side of pragmatic naturalism. That is to say, insofar as a relational ontology purports to offer the conceptual categories appropriate to an understanding of "whatever is," it has been necessary to show that it is at least possible, perhaps even sensible, to regard the "things" of the world as relational. If particulars cannot be relational, as the early Russell and Armstrong suggest, then a relational ontology is a nonstarter. But as we have seen, there is no reason to accept that claim. The complexes of the world, or of nature, if one prefers, can indeed be understood relationally.

However, the objectivist side of pragmatic naturalism is one of two basic moments, the other being its constructivism. I turn now to a consideration of a relational ontology and its implications for what I shall refer to as world making.

FIVE

MAKING SENSE OF WORLD MAKING

Creativity and Objectivity in Nature

In 1978 Nelson Goodman in *Ways of Worldmaking* wrote that both objects and knowledge are in important ways constructed: "If worlds are as much made as found, so also knowing is as much remaking as reporting."[1] Goodman at the time was concerned primarily with art and the senses in which "world making" makes sense in the context of artistic creation.[2] His remarks, like the one just quoted, often suggest that he is willing to extend the point beyond the arts, but he does not develop that thought in the book. Since Goodman's book was published, however, the notion that our world is in some ways and to some extent our own creative construction has been expanded far beyond the realm of artistic creation, and it has gained a currency it lacked even as recently as 1978. Since Goodman, what I will refer to broadly as postmodernism has vigorously argued for "constructivism," in the sense of the creative construction of our worlds and their meaning for us.

To a considerable extent pragmatism belongs to this tendency, though obviously it long predates Goodman and the postmodernism of recent decades. We have to be careful not to overstate this point, however. The point is not that pragmatism is "wholly" constructivist, whatever that would mean. Some philosophers do appear to overstate the extent to which we construct our worlds, but this view has never been maintained by pragmatists, and certainly not by the classical pragmatists. Of the latter, James may come the closest in his concept of pure experience, but he never suggests that we somehow construct our worlds out of whole cloth. James would never have claimed, to use other language, that making does not also involve finding. Classical pragmatism, especially in James and Dewey, was an effort to merge making and finding into a coherent philosophical view, which is one of the reasons it may have puzzled some of its detractors. This desire to have it both ways, so to speak, is part of its strength, and it is what makes the integration with naturalism possible. For its part, naturalism as it developed came to approach the constructivist side of pragmatism, most notably in Buchler with his merging of the natural definition and relationality of complexes and a broader, richer theory of judgment. Thus, pragmatic naturalism, as we have been developing it, bridges objectivism and constructivism.[3]

But constructivism there surely is. We have seen in the previous chapter's discussions of particulars and ordinality how a relational ontology may understand the complexes of nature as found, so to speak. Now we need to look more closely at the other side of pragmatic naturalism, at its predilection for constructivism or world making, as Goodman would have it. I have argued that an ordinal, relational ontology allows us comfortably to merge these two perspectives, but more is needed to render the approach more than simply possible. For it to be plausible it is necessary to indicate the reasonableness of its approach to what is found, as I have tried to do in the previous chapter, and to what is made, as I shall do now.

The Appeal of Objectivity

The opponents of the constructivist tendency in philosophy, whatever we might call them, have objected that by now the rejection of objectivity has gone too far. It may be appropriate to refer to these critics as modernists, and their view as modernism, in that they tend to support the two central assumptions of seventeenth- and eighteenth-century thought. The first is that "reality" has its traits independently of human interaction with it, and the second is that reality can be known, or discovered. I have placed the word "reality" in quotation marks because the use of the term is itself charged with meaning and implications, and if not handled carefully can create problems, as we have seen. Most important is the fact that in this context reality is defined as objectivity, which is to say that something is real, or "really real" as writers in this vein are occasionally inclined to say, if it exists independently of people. The rest is mere fiction, or even worse, mere appearance. This idea that the real is only that which is independent of people has played havoc with philosophy, causing far too much ink to be spilled in the attempt to distinguish between reality and "appearance." This has in turn created additional confusion over how to understand experience. Since experience is by definition human experience, and therefore has something to do with human interaction with whatever might be objective, it fails to meet the definition of "real," which in turn has caused countless philosophers to concern themselves with the relation between experience and reality.

The definition of reality as the objective, in the sense of being in possession of traits independently of human interaction, has, as I have indicated, inclined many thinkers to regard the products of human activity as "unreal." Thus, fictional characters, to consider literary creation as an illustration, would be considered unreal, despite the fact that they have some traits and not others, and that they can be decidedly influential in experience. The modernist assumption that the real is to be defined simply as the objectively determined has created for philosophers many of their own problems, like the problems of the relation between reality and appearance, between reality and experience, and the question of the ontological status of human products. The suspicion that these problems are themselves artificial is in part what has allowed the postmodernist interest in creativity and constructivism to flourish, not to mention the pragmatism that preceded it.

If the ideas of world making and the creative construction of meaning, indeed of experience, have received their impetus in part from a suspicion that modernist assumptions are misguided and therefore have led to more confusion than clarity, the modernist assumptions in turn receive their most plausible justification in the natural sciences. Modernism, in the sense I have been using the term here, argues for discovery over creativity, for finding over making, and points to the sciences as the clearest cases of inquiry in which the world is not made but discovered.

There are two aspects of the modernist defense of discovery in science that need to be highlighted. The first is that in early modernism (in fact, beginning much earlier in classical Greece) the assumption of objectivity and the possibility of discovery were extended far beyond the material world to include ethical and aesthetic values, social and political relations, art and literature, and mathematical entities and relations. When I use the expression "the assumption of objectivity" here I mean the assumption that there are facts, conditions, or states of affairs true of the world regardless of us—that is to say, facts that have certain determinate traits and not others, despite whatever we might say or think about them. On the face of it this assumption is easy enough to maintain in reference to rocks, trees, animals, and chemicals, that is to the more or less brute material world, though even in these cases ordinality, as we have seen, enables us to recognize their possible location in other, more constructed, orders as well. The classical and modernist impulse, though, was to apply this objectivist assumption to virtually everything. On the assumption of ontological objectivity, it was taken simply as a given that there is an objective truth to be discovered in all fields of inquiry, so that the vast bulk of philosophical writing for more than two thousand years has been an ongoing attempt to discover the objective truth in ethics, aesthetics, social and political theory, art, and mathematics.

The assumption of objectivity in all these fields of inquiry has had ramifications beyond the purely intellectual realm, and it continues to be influential in, for example, practical politics. I will offer one fairly recent and socially significant illustration of this point. As we all know, the events of September 11, 2001, had a profound impact on social and political life in the United States, the extent of which is still being seen. The more socially and politically conservative forces in American life, which is the say the forces that through most of the 2000s had by far the greatest influence on public policy, used the event to advance their social agenda in ways that most of us would never have imagined possible earlier. The USA Patriot Act was rushed through a compliant Congress, so that there are now, even at the time of this writing nearly ten years on, by law an extensive series of challenges to the civil liberties of people in

America, both citizens and noncitizens. In the same spirit, then Attorney General John Ashcroft announced the creation of an organization that was to recruit citizens to spy and report on the activities of their neighbors, all in the spirit of preventing "terrorists" from acting again.

I mention this in the context of a discussion of the extension of the assumption of objectivity to the nonmaterial world because it is precisely this assumption that has been used to defend the Patriot Act and the whole range of actions that were taken by the George W. Bush administration during its tenure. One of the more prominent of the social conservatives who supported this general direction is William Bennett, who in the past has served as US Secretary of Education and as the chairman of the National Endowment for the Humanities. Bennett published a book titled *Why We Fight: Moral Clarity and the War on Terrorism*,[4] in which he attempts to justify both then current policy and his version of "Americanism" in general. In the process he of course criticized American liberals and radicals, which he takes to include most of those teaching in American universities. More to our purposes, though, he goes to great lengths to attack what he calls "pseudo sophisticated relativism," by which he means what I have here referred to as postmodernism, that is to say the general idea that the world is in important ways not objectively determined but creatively constructed. Among the prime targets for Bennett's attack is Stanley Fish, a specialist in Milton and a prominent "postmodernist" in literary and cultural theory. Bennett attributes to Fish the idea that "everything is relative, everything can be justified and all is permitted." This is a distortion of Fish's far more sophisticated ideas, but Bennett is right that Fish does indeed criticize the assumption of objectivity. The reason Bennett is so critical of Fish and others who challenge the assumption of objectivity is that by rejecting objectivity in values and social relations generally they call into question what Bennett takes to be the foundation of civilization and culture. For example, Bennett says that September 11 was an event through which good and evil were starkly contrasted, in which "Good was distinguished from evil, truth from falsehood." For Bennett and many that share his general opinion it is no more complicated than that: There is good and evil, truth and falsehood, and of course America represents "good and truth." The point is that Bennett's view of the situation—in fact, his whole justification of "why we fight"—requires the assumption of objectivity. It is inconceivable, and nearly criminal, to him to reject the traditional assumption of objectivity in values, because without it there appears to him to be nowhere to stand, no way to distinguish right from wrong, better from worse. And that in turn is why he is as critical as he is of Fish and postmodernism in general. Postmodernism is a threat to the American establishment's ability to justify itself. The American establishment and its foreign and domestic policy appear in Bennett's view to require the assumption of objectivity.

So the extension of modernism's defense of discovery in science to other fields of inquiry has both theoretical and practical implications. But in addition to the objectivity of values, there is a second aspect of modernism's defense of discovery and the assumption of objectivity that bears mentioning. In the twentieth century and since, the development of the social sciences has reflected the modernist assumption. On the model of the natural sciences, sociologists, anthropologists, psychologists, political scientists, and economists have made extensive efforts to discover the objective truths of their respective domains. Many have carried this so far that they reject any methods in their disciplines that do not mimic the natural sciences. Thus, the social sciences have become increasingly descriptive and quantitative. There is some virtue in this, but the determination to discover objective truth makes it unlikely that the social sciences will be able to recognize, never mind appreciate, the extent to which people's relations are creative and constructive of their worlds and their lives. The assumption of objectivity and the methods of inquiry based on it simply preclude the creative dimension of people's lives.

Finding and Making

The big issue here is the tension between discovery and construction—how, in what sense, and to what extent, is our world found or made, discovered or constructed? Some scholars have attempted a middle ground between pure discovery and pure creation. In the American tradition, as we have said, pragmatism is the most outstanding example, and the most prominent and influential among the pragmatists in this respect has been John Dewey. If one had to choose only one example of his many writings on this score, it might be Chapter 10 of *The Quest for Certainty*, titled "The Construction of Good," in which he argues that the choice between objectivity and relativism in values is a false choice. The good is neither simply discovered, nor is it arbitrary; rather, it is the ongoing and fluid result of experience, which is to say of the interaction of people with one another, with their environment, and with their individual and collective purposes. The good is neither found nor chosen, but constructed.[5] More recently, Pierre Bourdieu attempted something similar. In *Le Sens Pratique*, for example, which is translated into English as *The Logic of Practice*, Bourdieu objects to both of the prevailing approaches in anthropology, which he identifies with the assumption of objectivity on the one hand and the assumption of subjectivity on the other.[6] Bourdieu rejects the anthropologists' objectivist assumption, and the subjectivist alternative, in favor of what he calls "habitus," by which he means, if I understand him correctly, the dimensions of social and cultural life, which include the full range of cultural practices and values that define a society and that contain and convey the culture's most meaningful dimensions. The reason he rejects them is that neither the objectivist nor the subjectivist assumption allows the anthropologist to understand the collectively creative dimension of cultural life. The assumptions themselves preclude access to what turns out to be the most important dimension of individual and social activity, which is the creative construction of value and meaning, and the cultural practices through which that creation takes place.

I have mentioned Dewey in connection with the response to the modernists' assumption of objectivity, and one could indeed point to the entire pragmatic naturalist tradition from which Dewey emerged. Long before Richard Rorty, for example, and in fact several years before Dewey's *Quest for Certainty*, George Santayana (though not a pragmatist in any explicit way) rejected the metaphor of reflection in his understanding of inquiry and knowledge.[7] Both Santayana and Dewey, as well as many other pragmatists and naturalists, regarded the world of experience, which is to say nature itself, including both the experiencer and the object of experience, to be the result of an ongoing and changing relation of interaction.

Thus, in the social sciences, and in the study of values, the assumption of objectivity has been questioned and in intriguing ways rejected.

We may also approach the larger question in another way, through a consideration of recent objections to constructivism along epistemological lines. A particularly strong illustration of such an objection is Paul Boghossian's *Fear of Knowledge*.[8] Boghossian's concern is to demonstrate that the apparent relativism of social constructivism is untenable, and therefore there is no reason to accept the constructivist view. Of course he is aware that some entities are what they are by virtue of social convention, money being an obvious example. Others are what John Lachs has called "choice-inclusive" facts—for example, that a particular body of water is a gulf and not a bay.[9] Boghossian is concerned not with these phenomena but with the more controversial claims made by philosophers who would identify themselves as social constructivists.

He identifies three forms of constructivism that he believes are ultimately unacceptable: constructivism about facts, constructivism about justification, and constructivism about rational explanation. The latter two categories concern the degree to which we are entitled, if at all, to justify one set of beliefs or epistemic principles against another without circularity. Or, is Rorty right when he says, for example, that Western liberalism needs, and in fact can have, no justification beyond saying that this is the way we think and live; for that matter, is the anthropologist right when he says that science is simply one among any number of possible systems of explanation, in general no better or worse epistemically than others? As interesting and important as these questions are, it is more relevant for us to focus first on the initial form of constructivism that worries Boghossian—constructivism about facts.

Boghossian illustrates what he means by fact-constructivism through examples taken from prominent constructivist philosophers. For example, he refers to the comment made by Bruno Latour, in reference to the apparent discovery that Ramses II may have died of tuberculosis, that such a claim makes no sense because tuberculosis had no existence before its discovery in 1882. Another example that Boghossian cites is Foucault's assertion that before the concept "homosexual" came into common use there were no homosexuals, only men who preferred to have sex with other men.[10] Boghossian argues that these and claims like them, which is to say fact-constructivist claims, cannot be true.

This point is relevant for us because we have claimed that pragmatic naturalism is both objectivist and constructivist, and if we are right then we should be able to address the kinds of misgivings to which Boghossian gives voice. He develops a number of arguments to support the conclusion that fact-constructivism is untenable, but like so much of otherwise strong analytic philosophy, the problem is not in the arguments but in the assumptions that precede the arguments and often go unexamined. Thus, I will focus not on his arguments, which are nevertheless interesting and deserve to be read, but on the more general conceptions at work in this debate.

What bothers Boghossian is that there is something perverse on the face of it in saying that the tuberculosis bacillus did not exist before it was "discovered," or that there was no homosexuality until we began to talk about it. At the common sense level he is right to think, in our terminology, that there are many complexes of nature that have any number of traits entirely independently of any relation with us. But if he means to say that there are no relevant senses in which relations with us construct such complexes as tuberculosis or homosexuality, then he is wrong. The problem is, and here his common sense instinct is on the mark, it is equally wrong for Latour or Foucault to say, if this is indeed what they meant, that there are no relevant respects in which such complexes as tuberculosis and homosexuality have traits independently of us. So there appears to be a problem in the very meaning of the relevant assertions. Let us try to clear this up.

The problem is that both constructivists like Latour and Foucault, and objectivists like Boghossian, seem to think that things are either one way or the other; complexes that have objective traits have only objective traits, or that complexes that are socially constructed are only and entirely socially constructed. Underlying both of these approaches is a failure to appreciate the complexity and ordinality of the phenomena of nature. The constructivists seem to think either that there are no facts of the world that can truthfully be described in some ways and not others, or that if there are such facts, we have no way of knowing them. The objectivist's alternative is to say that we do and should defer to science as the reliable way of knowing facts about the world, and that what science adequately demonstrates can be justifiably regarded as objective traits of things, of facts of the world.

Several questions are raised here. First, why are we talking about "facts," as if there are no other features or traits of complexes that are relevant to our understanding of them? Are facts to be distinguished from meanings, for example? If so, why? Meanings are no less traits of complexes than are any of the traits that might be included in a "fact." And if facts are not to be distinguished from meanings, then clearly it is inadequate to say of any complex that it has its traits, or anyway all of its traits, independently of its relations with us. A second question of course concerns why we should regard science as the reliable means by which we obtain knowledge even of objectively determined traits of complexes. What, for example, of art? This is a question to which we will return in Chapter 7.

The pragmatic naturalist has the philosophical tools available to settle this problem. The only reason to think that a complex, let us say tuberculosis, is what it is entirely independently of us, or conversely that it did not exist until it was discovered, is if we assume from the beginning that complexes are absolute rather than relational. Once we adopt the ordinal relationality of pragmatic naturalism we are able to understand that a complex can be objective in some respects and socially constructed in others, and that neither set of traits is more "essential" to the nature of the complex than any other. No trait or subset of traits is more "essential" to the nature of the complex than any other, though some are always more relevant than others in a given respect. Thus, we are never forced to say of any complex that in its entirety or in all respects it is either objectively determined or socially constructed. It may in principle be possible for there to be complexes that have no socially constructed traits or that have no objective traits. That is, there may in principle be complexes that are entirely objective or entirely constructed, but our ontological categories are such that we are never forced in one direction or another. We will return to the discussion of both the reasonableness and advantages of a relational understanding of nature in the subsequent sections of this chapter.

But let us continue to look at the general issue of fact-objectivism vs. fact-constructivism. It is unfortunate that this debate has absorbed so much attention in recent years, unfortunate because it has been unnecessary. The fact is that Dewey had addressed the problem nearly a century ago, and he did so in the same spirit in which we are treating it now. Consider the following passages from *Experience and Nature*:

> Sometimes discovery is treated as a proof of the opposite of what it actually shows. It is viewed as evidence that the object of knowledge is already there in full-fledged being and that we just run across it. . . . That there is existence antecedent to search and discovery is of course admitted; but it is denied that as such . . . it is already the object of knowledge. The Norsemen are said to have discovered America. But in what sense? . . . Discovery of America involved insertion of the newly touched land in a map of the globe. This insertion, moreover, was not merely additive, but transformative of a prior picture of the world as to its surfaces and their arrangements. It may be replied that it was not the world which was changed but only the map. To which there is the obvious retort that after all the map is part of the world, not something outside it, and that its meaning and bearings are so important that a change in the map involves other and still more important objective changes.[11]

Dewey is basically making my point in this passage. He did not have the language of ordinality at his disposal, but if he had he may have said something like this: Certainly a body of land existed prior to anyone's stepping on it, whether Norsemen or people from Siberia long before. To that extent what we now call America possessed traits naturally defined, in this case defined independently of relations with us. But the discovery of America by Europeans changed the complex that is America, as it changed much else in history. The meanings with which America has become imbued, whether social, political, geographic, or psychological, are as much traits of the complex that was and is America as any alteration in the land mass may have been. The meanings of America consequent upon its discovery are no less constitutive of the complex than its physical topography. With respect to its meanings, America did not exist until it was discovered and subsequently constructed. With respect to its topography it did. And both respects are constitutive of the complex that is America. The situation is no more complicated or mysterious than that.

Regardless of what they actually meant, Latour and Foucault might have said much the same thing. Certainly a bacillus existed independently of its being discovered, but the range of meanings that tuberculosis came to have was in part a result of the discovery of the bacillus and the social relations that developed with respect to it. Those socially constructed meanings are no less constitutive of tuberculosis than the biological traits of the bacillus; tuberculosis is as much socially constructed as it is naturally defined independently of us. The same applies to homosexuality. There were same sex relations long before the concept and term "homosexual" developed, but the meanings of the concept and term, with respect to social, psychological, political and legal relations, are a social construction dependent in part on the development of the term and concept. Homosexuality is no less socially constructed and simultaneously objective than are tuberculosis and America, and for that matter anything else with which we interact. Boghossian wants to insist that there has to be at least some sort of basic stuff, some independent state of affairs, regardless of our descriptions. We agree in a sense, and we have the concepts of natural definition to enable us to identify objectively determined traits in the simple sense that complexes not related to us receive their character, their definition, naturally, which is to say by way of whatever relations constitute them. What Boghossian does not appreciate is that even objectively determined traits are relational, and for many complexes among their relations are socially constructed traits, and that the socially constructed traits of complexes are as much constitutive, though more or less relevant in any given respect, as anything that one may want to consider to be a complex's "basic stuff."

Boghossian begins his analysis with an example that especially bothers him. The archeological evidence indicates that the earliest human inhabitants in the Americas arrived on the North American continent from Siberia. The Cheyenne River Sioux, however, believe that they are descendents of the Buffalo people and that they emerged from inside the earth. Some anthropologists claim that there is no noncircular way to prefer the archeological account over the Sioux's own stories, and therefore neither account is more accurate or true than the other. Both are social constructions, on this view. This is the constructivism about justification against which Boghossian argues at considerable length.

The constructivist point of view with respect to justification concerns him because it has been taken up by a number of intellectuals in recent years, Rorty prominent among them, and Boghossian thinks that the view is indefensible and that it damages our ability to know and understand the world by undermining the commitment to science and the strength of the scientific mode of inquiry.

Here too, though, ordinal categories make it possible to make sense of the situation without undermining scientific inquiry and without denying the significance, even the cognitive significance, of multiple modes of generating knowledge. First, it is necessary to recognize that knowledge is not to be understood merely as justified true belief, indeed it is not to be understood as a matter of belief at all, at least not in all cases. This point will be developed in more detail in Chapter 7. Suffice it to say for now that knowledge has as much to do with the generation of possibilities and the pragmatic implications of meanings as it does with belief. In some cases it has nothing to do with belief at all, and everything to do with possibilities and meanings. Consequently, knowledge is generally knowledge in some respect and toward some end, and in that regard it is invariably conditioned by the knower's perspectives and purposes. Knowledge, in other words, like all complexes, is relational and ordinal.

The relationality and ordinality of knowledge does not, however, preclude the superiority of one mode of knowing over another in a given respect. If we wish to understand the natural history of the movement of the first North American peoples there is, given all the evidence, no better mode of knowledge than archeology and the associated social and natural sciences. However, if we wish to understand a people's sense of itself and the meanings that give its community significance, even the meanings of its own history, its stories are likely to be far more reliable than archeological evidence. If we assume that all orders or contexts have equal importance and value, then the constructivists are right to claim that no mode of knowledge is superior to any other. But such an assumption makes sense only because the importance of knowledge is itself always contextual, which is to say that knowledge is meaningful and significant in some respect and for some purpose. It makes no sense to speak of knowledge outside some context or order of relations. Therefore, though one context in itself is no more or less important than another, one mode of knowledge or another is always superior, or at least we can assume in any given case that some way of knowing will be more reliable. If we want to understand quarks or quasars, or the migrations of peoples, all the evidence points to science, a point that is unnecessary, senseless, and even perverse to deny. For other purposes and in other orders of relations other modes of knowledge may well be more reliable, also a point that is unnecessary, senseless, and perverse to deny. This point then need not worry the scientist because it in no way undermines the superiority of the sciences in the contexts in which they are superior. And we will see in a later chapter that it is also a point that need not worry the artist.

This analysis of the relation between objectivity and social construction, between discovery and construction, rests on the categories of ordinality, some of which I have developed in previous chapters. It also rests on the related insights that we find in Bourdieu and in the American pragmatic naturalist tradition generally. It requires, however, that it be possible to develop a sufficiently clear account of the construction of meaning and of the relationality that gives it sense. I propose now to explore the issue along these lines.

The Creative Construction of Meaning

There is a tension between discovery and creativity because both modernism and postmodernism are partially right, as I have pointed out in this and previous chapters. The fact is that both discovery and creation, finding and making, are true of the world and of human query and inquiry. The tension between them is due to the fact that the modernist and postmodernist traditions have tended to exaggerate their claims, as we have seen. Modernism has emphasized objectivity to such an extent that it has obscured the many respects in which people in fact do create our lives, our societies, and most importantly the respects in which our lives have meaning. This is done implicitly in daily life. More formally, it is done through the arts and the humanities, more than anywhere else. Literature, music, the visual arts, the performing arts, history, and even philosophy each work with their own materials and in their own way, but they have one important trait in common. They all select aspects of their subject matter and relate them in new ways, whereby they generate, and reveal to an audience, new relationships, new meanings, and new experiences. These activities are all creative of our world precisely in that they bring to our attention ways of seeing and thinking that had not been available before. Furthermore, in doing so they are not simply revealing something that has all along been hidden, waiting to be discovered. On the contrary, they are creating new properties of the world, novel characteristics of the subjects they study and of the lives of those of us who interact with them, as either observers or participants. We will return to these points in more detail in a later chapter.

One of the traits of human query that makes this possible, both inquiry through science or philosophy and production through art and making in general, is that the modes of articulation, of judgment if you will, do not simply assert. When we write, or paint, or compose, we do not merely report the world. Human judgment, in addition to being assertive, is also exhibitive and active. In its exhibitive dimension we reassemble traits of our subject matter to create new relationships and to reveal those with which we are already familiar in fresh ways. In other respects, our judgment is active in that we bring into being something that did not exist before, and in so doing change the world, sometimes trivially and sometimes profoundly. Human judgment and query, in other words, do not simply report, find, or discover. In its selection of traits of its subject matter for emphasis and development it engenders and creates.[12]

I have mentioned the fact that the social sciences have too often slavishly followed the model of the natural sciences, and in so doing have made it difficult if not impossible to notice, let alone to understand, such creative dimensions of human activity. Given the degree to which human judgment is creative, implicitly in daily life and explicitly in the arts and humanities, the social scientist is at risk of failing to grasp crucial dimensions of individual and social life if he too vigorously insists on the modernist assumption of objectivity, notwithstanding the important value of the social sciences in their proper spheres of activity. It would benefit the social scientist, and the rest of us, to realize as well that even in the natural sciences there is sometimes a deep dimension of creativity that is too often overlooked. The development of theory is itself a creative act, which can be especially obvious in the case of theories that attempt to explain a broad range of phenomena. The theory of evolution, for example, or of plate tectonics, or M-theory, are examples of intellectual constructs that, like their counterparts in the arts and throughout the sciences, select traits of their subject matter for new emphasis, and in so doing create relationships that were simply not there before. A similar process occurs when scientists and mathematicians create new mathematics in order to solve a problem. Newton and Leibniz were not simply reporting the world or discovering its traits when they developed the infinitesimal calculus, nor was the new mathematics created to solve Fermat's Theorem merely a report. Similarly, the complex geometries of multiple dimensions currently at work in M-theory are not so much a discovery as a creation, or in fact they are both. The modernist assumption of objectivity and its focus on discovery as against creativity has overstated its case to such an extent that on its basis we miss much of what is most valuable not only in the arts and humanities but in the sciences and mathematics as well.

At the same time, the emphasis on making and creativity in much of postmodernist thought has undervalued objectivity and discovery. First, of course, there is the psychological fact that discovery is in itself thrilling, as any working scientist will tell you. But more generally, the role of creativity in human action and inquiry has been so exaggerated that the fact of objectivity has itself been obscured. To offer a couple of anecdotal examples, I have found myself in conversation with philosophers who are so nervous and squeamish about objectivity that they say things like "the world is whatever we say it is," or who have trouble granting what to me is the obvious point that, to repeat an example we have used before, a door in the wall is where it is and not somewhere else, and no amount of redescription will allow us to walk through it at any other point in the wall. There are, to make the point again, aspects of the world that are indeed independent of our descriptions of them. In some cases they are independent of us altogether, as, for example, the chemical reaction in a particular cloud nebula at some remote point in space. In other cases there are traits that we can influence, but only in ways and to the extent that the objective traits allow—for example, the structure of certain chemicals. And even in those cases where the "object" in question is a human product, say a piece of music or a fictional character, the products, as created, have certain traits and not others, and so our creative interactions with them are limited by the constraints imposed by their objectively determined properties. The assumption of creativity, then, like the assumption of objectivity, can be as detrimental as it is liberating. This is a fact that we cannot honestly ignore, such that an understanding of both objectivity and creativity requires that we appreciate their legitimate standing in human query and inquiry, and indeed their interrelation with one another.

Relationality

In the end, then, the most fruitful understanding of creativity and objectivity is that they stand in a symbiotic relation with each other. Objectivity provides the framework in which creativity occurs, and creativity is the developmental process of the world, and the generation of whatever meaning and value objectively determined aspects of nature might have. Objectivity and creativity are each senseless without the other.

This point returns us to the transcendental question that we posed earlier: What must the world be like—or more modestly, what may it be like—such that both objectivity and creativity seem to require one another? Or more generally, is there a specific ontology that best captures this fact about nature and the human activity within it? The answer, which by now should not surprise a reader who has been with us since the beginning of the book, is that we are best served to understand nature ordinally. The modernist assumption of objectivity came complete with an ontology of substance, in which all "real" objects or entities, material or spiritual, exist by virtue of a completely determined and immutable substance. Such relations and changes as the entity might undergo are merely attributes, and secondary attributes at that, of objective and immutable substance. With such an ontological point of departure it is hardly surprising that the modernist, objectivist tradition would have difficulty ascribing a significant place to creativity.

Far too often, however, the postmodernist, constructivist rejection of objectivity is accompanied by a rejection not only of a substance ontology but also of ontology altogether. The result, again not surprisingly, is a world in which things are "whatever we describe them as," either individually or collectively, through one or another medium—for example, wealth or power. Neither a complete embrace of objectivity nor its abandonment is adequate, nor is a substance or atomistic ontology or the rejection of ontology adequate either. The alternative is a conception of nature in which things, entities, objects, or the preferable term "complexes," are understood to be constituted by their relations with one another. Because so much of this concept that threads through our entire analysis is initially the work of Justus Buchler, it is probably appropriate to let him speak a bit more for himself. The first lines of his *Metaphysics of Natural Complexes* provide a good sense of the scope of Buchler's idea:

> Whatever is, in whatever way, is a natural complex. . . . Relations, structures, processes, societies, human individuals, human products, physical bodies, words and bodies of discourse, ideas, qualities, contradictions, meanings, possibilities, myths, laws, duties, feelings, illusions, reasonings, dreams—all are natural complexes.[13]

First, then, the claim that all complexes are to be understood relationally, as constituted relationally, means to apply to anything and everything that can be said to exist or to prevail in any way. Of course not everything simply exists in whatever way we might say it does. We are capable of being mistaken. This view does not, for example, mean that God exists in the traditional sense of the term simply because it is verbally identified, as we will see in the following chapter. It does mean, however, that as a complex with a pervasive presence in history and culture, and in many people's individual lives, God exists in some way or other. The "some way or other" is critical here, because it means that not only do all complexes prevail, but they prevail in some respect, in some set of relations, or more technically, in some order or orders of relations. To take the example of God, which is one of the more difficult cases, we can rightfully say that God prevails in any number of orders—for example, in the order of human history, in the order of literature, in the order of objects of veneration. Whether God also prevails in the orders of relations commonly attributed, as creator or savior of humanity, is another question. The important point is that it makes no sense to speak of a complex outside of any order, so that the specific spheres of relations in which a complex prevails are the determining factors in a complex's existence and identity.

I have offered several examples in the preceding chapters, and there is good enough reason to go over some of that ground again. To help to clarify the point we might expand on the example of a person. A particular human being is a complex that prevails in numerous orders of relations—as man or woman, father or mother, son or daughter, perhaps as teacher or bookkeeper, as citizen, as neighbor, as artist or plumber, or as the center of a particular personal trajectory. Each of these sets of relations contributes to the identity of the particular person, and collectively they define who that person is, and what his or her possibilities are. And it is important to note that it is the relations, or better the orders of relations, that define a person's identity and parameters. There is no need in such a conception, such an ontology, for the traditional modernist conception of substance or any other version of a permanent core or essence of the person through all his relational locations. The person is what he is by virtue of his relations, or to put it another way, a person's relations constitute his being. This is the sense in which this is a relational ontology. And keep in mind that this point applies to "whatever is, in whatever way." It is true of a book, or a poem, or a piece of music, or a mathematical proof, or a tree, or any other complex whatsoever, that it prevails, if it prevails or exists at all, in an order or orders of relations.

Thus, the nature or character of a complex is defined by its relations, its relational or ordinal locations, whether those relations involve people or not. Certainly for a human product like a poem, or a piece of music, or a building, there are relations, extremely important ones, to at least one human being. But even for a human product there are other relations as well. A building, for example, inhabits different orders of relations depending on the material out of which it is constructed, or the ongoing movement of the earth on which it is built. And of course there are complexes that bear no meaningful relation to human beings at all, such as an object or event in remote space. All of these relations provide what, following Buchler, I have called the natural definition of a complex. Complexes are "defined," which is to say they have the nature, character, and traits that they do by virtue of their relations. And their relations are the natural occasion, if you will, of the existence of the complex.

There are two important points to make here. First, the idea of the natural definition of relationally constituted complexes is important for our purposes because it is the way to understand objectivity and creativity in nature. Complexes, whether understood as orders that locate traits or as traits of other complexes, are objective precisely in the sense that they are defined by their relational locations and that those relational locations may be independent of any of us. There is no more to it than that. However, as we have seen in the treatment of Boghossian's concern with constructivism, because objectivity is defined in terms of relations, it becomes possible to understand how creativity is also possible. As complexes enter new relations, new orders of relations, they take on new traits, new characteristics. They can be said to prevail in new orders. When a complex comes to prevail in a new order, which is to say that it takes on traits that it did not have previously, there is an instance of creativity. When such a prevalence occurs as a result of human action of any kind, it can properly be said that such human activity has created, or constructed, or simply made, something new, something novel. By understanding creativity this way we can see that it is not a superfluous process, nor merely appearance as opposed to reality. On the contrary, creativity reaches deep into nature in the sense that it is an alteration of the relations that define a complex.

This is not to say, as some ontologies do, that nature is always changing. As we saw in an earlier chapter, change is not a basic category in an ordinal ontology. Many complexes change regularly, and they do so in various ways and with varying degrees of relevance. For others, change is not a defining characteristic. A logical principle, for example, is for all practical purposes available to us in a stable form. And in any case, it makes little sense to talk about a complex changing in general. Change—or better, the more general category of alescence—occurs with respect to a specific ordinal location or a set of ordinal locations. Even a logical principle, the stability of which is what makes it available to us over long periods of time and in many differing contexts, may enter into new relations, may prevail in new orders, and in that respect changes without altering its availability to us as a logical principle. It may, for example, be used to illustrate a philosophical point, as is happening here, which creates a new relation for it. It does not do to say that this new relation is extrinsic to its nature. On the contrary, the new ordinal location of the principle creates a new trait that is no more or less constitutive of the principle. It may be minimally relevant to the potential of the principle to serve as a principle of logic, but it is no less constitutive for that.

The point is that the ordinality of the complexes of nature does not indicate ubiquitous change, but it does indicate the regular potential for or availability of alescence. Because we no longer think in terms of an entity as fixed in its nature, with attributes coming or going without affecting its nature, complexes may and do acquire new ordinal locations, new traits. It is this fact that indicates creativity in nature. If complexes are defined naturally by their traits, their ordinal locations, and if complexes may come to prevail in new orders in many different ways at any given time, then the natural definition of complexes is regularly generated anew, or at least the potential for such creativity prevails. Ordinality enables us to understand what creativity in nature is, the sense in which it is potentially available to the natural definition of complexes, and perhaps most importantly how it is fully consistent with objectivity, as long as the latter is understood as natural, ordinal definition.

The second point to emphasize has to do not with the fact that all complexes are *relational*, but with the fact that *all complexes* are relational, that ordinality characterizes whatever is. The universal scope of a relational ontology, which is to say that it applies to all "the things in heaven and earth," whatever they may be, indicates the centrality of creativity in nature. The creative dimension of complexes is not something that applies only to human beings and it is not something to be found only in experience. The human construction of our world or worlds occurs as a normal dimension of the relational character of complexes. The character of human judgment, however, gives creativity in experience unique dimensions, and it is this that we acknowledge in constructivist philosophies. The interactional character of experience as Dewey describes it indicates the ordinal, constitutive nature of the relations between people and their surroundings.

That human beings are related constitutively to our environments indicates that like all complexes we constitute our surroundings by virtue of our complex relations to it, just as our surroundings, or more technically and generally our ordinal locations, constitute us. Like everything else, we are creatively related to the worlds we inhabit. But we also order our environments through judgment, through the countless selections we make in our lives, whether they be purposeful or habitual. Dewey's culture, Bourdieu's habitus, and Buchler's judgment, though they are not equivalent concepts, are all pointing to the same general feature of our condition. The decisions I make and the actions I take in writing this book, for example, construct my world, and yours as reader. The degree of relevance this particular construction has for each of us is impossible to specify in advance, and may even be impossible to specify at any point. If this book emerges "stillborn from the presses," to use Hume's wonderful phrase, if you are one of the few readers it ever has, and if the copies of the book do little more than collect dust on library shelves, then its relevance is likely to be minimal for any of us. But perhaps it will be otherwise.

Any other of our countless judgments illustrates the point equally well: when we drive to work or fix the wiring in our house; when we compose, perform, or simply listen to a piece of music; when we write a letter to the editor or simply read the paper. In all these cases and the innumerable others like them we are constructing and reconstructing our worlds; we are engaged in world making, usually in mundane but occasionally in profound ways.

One of the more profound ways in which we engage in world making (profound, that is, for each of us as individuals) is in the creative construction of meaning. Here is a case in which we can truthfully say that "the world is whatever we describe it as." Like all other examples of human judgment, the construction of meaning is not done arbitrarily. The creation of new relations or ordinal locations in our attribution of meaning to a specific event, for example, is a creative alteration of that event. Meaning, in other words, is one among the innumerable constituent complexes that taken together and in their specific relations are the event. When we ascribe a meaning to an event that bears little or no relation to the other traits of the event we can accurately be said to be delusional—for example, if I detect a likeness to a prominent religious figure on my morning toast and declare this to mean that God is communicating with me. But we are usually not delusional. That is, when we draw meaning from or ascribe meaning to the experiences and events of our lives we generally maintain some reasonable degree of relevance between the experiences or events and their meaning.

The important point for our purposes is that it is *we* who draw or ascribe the meaning. We may do so as individuals or as members of a community with shared assumptions and expectations, but it is nonetheless we who construct meaning. In doing so we are not overlaying the event or experience with an extrinsic element, as if meaning is somehow inessential to the nature of the event or experience in question. We are, rather, creating new relations, new ordinal locations, and thereby recreating the event or experience. It now has a new constitutive trait, which is to say its meaning in relation to us either as individuals or as members of a community.

It is common for people to wonder in the face of a specific experience what it means. This verbal formulation suggests that the experience possesses its meaning intrinsically, regardless of how it fits into the broader scope of our lives, either at the moment or in a longer run. One of the reasons this sort of formulation is serviceable is that often enough we are as if compelled to draw a certain meaning from something because, on pain of being delusional, we cannot ignore those of its traits that urge that specific meaning. It wears its meaning on its sleeve, we might say. Even in such a case, however, meaning is no less a relation between an event or experience and judgment. We may feel as if we simply acquiesce to a meaning that comes already packaged with the event or experience, but that feeling should not drive our ontological understanding. We may tacitly agree to or accept a specific meaning when we feel as if we have little choice, but meaning remains a relation with us.

So in a literal sense, when we wonder what a particular event or experience means we are in fact wondering which meaning we shall construct. This point is important because meaning is a crucial and probably distinctive feature of human life and experience, perhaps even the most important distinctively *human* feature of our lives; and because here at the point where our lives are most importantly human, we are engaged in an act of creative construction, of world making. The worlds we inhabit, so to speak—or better, the worlds of our experience—are suffused with meaning, and they are worlds of our making. There is nothing mysterious or incongruous about this. The creative construction of meaning is a moment, admittedly a critical moment for human life, of the creative dimension of a relational, ordinal nature.

To summarize: From the point of view of a relational ontology, both objectivity and creativity have a central role to play in nature, and in our understanding of human interaction with other complexes of nature. The tension between objectivity and creativity that we identified earlier is the result of a failure on the part of both modernism and postmodernism, and of the standard objectivist and constructivist, to understand how nature works. Once we approach nature relationally, we can see that far from being in tension, objectivity and creativity are complementary characteristics of natural processes. This in turn can help us appreciate the fact that the creation of value and meaning in our individual lives, and in culture generally, is not a mere accretion on reality, but a constitutive characteristic of reality itself. Nature simultaneously is what it is, whatever that is, and it is what we describe it as.

SIX

GOD AND FAITH

One of the thornier problems for pragmatic naturalism is how to understand religion and God.[1] On the one hand, naturalism rests on the assumption that whatever there is, it is fully a natural entity. This means, among other things, that neither nature in general nor anything in or of it requires for its being or explanation anything that is not natural. This on the face of it rules out the possibility of any traditional conception of the divine wherein the divine is nonnatural, or supernatural, or the cause of nature, or the sustainer of nature, or for that matter the redeemer of nature. So much, one would think, for God and religion.

The problem is "the other hand," which is to say that if naturalism takes the view that whatever there is, it is fully encompassed within nature, then there seems to be a necessity to understand both God and religion as natural phenomena. Religion is certainly a reality, and naturalism must be able to understand it given its character and role within orders of nature. God is a trickier matter. If we say that God exists, then we need to specify the characteristics of that whose existence we are affirming. If we say that there is a God that is the first cause, so to speak, whether in time or in being, then we have posited a nonnatural entity and have moved outside of naturalism. If we say that there is a God but that God is fully a natural being then it is not clear that we are talking about the God that appears to motivate believers within the major monotheistic traditions. This fully natural God, for example, could not be a first cause in any sense.

One way around the problem of God is simply to deny God's existence, i.e., to say that though millions of people assert and through history have asserted the existence of God, and claim in a wide range of ways to feel God's presence in their lives, they are all simply wrong. It is of course possible that they are all wrong, and there is no logical inconsistency in the idea that most people, or even all people, hold a view that is false. And in fact a naturalist has to say something like this, i.e., that the God in whom millions of people have believed and continue to believe does not now and never has existed.

But there remains something unsatisfactory about this because to talk about God in this way seems not to take account of the significance the belief in God has for many people. To talk about God's existence is not simply to make one more existential claim, on a par with, for example, the monster in the closet. The meaning and significance for people's lives of the belief in the existence of God is a dimension or trait of God itself, it is a dimension of the complex relation between believers and the object of their belief, and therefore God's existence can not be breezily waved aside without equally breezily waving aside the power that belief in God has. It is precisely here that the naturalist has to be careful. The power and significance of the belief in God is a dimension of the phenomenon that is to be accounted for on natural terms, and so cannot simply be dismissed.

The focus of this chapter is to consider some of the many aspects of religion such that we understand them within a pragmatic naturalist framework without simply dismissing them or distorting their character. This is important because I have argued that one of the virtues of pragmatic naturalism in general is that it is capable of encompassing the many dimensions of experience, and of nature generally, without the reductionism that is all too common in much of philosophy. It would not do at this point simply to dismiss the belief in God as an illusion, as we have said. It will also not do simply to reduce religious commitment and faith to social or psychological conditions. Freud may or may not have been right that religion is an illusion, or that belief in God is a craving for a father figure, but even if he were right, religious belief and faith are too central to individuals, communities, and societies to be explained away. It is more reasonable, and more consistent with the tenor of pragmatic naturalism, to attempt to understand them, to the extent possible, on their own terms. That "their own terms" tend to be supernatural sets the philosophic challenge for us.

Religion is a huge topic, most of which therefore has to fall beyond the scope of this chapter. But to avoid the charge that I have taken an easy way out, I will address what for pragmatic naturalism must be the two most challenging aspects of religion: the nature of God and of religious faith. I shall begin with God.

An Ordinal God

Over the years there have been various approaches to an understanding of God and religion as natural phenomena. Before we look at those attempts to understand a natural God, I need first to clarify the implications of an ordinal, relational ontology for a concept of God. I shall stipulate, first, that God prevails. This is a rather bald acknowledgment, though, in that it says nothing about the traits that we may reasonably ascribe to God. It says simply that there are ordinal locations of which God is a constitutive trait, which is a more technical way of saying simply that God prevails in some order or orders. This may appear to beg the question of God's existence in that it seems to assert the very thing that is at issue when one asks whether God exists. As we have seen earlier, though, the term "existence" is a tricky one. For us it has to mean simply prevalence in one or more orders of relations. As we will soon see, if it is not clear already, when one asks whether God exists one typically is not simply asking whether there are any ordinal locations at all in which God prevails. When we translate the traditional question whether God exists into ordinal terms, it turns out to be asking whether God prevails in certain specific orders. To say, then, that God prevails in some order or orders is not necessarily to respond in the affirmative to the standard meaning and significance of the question of whether God exists; it is not question begging.

It does, however, assume that we cannot simply dismiss God altogether, if only because our experience refuses to allow it. God has been a factor in countless lives and events for thousands of years. Human history and individual lives would be radically different if there had not been a God motivating people to do this or that, or to act one way or another. From the rapturous to the despicable, God has been involved in much of what the human race has undergone, accomplished, and committed.

Notice that I did not say that the concept of God has motivated people, but God itself. In doing so, am I not smuggling in through the back door a kind of ontological argument? Or less grandiosely, am I not equivocating between God and the concept of or belief in God? The answer is that I am not, and the reason I am not may be one of the more important philosophical points to be made here. First, I should distinguish between concepts and beliefs. Concepts do not generally have much motivating power. For example, I might have a concept of right and wrong such that doing *x* is right and not doing *x* is wrong. However, if when faced with having to chose between them I do *x*, I do so not because I have a specific concept of right and wrong in this case but because I have a commitment to doing right, or because I believe that doing right is the appropriate thing for me to do. It is the belief or commitment that has the motivating power in such a case, and not the concept. Similarly, if I am a Justice of the US Supreme Court and I have a certain concept of the US Constitution I will rule in certain ways and not others. But it is not the concept that drives me as much as it would be my commitment to the Constitution as the foundational law of the country and the final arbiter of the legitimacy of state and federal law. My concept may provide the criterion for my decision, but it is not what motivates me.

The case is similar for religious motivation. It is not having the concept of God that inclines us to go to war or to make peace, to found a city or to follow a particular way of life. It seems more reasonable to say that belief or faith may have this power than to say that a concept does. I will deal further on with the difficult question of how to understand religious faith. At this point we need to consider the question of whether it is more sensible to say that God has figured in human behavior or that the concept of or belief in God has done so. The distinction is important because if the former is the case then we have sufficient justification to talk about God as prevailing without having to make any prior arguments about God's existence.

Let us face the question directly. Neither concept nor belief nor commitment are themselves sufficient to imply the prevalence of anything, at least beyond the order of intension or objects of belief, but it is fair to say that belief or commitment has greater functional power with respect to the prevalence of the object of belief or commitment. Nevertheless, God and the belief in God are not the same thing. The latter is a mental or psychological condition, or at least a predisposition to behave in certain ways under certain conditions, while the former is a complex that might in principle be located in, or is locatable in, any number of orders beyond the psychological or behavioral. But belief and commitment point to their objects in ways that have ontological relevance. When people pray, for example, the object of prayer is not their belief in God, but God itself. When people write religious poetry or music, it is in praise not of the belief in God but of God itself. God is the object of these activities, not the belief in God. To say that the object of such activities is a belief or a concept is to twist them into something they are not. In the same way, Biblical or Koranic stories are stories about God, not stories about the concept of or belief in God, just as *Hamlet* is a play about a Danish prince and "Kubla Khan" is a poem about the emperor and his Xanadu. The pragmatic naturalist has no more reason to be unnerved by the object of Biblical stories than he or she does about the object of the works of Shakespeare or Coleridge.

If considerations like these are not sufficient to make the point that we may reasonably talk about God rather than simply the belief in or concept of God, perhaps a stronger way to make it would be to emphasize the phenomenological dimension of the experience of God. Though this does not and never has applied to me, there are many people for whom God is a presence in their lives. William James more than anyone has demonstrated the many ways that such an experience can occur. There are no doubt psychological dimensions to religious experience, but if we are to avoid the kind of reductionism that we have been critical of elsewhere, it is not sufficient to content ourselves by explaining away religious experience in psychological terms any more than we can legitimately explain away the relatively large in terms of the relatively small, or the biological in terms of the chemical, or the social in terms of the individual. Religious experience has an integrity that is not to be denied and there is no philosophical justification for attempting to do so. Just as religious stories have an object, so religious experience has one or more constituents that cannot justifiably be written off. Religious experience is to be taken at face value, and such experience invariably includes some sense of the divine. In some way or other such experiences are about or include God, understood in various ways. They are not simply about beliefs or concepts.

That is not to say that every possible interpretation of religious experiences is equally valid, because interpretation involves other epistemological moves: Analogies may be more or less adequate; inferences may be valid or not; references may be more or less accurate. It is surely the case that in many religious experiences the inference to an appropriate understanding or explanation is replaced by wishful thinking and jumping to conclusions. The phenomenological dimension of religious experience justifies talk about God, but it does not by itself justify the attribution of any specific traits to God. The most we can say based on the reality and integrity of religious experience, which is to say, based solely on the phenomenological level, is that God prevails. To specify the orders in which we may reasonably say that God prevails requires more careful philosophic analysis.

God, we may then say, is discriminated, identified, picked out, and to that extent we are justified in talking about God directly. And the orders in which God is so discriminated indicate the respects in which it is appropriate to say that God prevails. To do so is not to equivocate between God and belief in God. It is, on the contrary, to take seriously the fact that it is God about which people write and speak, to which people pray, and which people experience. We are well served to remind ourselves at this point of Randall's observation that the important question is not whether this or that exists, but how and in what way it exists. In no case is that insight more important than with respect to God.

So God prevails. But in a relational nature, in what order or orders can we reasonably say that God is located? We can readily locate God in the orders of myth, of symbol, of literature, of historical events, of many people's experience, of piety, and of many others in which God has figured. The critical question is how we might understand other religiously important traits that are traditionally ascribed to a monotheistic God: creator, redeemer, ultimate ground of reality, etc. We need to take up these attributes and consider whether they can reasonably be ascribed to God given the demands of an ordinal, relational nature.

We may begin with the traditionally ascribed attribute of God as creator ex nihilo. If God is a creator ex nihilo, then certain things must be true. It must be true, for example, that at the point when God had not created the world, there was nothing other than God alone. If an ordinal ontology allows for this possibility, then it may allow for the possibility of God's being located in the order of complexes that create, or create ex nihilo. If this characteristic of God is found not to be possible in an ordinal, relational nature, then it is not possible that God is located in the order of complexes that create ex nihilo. In fact, because God can by definition be the only complex located in such an order, it would mean that there is no order of creators ex nihilo, which is to say that creation ex nihilo does not occur in nature. If God cannot be located in such an order, or if there is no such order, then God cannot be a creator, at least not a creator from nothing. The same methodology must be applied to the other prominent and distinctive characteristics traditionally ascribed to God. Once that is done a picture will emerge of the sort of God that can prevail in a relational nature.

Reference to some of the technical details of an ordinal ontology is relevant at this point because we have need to translate traditional attributes of God into ordinal, relational terms. For example, if God, like everything else, is a natural complex, then by definition God is not simple or indivisible. God, like every other complex, is composed of constituent complexes; it is itself an order of relations. This is already contrary to one of the more prevalent features of the God of much of monotheism—namely, its simplicity. One of the consequences of this general ontological point has to do with God as creator. If God were a creator ex nihilo, then there was a point at which God had not yet produced its creation, or at least this is the popular conception. Leaving aside the obvious question of how there could be a "before" if time was not "yet" created, there are other difficulties with the notion of a creator God. Presumably, when God had not yet created nature, there was nothing in existence other than God. But if God is a natural complex, as it must be in a relational, naturalist ontology, then this complex locates other, subordinate complexes. That is, it has constituents. These constituents cannot be the same as God, since God, as a complex, is the order in which they are located. In order for God to "be" at all, certain subordinate complexes must be as well.

In nature ordinally understood there are further stipulations on the character of any given complex. Not only must a complex locate subordinate subcomplexes, but it must itself also be a subcomplex of another, perhaps more pervasive complex. All complexes both locate and are located. If God is a complex, then God is located in at least one order. Here again, the image of God (as cause) standing alone, prior to everything else (its effects), is untenable. An order necessarily distinguishes complexes in certain ways and along certain lines; it necessarily delimits complexes and the relations among them. Complexes are what they are by virtue of their ordinal locations. The multiplicity of orders, and the function of orders as that which delimits a complex's traits and scope, provide the many faceted nature of complexes. The ordinal location or locations of a complex are what provide, or constitute, its integrity or integrities. The general contour or scope of a complex is what determines it as that and just that complex. As we have seen earlier, this categorial apparatus is necessary for an ordinal ontology because it is the relation of the overall contour of a complex with any of its specific integrities or traits that constitutes the identity of the complex. The identity of a complex, in other words, is a function of its ordinal locations, and therefore the ontology requires the stipulation that every complex must both locate traits and be located in one or more orders of traits. For God to obtain at all, it is necessary that it both locate traits and be itself ordinally located. Neither of these structural requirements is compatible with a creator ex nihilo.

Even the principle of ontological parity, which is the stipulation that no complex is more or less real than any other, that there is no sense to the traditional idea of degrees of reality, creates trouble for a creator God. Much if not all of the more Platonic strain in the history of Christian thought turns to a large extent on a principle of ontological priority, but this is not the source of the trouble here. Even though the principle of ontological priority has played such a crucial role in our philosophic and theological development, there is an equally strong tradition wherein the notion of degrees of being does not figure quite as prominently. The point at which the principle of ontological parity interferes with a creator God is in the context of the idea of existence itself, more specifically what can reasonably be said to exist. As we have seen, many things, and many different kinds of things, can be said "to be." It has become traditional philosophically to erect as a model of existence a rather crude spatiotemporal paradigm. But this is clearly too restrictive because there are many kinds of complexes that can be said to be but do not fit this paradigm. Possibilities are one such kind of complex, as we have argued previously. There has also been a strong tendency in philosophy to consider being as in some sense equivalent to actuality, a conception that places possibility in some sort of ontological limbo. A more coherent way to look at all this is to say that actuality "is" no more than possibility "is." A possibility is no less of a complex, with all of the appropriate ordinal conditions, than is an actuality. Both are complexes located in orders of relations. If either can be said "to be," then so must the other.

If God were a creator, then the possibility of what it creates obtains along with it. It would not do to suggest that God creates this possibility as well, since that would only push the question back a step. The question would then have to do with the possibility of *this* creation, and we are off on an infinite regress. The possibility of creation must be understood as a complex, located in certain orders, and as obtaining along with, and in relation of some kind to, God. Again, the idea of a creator ex nihilo is severely hampered by the categorial demands of a nature understood relationally and ordinally.

God, as this analysis demonstrates, cannot be a creator ex nihilo, regardless of other orders in which it may be located and other traits that may be attributed to it. A similar situation results from an analysis of other critical characteristics that have been attributed to the divine. For example, God is sometimes referred to as that which grounds being, as that which makes everything else possible, as the "sustainer" of nature. But for the same reasons that it cannot be a creator ex nihilo, God cannot be that which makes existence or nature possible. This traditional trait of God makes a bit more sense than the idea that God has created from nothing, but that is only because it avoids the strange temporal paradox that a creator God generates. Nonetheless, to be that which grounds everything else, God would need not to be ordinally located, and that is impossible. For ontological reasons, then, God cannot possess these significant traits that have traditionally been ascribed to it. In fact, God cannot stand in any specific relation to nature in general for the simple reason that God is among the complexes of nature.

This fact does not, however, preclude the possibility that God may have other traits of religious significance. For example, it is impossible to ascribe to God the role of redeemer of nature overall, but it may still be possible for God to redeem individuals. At least the ontology does not preclude such a possibility. God, or an individual's relation to God, may also in principle be a source of profound meaning and provide an individual spiritual sustenance of a profound kind. Such possibilities as these allow those naturalists with the inclination to develop a naturalist theology of one sort or another without necessarily violating the naturalist assumption that nature is all-inclusive. Whether there is sufficient reason to do so is another question. I can think of no reason to assume that nature cannot account for itself. With respect to those aspects of nature available to scientific inquiry, we have over the centuries come to understand in more and deeper detail the natural principles that govern the behavior of material, and to some extent nonmaterial, phenomena. The one set of questions about which natural science has little to say has to do with origins. Thanks to Darwin and his successors we know quite a bit about the origin of species, but we know far less, and therefore at this point can explain far less, about the origin of life. Cosmology has helped us to understand more than we recently did about the conditions and forces that prevailed in the earliest moments of the Big Bang, but we know little to nothing about what preceded that event, or indeed why it occurred at all. If we slide from that question about the universe in general into the related but nonscientific question why there is anything at all, we have no adequate answer to give. But to introduce God as the explanation, beside the fact that it would require a violation of the categories of a relational ontology, still provides no adequate answer. If we are entitled to ask the question of why there is anything at all, then we would be equally entitled to ask the same question about God. If the answer with respect to God is that we do not know, then we have not advanced our understanding of nature by introducing God. If the answer is that God somehow explains itself, then we are entitled to wonder why we cannot make the same claim about nature. God in the end has no explanatory power with respect to nature in general or to specific natural, material events.

But God has traditionally been much more than an explanation for that which we otherwise do not understand, and it is these other characteristics of God that naturalist philosophers within the American pragmatic naturalist tradition, and long before it, have emphasized in their efforts to develop a naturalist theology, or at least a conception of God that can sit comfortably within a naturalist world view. Spinoza, perhaps the most important pre-American example, equated God and nature, and for doing so he was attacked for atheism. But Spinoza did manage to maintain a degree of the humility and piety before nature that is characteristic of the humility and piety common in religious experience and observance. Such a sense of piety is often associated with a religious sensibility, and Spinoza's example indicates that what in his case is a natural piety nonetheless captures something distinctive about religious experience.

In the American naturalist tradition the first key figure is Santayana, who sought to preserve the power and significance of religion and God, one consistent with naturalist assumptions, through an aesthetic reading of the nature of God and religion.[2] Dewey, in a more instrumentalist vein, offered an ethical reading of God and religion, understanding and even maintaining the significance of both while at the same time redefining them. In Dewey's hands God comes to represent the unification of the ideals that we hold in highest esteem: justice, truth, beauty, wisdom, and benevolence.[3] Randall took a still different approach, wherein both religion and God are understood through the function they serve to provide coherence, meaning, and direction for people's lives. In this respect Randall's treatment of religious and theistic themes is consistent with his ontological insight that the important question is not whether this or that exists, but how.[4]

A fourth approach is taken by John McDermott, who gives the whole set of issues what we might call a literary twist. McDermott often makes the claim that there is no "canopy of explanation." This is very much a naturalist's point of view in that it denies that there is an overarching story that neatly ties reality in a bow and provides whatever meaning we may seek or need. But meaning and significance there still must be. So what exactly is McDermott rejecting when he denies a canopy of explanation or an overarching story? It is not the explanation or the story that he rejects but the canopy. In fact he insists on a multiplicity of stories, and it is in the stories that the important insights and understandings are to be found. And the stories can be anything and come from anywhere; they can be mythical, or heroic, or personal; they can derive from memory, invention, or the will, individual or collective. Whether God survives in this approach is an open question in that the stories may or may not be stories about God, but the function of God surely survives, as does the significance of a more traditional religious understanding.[5]

Another approach to the questions of God and religion within a pragmatic naturalist framework has come from Robert Corrington, who constructs a theology, in the traditional sense of an articulation of the nature of God and spirit, with the help of the categories of an ordinal ontology. Corrington casts a wide net, and consequently his theology, though rooted in ordinality, crosses a number of lines of thought, including Spinoza's pantheism and Whitehead's process theology.[6] Another conception of and approach to a naturalist theology has been developed in recent years by Donald Crosby.[7] He refers to his as a "Religion of Nature," the basic point of which is to develop a way of achieving for our lives the ends that theistic religion serves while acknowledging the natural context of our lives, our struggles, and the full range of possibilities we have for confronting and resolving them.

This is not the place to describe the details of the various approaches to God that have been and are currently being taken within the pragmatic naturalist perspective. Nor is it the place to criticize them. Our primary purpose has been to develop three points: (1) God prevails in various respects as a significant factor in history, in literature and other human products, and in the experience of many people; (2) the relational ontology of pragmatic naturalism does not allow for some of the traditional and religiously important attributes of God, most notably as the creator and ground of nature; and (3) because pragmatic naturalism respects religious experience no less than other sorts, there is a place within it for a meaningful conception of God, should someone find such a thing valuable.

One of the more surprising results of our analysis of God is that in the end God turns out not to be very difficult to handle. As an explanatory device it is pointless, and as a meaningful dimension of experience it presents no special philosophical problems. Religious faith, interestingly enough, is a more difficult matter.

Faith

Religion has dimensions that concern cosmology, aesthetics, ethics, politics, meaning, and purpose. It is small wonder that it has played a central role in the lives of individuals, nations, and whole cultures for, it appears, as long as there have been people. Its centrality ebbs and flows, from the more secular character of modern European societies to the theocracies, real and desired, of the Middle East, to the Christian fundamentalism of the United States, to the political commitments of Zionism. In one way or another, religion and religions have been and continue to be prepared to explain and govern every aspect of the lives of individuals and of societies.

Though it may seem ironic, we have suggested that among the easier of the many dimensions of religion for the naturalist to deal with is the cosmological and ontological. With respect to cosmology, there is nothing gained in our understanding of the material universe by positing an eternal, supreme being. We understand enough about the workings of physical laws to do a fair job of accounting for physical events in the universe, and we get better at it as we go along. Of course physical laws do not explain the origins of the universe, but then neither does an eternal being. If we can posit an eternal being outside nature then, as we have said, we can just as easily posit the eternality of nature. The one is no easier to understand than the other, but for the sake of simplicity of explanation and with a nod to William of Ockham, there is no point in multiplying entities unnecessarily, or to paraphrase the same William, there is no point in multiplying ordinal locations unnecessarily.

Ethics presents no great difficulty either. It is common for nonphilosophical theists to assume that ethical principles must have a divine source for them to have any legitimacy, but we know that there is no reason to accept that assumption. Those who assume that there must be a divine or at least absolute source of ethical principles make one of two mistakes: Either they assume that without an absolute source ethical principles are arbitrary and therefore without sufficient justification, or they reason that without the threat of punishment from a divine source there would be no sufficient reason for people in adequate numbers to take ethical principles seriously.

The response to the first point is of course that there are at least several bases for the justification of ethical principles other than an absolute source, the most obvious of which is consequences. Another is purposes. It is a given of pragmatist thought that we act to achieve something, or as Dewey would put it, with ends in view. In many cases those ends or purposes are related to ideals, and our ideals are in one way or another constructed both individually and collectively. Actions and their purposes, or means and ends, are constitutively related to one another. Ethical principles, like everything else, are complexes the characteristics of which are determined relationally. Both their justification and their force are a function of their relations.

The second point is more easily dispensed with. First, as even theological ethicists will acknowledge, the threat of punishment is not an ethically valuable reason for taking ethical principles seriously. That many people seem to think that it is reflects more the inadequacy of education or the relative thinness of many believers' understanding of theology than the nature of ethical principles. Second, experience demonstrates otherwise because there are many atheists who live normally ethically informed lives. It is safe to say that theists and atheists are equally capable of embodying and transgressing ethical principles.

This is not to say that a pragmatic naturalist ethics is a simple matter and presents no difficulties. But quantum physics is not easy either and presents all sorts of difficulties, a fact that does not incline us to infer that the better explanation of quantum behavior is divine. The examination of ethics is no less a natural enterprise than is the examination of material nature.

Certain other aspects of religious belief and life present a range of problems, though they are not philosophical problems. I have in mind psychological questions and social and political issues. The latter can of course be usefully considered by philosophers—for example, the relative advantages of secular democracy, or at least a secular polity of some kind, over theocracy. But these questions are also grist for the mill of sociologists and political scientists. In other words, they pose no special problem for naturalist philosophers.

There are, as we have already suggested, questions of meaning and purpose that are in no way trivial. To provide purpose and meaning is perhaps the most important function religion serves. And it is not only a psychological matter. Religious faith can and does provide the glue, we might say, or the general framework that sustains individuals, families, and whole communities. The institution of the church or any religious community plays a role here, but it is the belief of its members that conveys the moral authority on the church or community to serve the institutional function that it does. In other words, it is religious faith and belief that serve as the source of meaning and purpose more than the church.

We know of course that meaning and purpose do not require religious belief, if only because there are many of us who live purposeful and meaning-filled lives without it. But that understanding is shared by relatively few of us, especially in the United States and other societies in which religion remains a potent force. Secularism may be more widespread in Europe and China, but from a global perspective it is still more the exception than the rule. And in any case meaning is, as we have discussed in the previous chapter, a matter of creative construction more than a given of nature.

So the pragmatic naturalist can handle the bulk of issues that arise around religion. With respect to ontology and cosmology, ethics and aesthetics, society and politics, and meaning and purpose, pragmatic naturalism can make sense on its own terms of the religiously oriented questions that have traditionally been posed. But there remains one outstanding question: What do we do in the face of straightforward religious faith?

It is worth taking a moment to think about what religious faith is. I suspect that we typically think of it as rather like any sort of belief, even if more fundamental to people's lives than most or all other beliefs. But this is probably not right. Why, we might ask, do people believe things?

In some cases it is a matter of desire. We might believe that our favorite team will win the championship because we wish it to be so. In other cases we might believe something because we judge that there are enough good reasons to think it true that we draw our belief more or less like a deductive conclusion or some less rigorous inference. In yet other cases we may believe something because our experience points toward it. But none of these kinds of situations adequately describe religious faith. It is not embraced by believers as a conclusion to an argument, deductive, inductive, abductive, or pragmatic, nor is it an inference drawn from experience. There is, however, one sense in which faith is wishful thinking, so to speak, and that is the sense in which James deals with it in "The Will to Believe." James makes a compelling case in that essay not for the claim that we ought to believe but for the more modest but nevertheless important claim that given the conditions that apply in the case of religious faith we are rationally justified in doing so if we are so inclined, despite the absence of sufficient evidence. The appropriate conditions, however, do not apply to most cases of belief, and so even with respect to "willing" to believe, religious faith is unlike most other forms of belief.

Anselm understood this fact about faith when he described his argument as a case of "faith seeking understanding." James understood it in "The Will to Believe" and in *The Varieties of Religious Experience.* Randall understood it in his many efforts to provide an account of the function of religious ideas and beliefs in people's lives. And Santayana understood it when he said that myths are conceived, i.e., that mythical thinking is its own conceptual framework. Religious faith, it appears, is not a conclusion but a point of departure, a general framework for dealing with whatever one faces. Interestingly enough, one might also describe pragmatic naturalism in these terms, along with the general humanism that accompanies it. This is not to say that naturalism or humanism are secular religions, but they do have in common with religious faith the function of serving as a framework within or through which one lives.

Neither the secularism of humanism and pragmatic naturalism nor religious faith can "best" the other, so to speak, because neither is an inference. Argument is not relevant at this conceptual level. It is senseless, in other words, for pragmatic naturalism to seek to refute faith. To attempt to do so is to betray a failure to understand what it is. What it must do, on the contrary, is to recognize as a fully natural phenomenon the fact of religious faith as an alternative framework for many people's lives. This, however, simply sets the problem for us: Pragmatic naturalism must recognize religious faith as a natural phenomenon, but religious faith, by virtue of some of its content, is inconsistent with the naturalism that wants to acknowledge it.

But perhaps this overstates the problem, or suggests more of a problem than there really is. If there is an inconsistency between faith and naturalism, it arises only insofar as religious faith includes the belief in a being that naturalism cannot incorporate, an absolute God. On the point of this particular belief, however, there is nothing to prevent the naturalist from simply disagreeing and claiming that the belief is mistaken in that the object of the belief does not exist, at least not with the traits that the theist typically wants to ascribe to it. That is to say that there is not a God that prevails in the orders of creator ex nihilo and ground of nature. To make such a claim would be no different in kind than objecting to any other specific belief, no matter what its object. This would be a problem for naturalism's interest in acknowledging religious faith only if faith were reducible to these specific beliefs. But faith cannot be so reduced.

First, it is possible for faith to involve a belief in a God that is not absolute, in which case there would not necessarily be an inconsistency. If God can be construed as Dewey, Randall, or Corrington have done and remain religiously meaningful, then faith that includes such a belief poses no special problem. The possibility and significance of faith in such cases, of a faith that incorporates such a God, becomes a theological rather than a philosophical issue. Second, religious faith involves much more than a set of beliefs, regardless of the traits attributed to the objects of belief, and faith more fully understood presents no problem for pragmatic naturalism. This is the point that needs development.

We can put the point in a slightly different way. If faith is primarily belief in an absolute creator that stands outside of nature, then it is fundamentally flawed because its defining constituent is a false belief. But must a life lived in faith be a mistake, however psychologically satisfying it may be? This is the question we need to explore if we wish not to dismiss a life lived in faith but to understand its place in nature and in experience.

In what does a life lived in faith consist? The first point to note is that a life of faith is a way of life in the sense that it is about how one lives rather than simply what one believes. There are several characteristics of such a life that taken together make it clear that faith involves much more than simply this or that belief, even a belief in God. Among the characteristics that should be noticed, a life lived in faith is characterized by trust in other people, by the sense of the actual or possible general "rightness" of things, by a belief in salvation and redemption, by a sense of and commitment to justice, and by a general posture of humility and piety.

There is of course a sense in which social life in general requires some degree of trust. If, for example, we did not trust the other drivers on the road, or the pilots of the airplanes we fly in, or the teachers in our children's schools, then our lives in anything like their present form would not be possible at all. But the trust that characterizes a life of faith goes much deeper. A life defined by trust in other people is not primarily self-interested, or at least is not a selfish life. If we trust others, for example, then we do not look to manipulate them to meet or fulfill our own interests. That is not to say that religious faith makes us indifferent to our own interests, but it does incline us to understand or pursue our self interest within the context of the interests of others. To trust in other people is to act in ways that take for granted the moral significance of those around one. It also inclines us to assume, with or without evidence, that for the most part those around us to some extent take our interests to heart. It is to assume a community that is based, usually in unspecified ways, on common concerns and aspirations. For some, such a community can be fairly limited in scope, in the sense that it includes a limited number of other people, while for others it can cast a much wider net. Thus, for some people their "faith community" is limited to those who share a common confession, while for other people it can genuinely encompass much or all of the world. People whose faith moves them to work in distant and underdeveloped places in the world, for example, can be understood to be moved by a trust in and commitment to others in the latter, broader sense. Whether narrowly or broadly understood, the trust in others that characterizes a life of faith is of this deeper sort that not only enables social life but also defines one's responsibilities within it.

A sense of the "rightness" of things is a second characteristic of the life of faith. What does this mean? Presumably one of the virtues of belief in a God that orders the world is that one can assume that sooner or later, if not already, things are ordered as they should be. This is what Leibniz meant, though he offered the point in technical terms, when he said that this is the best of all possible worlds. Given all the serious problems we habitually face, from the mundane to the global, it is easy to regard such a view as hopelessly naïve. Voltaire had himself a good time doing just that. It is easy to laugh with Voltaire at Panglossian foolishness, but we ought not to laugh too hard. It is not silly, or even entirely unreasonable, to understand the world as in a process that ultimately will work itself out for the best, either through God's actions or our own. In fact there is a sense in which we must take such a view, at least in a moderate form. Our lives would be dismal indeed without some degree of hope that the future can be an improvement on the present. Without the assumption of such a possibility there would be little reason for us to attempt to do anything constructive at all. It seems that when we act to solve any problem big or small, we necessarily assume that the world and our lives are meliorable. The difference between this common assumption and the person of faith's sense of the "rightness" of things is the difference between meliorism and perfectibility. For most of us we need assume only that our actions can achieve some desirable effect. For the person of faith, however, the world is not only capable of becoming better; it is inevitably becoming perfect, if it is not already. In the abstract this is a very big difference, but it is worth noting that for practical purposes it is more a difference of degree than of kind.

Another dimension of a life lived in faith is the element of salvation or redemption. This is the personal corollary of the previous point. Not only is the world in general capable of perfection, but we as individuals will, in one way or another, be redeemed. Theological traditions have differed on this point. For some, salvation is a result of what individuals do, and for others it is a matter for an omnipotent God to determine. Either way, for the faithful, personal salvation is a possibility, and something either to be worked toward or hoped for. A world in which one is not irredeemable is one in which there is hope. A life of faith is a hopeful life; faith imbues life with hope—for oneself, for the future, for "things" in general. As with the other characteristics of a life of faith, there are obvious virtues to a life lived in hope: Hopefulness, even on purely pragmatic grounds, is preferable to hopelessness.

Yet another trait of faith is a sense of a pervasive justice in the world. God itself is typically understood to embody justice, and divine justice is understood by the faithful to pervade God's creation. Those who live a life of faith take it as a given not only that things happen for reasons, but that the reasons are good ones because the events in the world, and in one's life, add up to something morally desirable. For many people this sense of a cosmic justice is also translated into a personal commitment to justice. Much of classical scripture in many religious traditions is read this way, and whole theologies have been built around the commitment to justice, social and individual, as the cornerstone of a life of faith. In some cases—for example, in Christian Liberation Theology—the pursuit of justice that constitutes a life of faith has an overtly political dimension. In other cases the commitment to justice may have more personal and immediate implications than social ones. In either case, to live a life of faith is to take seriously justice as a trait of creation itself and the commitment to justice as a defining trait of one's life.

We have also mentioned humility and piety as characteristics of faith. A life of faith will be one that avoids an arrogance and aggressiveness toward nature itself and toward other people. If nature is understood to be a divine creation then no other stance than humility toward it can be appropriate. Natural piety, we may say, has a comfortable home in the faithful life. Humility in one's relations with other people is no less a defining trait of faith. From a religious point of view people are no less divine creations than the rest of nature, and that alone calls for humility. In addition, if one is to take seriously the other traits of a life of faith that we have discussed—for example, justice and redemption—then consistency if nothing else calls for humility before others, even if one does not posit a divine source of oneself, others, or nature in general. Both humility and piety are expressions of a faith in the importance and inherent value of one's surroundings, of the environment in which one finds oneself. If I approach the world around me, and the people with whom I share it, as inherently valuable, then I can have no other attitude than humility toward them.

Religious faith, then, is far more than a particular belief or even set of beliefs. It consists in addition of a set of attitudes toward the world, toward other people, and toward one's own life that govern the decisions one makes, the actions one takes, and in general the life one lives. Faith is, therefore, not so much a set of beliefs as a way of life. Specifically, it is a way of life that embodies trust, hope, justice, rightness, humility, and redemption.

For traditional religious faith this way of life and the traits that constitute it are bound up with a belief in a creator God. If a creator God, indeed anything nonnatural, is impossible, as we have argued, what happens to our understanding of a life lived with these characteristics? Or to ask again our overarching question, how are we to understand faith?

There are three logical possibilities: (1) A life so lived is impossible without a creator God; (2) such a life can be coupled with a God differently understood, one that makes sense within a natural world; or (3) such a life can be lived without any conception of God. The first of these possibilities is false on the face of it. It is certainly possible to live a life of trust, hope, commitment to justice, humility, and redemption without a creator God, or without belief in one. It happens all the time, and the fact that it happens all the time is the basis, we might add, for the common ground that believers and nonbelievers have with respect to many important individual and social issues.

The second possibility speaks to the whole field of naturalist theology to which we referred earlier. Whether any of the various conceptions of God that have been developed by naturalist theologians are religiously compelling is a question for others to answer. There is, as we have said, nothing necessarily inconsistent about a theology developed within a naturalist philosophical framework. It remains the task of the naturalist theologian to indicate both the nature and value of a natural God and the character of the religious life, or faith, within such a conceptual framework.

The third possibility is, as we have already hinted in our response to the first, the central point that needs to be made about an understanding of faith appropriate to pragmatic naturalism. A life of faith is both possible and can make perfectly good sense independent of religious belief. Faith, in other words, is not something the pragmatic naturalist needs to ignore, dismiss, explain away, or in any way fear. The point is not that we *ought* to live a life of faith. One lives one's life as one sees fit, and other things being equal there is not much to be gained by dictating to people how they ought to live. The point is, rather, that the way of life that we have described as constituting a life of faith makes perfectly good sense on naturalist principles. There are, if nothing else, good pragmatic reasons. A life that is hopeful and committed to justice is more likely to achieve some measure of satisfaction and "rightness" than a life of despair and cynicism. Redemption and salvation too have pragmatic value. Even when divorced from their more cosmic and eternal religious forms of expression, to understand ourselves, our lives, and our world as savable, as redeemable, is in fact a necessary condition for acting such that we bring about better conditions than we currently have. And humility and natural piety are not only possible independent of religious belief, but given the current state of our environment and our social and political relations, they may be necessary if we wish not to destroy ourselves and our world.

Faith, in other words, makes perfectly good sense, and a life so lived is one that a naturalist can comfortably recommend. We recognize of course that for the traditional religious believer the meaning and import of his faith is related to a belief in a divine creator and presence. To that extent a religious life of faith and a similar secular life are different. But they are not as different as one might have supposed. In fact they are similar enough that the pragmatic naturalist and the believer have a great deal of common ground. Thus, despite the rejection of a religious belief in God, the pragmatic naturalist can recognize without difficulty the character, meaning and import of faith as a constituent of nature and of a life understood and lived on naturalist principles.

SEVEN

ART AND KNOWLEDGE

I have made the case in previous chapters that nature is to be understood as a term or concept of the widest possible scope, which is to say that it is understood to be all-inclusive.[1] Whatever there is, in other words, is natural. In the effort to put some flesh on such a bare-bones concept we have claimed that nature is to be understood as pluralistic, which is to say that nature consists of whatever we find in it, and in experience, itself a fully natural process, without any need to reduce one kind of complex to another. Thus, nature consists, among other sorts of things, of material objects, time, mathematical entities, fictional characters, histories, ethical principles, mind, consciousness, mental events of all kinds, illusions, delusions, natural laws, logic, language, science, art, selves, processes, God and gods, meanings, purposes, individuals, societies, institutions, relations, particulars, universals, atomic particles, ecosystems, life, death, actualities, possibilities, sadness, and joy.

Traditionally philosophers, especially when doing metaphysics, have understood their task as determining which of these and other sorts of entities or complexes are real and which are not, and they have tended to do so by explaining some or others away, or by trying to explain some in terms of others. For an influential form of contemporary "naturalism" this metaphysical approach has led to the association of nature exclusively with the material world, and the corresponding epistemological view that only those methods of inquiry that have access to material entities and processes, i.e., the natural sciences, are capable of providing knowledge of nature. Though not all philosophers engaged in metaphysics and epistemology would describe themselves as naturalists, the general thrust of the approach in which many philosophical issues are explored has tended to consist of an understanding of nature that limits it to material reality and to events in time and space, along with the corresponding epistemological points of view and methods of analysis.

This entire approach to metaphysics and epistemology is misguided, or so we are arguing. On the contrary, the task of metaphysics, indeed philosophy in general, is to take nature and experience at face value and to ask not whether this or that exists or is real, but to ask rather Randall's question "how and in what sense it is real." The previous chapter, in which we explored the existence of God and the nature of religious faith, particularly thorny problems for pragmatic naturalism, exemplifies this understanding of metaphysics and the task of philosophy. If nature is to be understood in this pluralistic way, and if one of the tasks of philosophy is to be understood as making sense of how this plurality of natural complexes may be comprehended, then there are significant implications for a naturalist epistemology.

Among the most important is that if nature is not to be reduced to material objects and processes alone, then there is no reason to think that the methods of the natural sciences represent the only cognitive access to nature. As powerful as they are, the sciences have a limited amount to offer with respect to our understanding of many of the complexes of nature. This is true even for those complexes whose aspects can be illuminated by science. For example, neurochemistry and neurophysiology can explain a great deal about how states of our neurological systems are related to events in consciousness, and perhaps even why we think in some ways and not others, but they cannot explain the meaning and lived importance of those events. As valuable as it is to know which regions of the brain are related to memories, for example, and the chemistry involved in the creation and retrieval of memories, something very different is needed for us to understand how and why this or that memory has the import that it does for the person having it, or why it influences a person the way it does. Similarly, there is a good deal of intriguing work underway in computer science, artificial intelligence, and their associated mathematics. Research on pattern recognition is an example, as is the interesting effort to probe the limits of the capacity of artificial intelligence to write literature.[2] Work of this kind can provide us with an enormous amount of interesting information about the mechanics of certain kinds of thought processes, and even about what we might mean by "thinking." It does not, however, help us to understand what to do with recognized patterns, nor does it help us much to understand of what literature is capable. And it certainly does not help us to define or redefine knowledge, or for that matter consciousness. In other words, once we take seriously the plurality of nature, we can no longer rest content with the sciences as the only or even primary access to it.

This is the context in which we need now to explore the arts. Just to be clear, the focus of our discussion is not a question about the relation of art to nature, in the common sense of that term. We are not concerned, for example, with a distinction between natural objects or processes and artworks as fabricated. There may well be a place for such a distinction, but it is not here. Art, like every other complex, is a fully natural activity, and artworks are ontologically no less natural than everything else. The issue here, rather, is the question of whether art is or can be cognitive, and the further question of how to understand knowledge such that art no less than science can be epistemologically embraced.

We should also point out that no systematic distinction will be made here between art objects or works of art and the experience of art. It is possible that a more thoroughly developed understanding of the cognitive dimension of art would require this distinction, but for our purposes it is not necessary. Of course it is obvious that knowledge is something that people have or achieve, in which case to the extent that knowledge derives from art it is, or it happens in, aesthetic experience. But the distinction between art and the experience of art cannot and should not be drawn too sharply. If we derive knowledge from art then a cognitive dimension is a trait of art itself, or objects of art themselves.

The relation between the experiencer and the art experienced is, after all, constitutive. It will therefore be possible for us to talk both about art and about aesthetic experience without concerning ourselves with otherwise relevant distinctions between them.

Art has many functions. It is expressive of points of view and emotions, and it is creative. And in its creativity, to make the point directly, it is, or at least can be, cognitive. Art, in other words, is one of the ways in which we have cognitive access to nature, no less than science. This is the claim that we shall now examine, and it is in some sense a modest claim. We are not proposing an entire theory of art or an entire aesthetic theory, nor do we wish to develop an entirely novel epistemology, though some novelty is called for. Aesthetics and epistemology have been woven together in many ways from Aristotle through Dewey to the present, and each such theory has its own contributions to make. We need not review them at this point.

We do, however, need to take another look at certain assumptions that have been made about inquiry and knowledge because in some respects those assumptions have contributed to the problem with which we are dealing. For example, if we assume that knowledge of nature is the product of inquiry, as epistemologists tend to do; and if we assume that inquiry is a matter of empirical and rational investigation, as epistemologists also tend to do; then we will be inclined to infer that only the process of rational and empirical investigation can generate knowledge, and only the products of such a process can qualify as knowledge. Or, somewhat more subtly, we may want to claim that art is cognitive, and even recognize that art and science are cognitive in different ways, but we may nonetheless end up with a distorted conception of both art and its cognitive character if we assume a traditional, Anglo-American epistemology.

Something like this is the case with James O. Young's *Art and Knowledge.*[3] Young thinks that art is cognitive—indeed, he thinks that good art *must* be cognitive, and in profound ways. Unfortunately, Young also thinks that to be cognitive something must be representational, as a result of which he goes to great lengths to try to show how good art represents. One of the results of this truncated understanding of knowledge is that Young is compelled to argue that art that does not represent—for example, a good deal of avant-garde art—is in fact not art at all. One might have thought that such a conclusion would be treated as a reductio ad absurdum of the epistemological assumptions, no less forceful for being unintentional. Young does not see it that way, perhaps because, as he makes clear, he does not much like avant-garde art anyway. The real problem in Young's analysis, which obscures a number of its virtues, is that he is operating with a thoroughly inadequate ontology and epistemology. With respect to ontology, for example, he assumes that fictional characters are not real, and therefore they cannot be the objects of representation. This in turn means that literary assertions about fictional characters cannot represent. At the same time, however, he wants to hold that fictional characters, apparently despite the fact that they are unreal, are capable of representing something else. On the epistemological side, Young assumes that literature, because it is linguistic, consists of assertive statements. Furthermore, literary assertions tend to be about fictional circumstances, and they are thereby false.

An analysis like this suggests the need to rethink our ontological and epistemological assumptions and categories. We have paid a good deal of attention to the relationality and ordinality of complexes in earlier chapters, thus dealing with Young's problem with the "reality" of fictional circumstances and characters. If we claim that art is or can be cognitive, and if we assume that art, whatever else may be said about it, is something other than rational and empirical investigation, then we must also revise to some extent our conception of the nature of knowledge. For this we take our cue from the pragmatic naturalist tradition and from Buchler's theory of judgment. First, though, we will consider some of the ways one can plausibly say that art is cognitive.

Art as Knowledge

By identifying knowledge with inquiry, as opposed to a broader understanding of knowledge that we will develop below, traditional epistemology has focused on propositional knowledge, or "knowledge that." But epistemology has also for long recognized that there is in addition "knowledge how," so in a sense to say that knowledge derives from more than inquiry traditionally understood is not to say anything that is not already generally acknowledged. We are, however, saying that knowledge needs to be understood more broadly still. Buchler, for example, talks in the context of a theory of poetry about "knowledge through," and Richard Shusterman about "interpretive knowledge," and both associate these similar sorts of knowledge with art generally.[4] In these cases we do not describe, or do not merely describe, nor do we simply exhibit a technical skill; rather, in Shusterman's words, we "develop and transmit a . . . meaningful response."[5] Other philosophers, Dewey, Susanne Langer, and Nelson Goodman prominent among them, have also acknowledged the cognitive dimension of art. In Dewey's case he did so through understanding both art and knowledge generally through experience. Langer understood art as capable of generating insight through its symbolic character. And Goodman, more in the spirit of Cassirer, Langer, and to a certain degree Santayana, though not from within their intellectual traditions, was also interested in the symbolic dimension of art and its cognitive power exercised through symbolic structure. Goodman, unfortunately, understood art as a form of inquiry and expressed its cognitive capacity as a form of symbolic structure and therefore much like science.[6] If he had had at his disposal the distinction between inquiry and art, and a theory of judgment and query adequate to the job, he might have saved himself a good deal of trouble. We will consider in a bit more detail Dewey's and Langer's more promising approaches below.

More recent discussions of the cognitive possibilities of art run into similar problems. There has been a fair bit of literature in recent decades, primarily by aestheticians rather than epistemologists, about how art may be cognitive and whether its cognitive dimension is an aesthetic, defining characteristic of art. It is interesting to note that in much of this literature it is assumed that, with the exception of "knowledge how," knowledge is understood to be propositional. Thus, the discussion has tended to assume a traditional conception of knowledge as the result of inquiry, which is to say the very conception of knowledge that we will here try to correct through the theory of judgment. Because this literature associates knowledge with inquiry, and because it does not have a broader concept of query through which to approach the topic, it tends to assume that nonrepresentational forms of art such as music are not cognitive in any significant way, or it assumes, as Young does, that knowledge is representational and therefore music, because it is cognitive, has to be representational. As a result, with the exception of Young and perhaps a couple of others, the focus tends to be on the possible cognitive capacity of literature.[7] Our approach is not limited in such ways. All forms of art, music included, are exhibitive judgment that explore relevant complexes of nature. Consequently, there is no reason to regard art as necessarily representational or to regard nonrepresentational art as any less able to generate knowledge than any other.

So there is nothing radically new about saying that art can result in knowledge. We will suggest, drawing largely from Buchler, that it does so through its distinctive form of judgment, though undoubtedly Santayana, Dewey, Langer, Goodman, Shusterman, and others have something to add to a fuller theory of aesthetic meaning and knowledge. But still, we may ask, what sort of knowledge does art produce? It certainly can describe, in which case we can derive "knowledge that." But if that were all there is to it, then art would be little more than the exhibitive form of propositional knowledge, which is to say a fairly weak and limited way for making declarative statements. This would be all right as far as it goes, but art would hardly be the powerful form of judgment that it is. Art does something, in fact many things, other than simply describe or render propositions. What is that?

There are libraries full of works that describe what art does, can do, or should do. Our interest is in the senses in which art functions to elicit knowledge and by extension truth, in which in some sense or senses it enables us to acquire "knowledge of" or "understanding of" or "insight into" something. That it *can* do so will become clear from the fact that art is exhibitive judgment and a form of query, concepts we will develop in more detail below. Exactly *what* it can do is clear enough if we take the time to consider the question. The following account of some of the ways in which art is or can be cognitive is intended to illustrate the point. The examples offered are not systematically presented, in large measure because there is no attempt here to make a systematic point, or to relate the ways art is cognitive to one another in a system of any kind. What we need are examples of cases in which art makes possible learning, understanding, insight, and knowledge. If the examples are compelling and taken together make a plausible case, then the point is made. Furthermore, the examples are themselves rather idiosyncratic in that they are drawn from my experience in and with art and artworks. Every reader, if pressed to give examples of this kind, would no doubt produce a different set of illustrations of the point. That the examples offered here are merely a small subset of the many more that are possible simply makes the point more strongly.

A Picasso painting, a Wilfred Owen poem, and a Remarque narrative make clear beyond any question the shock and moral inadequacy of war, to begin with examples that others have discussed. A philosophical, historical, or sociological disquisition on war can do the same thing, ideally with greater propositional precision, but in all likelihood with less clarity and force. A work of art can focus our attention in unique ways, thereby rendering its judgment more clearly than is otherwise likely, or perhaps even possible. When we describe the judgments of powerful works of art we are in effect translating an exhibitive into an assertive judgment, and usually a great deal is lost in the translation. That is why commentary on art is difficult to do well, and often has a somewhat artificial or strained feel to it. Assertive judgments when rendered carefully can generate knowledge of a profound sort, and exhibitive judgments uttered with skill and acute creativity can also generate profound knowledge. They are not, however, the same because each does something the other does not. An assertive judgment will rarely if ever have the cognitive force of *Guernica*, and an exhibitive judgment is unlikely to express the complexity and subtlety of a Platonic dialogue, except insofar as the Platonic dialogues themselves have an exhibitive dimension.

The knowledge we derive about the moral dimension of war from Picasso, Owen, and Remarque is an instance of "knowledge through," as Buchler has it, or "knowledge of"; it enables, in some sense imposes on us, an understanding of war. There is of course more to be said about war in its technical, strategic, tactical, political, and social dimensions, but without an understanding of its impact on people directly affected in so many ways, an understanding of the sort that works of art provide, our knowledge of war is fatally impoverished, and among other consequences such impoverishment more easily allows us to accept war when it may well not be called for or appropriate. Thus, for example, when former US vice president Cheney was told that the death toll of US servicemen and

-women in the war in Iraq had reached four thousand (not to mention the far higher number of Iraqi deaths), he responded simply by pointing out that they were all volunteers. One has to believe that Cheney had never taken seriously Picasso, Owen, or Remarque, because if he had had the benefit of the understanding their work provides us, it seems unlikely that he could have responded in such a dismissive way. If they have such potential, then what these works of art provide surely counts as knowledge, if anything does.

Most works of art are not political or social in this way, though many do advance our understanding of human experience. One of the contributions great novelists can make is to provide a look, sometimes in great detail, into the workings of human psychology, or, speaking metaphorically, into the soul. Shakespeare, Flaubert, Dostoevsky, and James, among a list of others, accomplish this in extraordinarily insightful ways. What we learn about human beings from the explication of the inner lives of Macbeth, Emma Bovary, Raskolnikov, and so many others, is not an irrefutable understanding of human psychology, but then neither for the most part is what experimental psychology offers irrefutable. All of the insights into human motivation and action, whether literary or scientific, enter our ongoing effort to understand ourselves as possibilities to be explored, extended, ramified, revised, or rejected. If the history of literature and scientific psychology is any guide, none of them simply by virtue of being literary or scientific can be assumed to be a more reliable source of knowledge than the others. Each provides something the other does not. Experimental psychology, for example, can give us statistical information about our behavior that no amount of even great literature can equal. By the same token, in the hands of a great writer, character development and exploration can plumb depths of psychological possibilities that are well beyond the range of even the best experimental and scientific psychology. Neither has any greater claim than the other to being a more valuable source of psychological knowledge.

Works of art may also produce knowledge of a more formal nature. Literature, both prose and poetry, may be an articulation of the possibilities of language itself, without reference to other subjects. One can certainly read *Finnegan's Wake* in this way, and many poetic styles are as much or more about the language used, its sound and the relations of words to one another, than about any extrinsic meaning. And much of twentieth-century visual art is formal in this sense. Albers and Rothko, for example, not to mention the Brücke, Blaue Reiter, and Fauvist schools, were interested in and investigated the nature of color and the relations of colors to one another, and there are numerous examples in modern and contemporary sculpture of the manipulations of shapes. Something comparable also went on in modern music, from the experiments in twelve-tone composition in Schoenberg to the rhythmic explorations of Varèse and Orff to the influence of the Institut de Recherche et Coordination Acoustique/Musique (IRCAM) and Boulez in Paris in the latter years of the last century. Such formal experimentation and problem solving is an exploration of the traits of the formal elements themselves, and to that extent produces knowledge. The nature of words, color, shape, sound, and rhythm are far better known and understood today than they were a century ago because of these formalist exercises and the many extraordinary works of art they have produced.

The significance of such developments in the arts is the more apparent when we attend to the fact that query and the knowledge that results is not so much a matter of producing information of the sort that belongs in data sets, or in systematic collections of propositions, but of teasing out the possibilities and potential of the complexes involved, in formal and other respects. The more purely formal developments in the arts were enabled by the earlier breakdown of representationalism in the visual arts and the traditional structures in literature and music, processes that were well underway by the middle years of the nineteenth century in Western art forms. Wagner stretched traditional tonality in an increasingly chromatic direction, thus enabling Schoenberg and others to go much further, and in so doing developed the expressive and dramatic qualities of music in ways that continue to intrigue us. At roughly the same time, the impressionists in France and the United States, and others such as Turner in the United Kingdom, developed ways to employ shape and color not so much to represent objects as to investigate the nature of light and its perception. These examples, and they can be multiplied many times, are cases of artists engaged in a process of ramifying the complexes of nature with which they were concerned. The results of this process demonstrate the capacities of color, shape, sound, rhythm, and words to an extent that was not available to us before. This is knowledge no less than data sets, facts, propositions, and the products of reason.

By revealing the potential of its elements, the formalists in the arts created possibilities that others could build on. Perhaps the most iconic image of the Russian avant-garde of the early twentieth century is Kazimir Malevich's *Black Square*, which for those who are not familiar with it is a painting of a black square. Malevich himself executed several such paintings, and among their more intriguing traits is the potential inherent in the black square; this is something we have become more aware of in the many ways that the color and shape have been put to use by artists since Malevich. An exhibition at the Russian Museum in St. Petersburg in 2007 gathered numerous examples of the experiments with the black square that have been undertaken in painting, sculpture, and installations by Russian and other artists in the century since Malevich produced the original. What appears to be a simple black, square shape on canvas has unleashed a remarkable range of experiments and permutations. The black square was pregnant with possibilities, and other artists sufficiently astute and creative have been able to unfold those possibilities in novel and interesting ways.[8] This is a clear illustration of the point that knowledge is as much and probably more about contributing and exploring possibilities and potential than it is about asserting propositions; it is an example of the cognitive dimension of art in the sense of participation in an ongoing process in which many people with similar interests and skills, which is to say a community of sorts, work through the possibilities of an idea. Here again is a case not of "knowledge that" or "knowledge how," but of "knowledge through," "knowledge of," and "interpretative knowledge." Buchler makes the point that any methodic utterance, any judgment, can stimulate further judgment, and in so doing may contribute knowledge. We can, he also points out, seek articulation of the gain acquired not by a translation into assertive propositions, but by tracing the impact of the art and its themes in other art and in other orders. In this respect knowledge through art, like other knowledge, is power. It can point us in new and richer directions. Absence of knowledge in this regard means discontinuity and impotence, as it also does in cognitively flawed judgments of science.[9]

Experimentation with form also engenders meaning and implications beyond form itself. Consider the examples of Picasso and Braque, Kirchner, Leger, and Cage. In their cubist experiments Picasso and Braque fractured the literal representation of objects by employing sharp-edged geometrical shapes, whose effect was in part to produce a subject matter that was less familiar to the viewer and to that extent less comfortable to look at. The visual dislocation and distortion of the subjects prompts the viewer to raise questions about the traits and character of the subjects, and to generalize those questions into a broader cultural query of his own. The German expressionist painter Ernst Ludwig Kirchner, a contemporary of Picasso and Braque, did something similar, though not in the cubist style. His street scenes of Berlin in the years immediately preceding and early in the First World War, in which the figures are depicted with sharp, angular, and somewhat elongated shapes, convey a disquieting and rather frightening sense of the street life, primarily that of prostitutes and their customers, of the German capital at that momentous point in history. In the later of these paintings one knows that the war is already taking its toll because some of the women are wearing clothes that were characteristic attire for war widows at the time, and the paintings are a revealing glimpse into the psychological and cultural dislocation that the war was causing in Berlin.[10] The creative use of form for the cubists like Picasso and Braque and the German expressionists like Kirchner generate insights into the people and culture of their time and place, and perhaps far more broadly than their own. Without them, our understanding of those people, times, and places—and of people, time, and place more generally—would be impoverished.

Leger is another case in point. Many artists of the modern period, particularly painters, sculptors, and filmmakers, were concerned with industrialization and its effect on society, culture, and individual psychology. For some the effect was largely positive, or could be positive. Lenin had famously said that communism meant Soviet power plus electrification, and rapid industrialization was a central goal in the early Soviet years. In a popular film of the middle Soviet period, Alexandr Zarkhy's 1957 *Vysota* (*Altitude*), a sprawling industrial facility under construction, which might look to the viewer to be rather ugly, is referred to, apparently without irony, as "man-made beauty." The futurists and much of the Russian avant-garde took a similar, though more sophisticated and nuanced, view. For others, however, the potential alienation of industrialization was the focus of their work. Chaplin expressed it clearly enough, but Leger made the most of the shapes of industrial objects in much of his work. Malevich had already explored the effect of the use of rounded and largely conical forms in his paintings of a variety of subjects, including Russian peasants, to great effect. Leger pushed the use of these shapes even further, such that in many of his paintings one sees the extent to which industrial modernity had become the very shape of individuals. When one looks at Leger's work one cannot help thinking about the possibility that industrial modernity had not so much influenced people as transformed them into something they were not before. He and the other artists with a similar concern may well have had a point, particularly when one considers the extent to which humanity had in the twentieth century transformed itself into ever-more-efficient killing machines. How much of this history can be attributed to industrial modernity is of course an open question, especially given the more recent experience of mass murder in less heavily industrialized parts of the world from Bosnia to Rwanda to Darfur. But the questions and possibilities raised by Chaplin, Leger, and others bring the issue into focus in a way that contributes to our ongoing struggle to understand ourselves in relation to the worlds we construct. To that extent the contribution of the arts to our knowledge, such as it is, has been critical.

Composers too have experimented with form in ways that raise questions about matters far beyond the forms themselves. The work of John Cage is a telling example. In their atonal compositions, composers long before Cage had broken down the traditional harmonic and tonal structures of Western art music. Cage, however, pushed the experiments further still by introducing new sounds in his music, particularly through his compositions for prepared piano. Cage invented the prepared piano by placing objects made of various materials—for example, pencils or metal screws—into the strings of a piano, the effect of which was to distort the sound produced when the strings were sounded. By so doing, Cage created yet new formal possibilities in composition. His most remarkable experiment, however, was the famous *4′33″*, in which the pianist sits at the piano with hands at the keyboard for four minutes and thirty-three seconds. The implications of this innovation are profound. Most obviously, Cage here raises the question of the relation between the normal sounds one hears, whether it is nervous coughing in the audience or sounds from beyond the room, to music itself. The piece blurs the normally assumed barrier between the two. One might in a traditional spirit want to insist on the distinction between music and noise, but the question of the nature of that distinction and where the barrier might lie, if indeed there is one, has been raised in a new and intriguing way. Cage focuses our attention on the possibilities and potential meaning of the quotidian sounds we hear, placing both our normal experience and our experience of music in a new context. For example, not long ago I was attending a concert of contemporary Polish music in a concert hall in Krakow, and had a seat near the door to the street. The music being performed had the dissonance, tonal vagueness, and rhythmic irregularity one expects from late-twentieth-century compositions, but I could also hear quite clearly the sounds of the automotive and pedestrian traffic from outside the door. Those sounds could easily be taken to be an annoyance and distraction from the music on the stage, but familiarity with Cage and *4′33″* colored that experience. The exploration of tonal dissonance and unexpected rhythmic patterns in the performed pieces already stretches one's sense of music and, coupled with the street sounds from outside the hall, one's conception of music and its relation to the rest of the world, to experience generally, is shaken rather deeply. The import of this juxtaposition is to raise questions about both music and aural experience as a whole. Cage's compositions, from prepared to silent piano, have enabled such experience, and to that extent have added to the possibilities of one's ongoing experience and interaction with one's world. And that, after all, is what knowledge does.

A very young Susan Sontag wrote in her diary that reading Romain Rolland gave her a "knowledge of aliveness." In a similar vein, Orhan Pamuk has recently said that though he regrets the "utilitarian" nature of the idea, he cannot help but think that "books exist to prepare one for life."[11] Pamuk has in mind books of all kinds, but certainly including prose and poetry. Both writers are expressing an important sense in which art, in their cases literature, contributes knowledge, which is to say that it has an import for one's life, how it is understood and how it is lived. This can take a variety of forms. It may be didactic, in the way that the ideologically driven paintings of medieval Europe taught the principles of Christianity to the population, or that much of the visual and literary art of socialist realism pointed to the values of the anticipated, bright, communist future. It can also parody such ideologies, as do some of Shostakovich's works, such as his early ballet *Svetli Ruchi* and his later operetta *Moskva Cheryomushki*.

But neither Sontag nor Pamuk has such didacticism or its parody in mind. Nor do they have in mind only the fact that we can learn about people, cultures, and times other than our own, though they would probably acknowledge that literature can do this. They have in mind, I imagine, the fact that literature does not so much offer information about the world, or something to which to aspire, as it exposes us to the range of experience and the possibilities inherent in it. Stories that occur in a setting with which we are familiar (our own time and place, for example) and that include characters we can recognize, thereby expand our own experience. They often involve events in which we can place ourselves and imagine our own reactions and behavior. But literature that places us beyond our own time and place can be, and usually is, even more expansive. Perhaps there are sufficient commonalities among people across cultures and through history that we are able to expand the possibilities of our own lives by engaging with them. We can feel, which is to say we can understand, both the romanticism and the hopelessness of Don Quixote's efforts, and we know what it means to "tilt at windmills," though none of us have ever lived or will ever live in early modern Spain. We can feel the internal struggle and trauma of Sensei in Natsume Soseki's *Kokoro*, though none of us have experienced the individual and cultural confusion of Meiji Japan's struggle to confront the modern West. And even a cursory reading of *Ali and Nino* brings into relief for us the trauma of a multiethnic, multicultural, and multireligious world in turmoil, though we have no direct experience with the complex struggles that characterized the Caucasus before, during, and after the Great War. In such cases we learn not so much about early modern Spain or Meiji Japan or Azerbaijan and the southern Caucasus in the early twentieth century as about the possibilities of experience; our own experience and its possibilities expand accordingly. Something like this, I take it, is the "knowledge of aliveness," and the sense in which literature can "prepare one for life."

Art, then, is cognitive in these and many other ways. Precisely how this works is something that studies in aesthetic theory, art history, musicology, and literary criticism can explicate, among their many other contributions. As we think through the breadth and depth of artistic creation and the impact it has on us, we wonder how it is that anyone could ever doubt its cognitive capacity. One reason is the overly narrow conception of knowledge that philosophers have allowed themselves to embrace. Another reason for the apparent persistence of such doubt is that there appear to be appropriate distinctions to be drawn among knowledge, beliefs, and opinions. Not every idea or conception we entertain counts as knowledge, we want to say. Therefore, simply because something serves as a source of thoughts and ideas it is not thereby cognitive; it is not necessarily knowledge. In the end, knowledge must have something to do with truth, such that a thought, idea, or conception must be true in order for it to count as knowledge. We are led, therefore, to consider both a more adequate understanding of knowledge and the relation between art and truth.

Pragmatic Naturalism and Knowledge

I use the term "epistemology" to mean any systematic attempt to understand knowledge and truth, so that it is intended to include the various forms of analytic epistemology, pragmatist approaches to knowledge, and other creative approaches such as Buchler's and Susanne Langer's. In the English-speaking world the most pervasive forms of epistemology in this broad sense have been the analytic and pragmatist approaches, so I will turn first to the implications of the cognitive dimension of art for epistemology in these senses.

An obvious problem arises when we consider what is commonly called naturalist epistemology, which derives its name from the fact that it is a series of developments from Quine's initial call to naturalize epistemology. The problem is in part a consequence of the fact that in this tradition the natural sciences hold a privileged position with respect to the understanding of knowledge. We should distinguish two ways this occurs. One of them is that naturalists of this stripe argue for turning to the results of the sciences, primarily to psychology and other cognitive disciplines, in our efforts to understand the nature of knowledge and its acquisition. This move amounts to an abandonment of more traditional a priori analysis in the attempt to understand knowledge. The second way the emphasis on science appears in naturalist epistemology is in its tendency to privilege the results of the natural sciences as the paradigmatic instances of knowledge. This is significant because the naturalist needs to have something in mind as to what counts as knowledge if he is to inquire into its nature, and his inclination is to point to the propositions that result from natural scientific inquiry and say: "That's what we mean by knowledge." This move can have a weak and a strong form. The weak version will say that the propositions of the sciences are the clearest instances of knowledge, though other sorts of activities may also generate knowledge in less clear and perhaps less reliable forms. The strong version is to say that the propositions of the natural sciences are the only instances of knowledge, which is to say the only way we can have knowledge of nature is through the sciences. Everything else may have some value, but it is not cognitive.[12]

Another observation worth making at this point is that naturalist epistemologists share with many of their nonnaturalist opponents an assumption about knowledge, which is that it is always to be understood as a belief. Thus, the question becomes "What kinds of belief count as knowledge, and why?" Naturalists will say that empirically derived beliefs either modeled on or rooted in the sciences are the only ones that count as knowledge, and nonnaturalists will allow for other, nonempirical or rationally derived beliefs to count. Either way, the analysis of knowledge is about which beliefs are cognitively acceptable.

Analytic naturalist epistemology in any of its forms cannot adequately handle the fact that art has a cognitive dimension. Nor, we should add, can any form of epistemology that understands knowledge entirely or paradigmatically in terms of propositions and/or beliefs. We must keep in mind the senses in which we have ascribed a cognitive dimension to art. The observation that art has a cognitive capacity has been made before, though usually by aestheticians rather than epistemologists. Even there, though, the tendency has been to ascribe to art the capacity to generate knowledge that is similar to the knowledge enabled by the sciences. So, for example, the cognitive capacity of literature has been debated in terms of the truth-claims that can be found in it or derived from it. And as we have pointed out above, even those who are inclined to defend art's cognitive dimension in these terms are reluctant to extend the point beyond literature to more abstract arts such as music or dance because these do not issue in propositions or truth-claims. In our ascription of a cognitive dimension of art we have been careful, it should be remembered, not to limit knowledge in art to propositions or to truth-claims of the traditional sorts. In fact we have not limited knowledge in the arts to beliefs that can be propositionally expressed at all.

If we are right in attributing to art the possibility of knowledge that is not propositional and not a matter of beliefs to which truth-value can be readily assigned, then any epistemological approach that understands knowledge as justified belief is inadequate to the cognitive capacity of art, and therefore will result in an inadequate understanding of knowledge. Naturalist epistemology suffers from the further disability of limiting from the outset its conception of knowledge to the propositions of the natural sciences, in either its weak or strong versions. With that point of departure naturalist epistemology can never generate an adequate understanding of knowledge. One might ask at this point whether it might be possible to recast naturalist epistemological approaches, or other, non-naturalist forms of analytic epistemology, by taking knowledge in art, perhaps alongside knowledge in science, as paradigmatic. The answer is that it is certainly possible, though we may find in doing so that the analytic tools characteristically used in this tradition are not up to the task. But we do not know the results of such an experiment until it is tried, and it would likely be an interesting project to do so.

Another approach at this point is to say that there are alternatives with rich histories to which we might turn. The most obvious of them for those of us who are inclined to do philosophy in the American traditions is the broadly pragmatist, or more precisely, Deweyan, approach. A weak version of this can be found in Rorty's interest in literature as being no less interesting and valuable than science, and in his overall rejection of the need for a theory of knowledge. The problem with Rorty, at least for our purposes, is that he nowhere discussed the arts in general in the context of our ongoing dialogue. In fact, he himself said that he had little feel for the arts, and therefore did not consider them in this light.[13] We may find greater possibilities, then, in turning to Dewey. Is there in Dewey's understanding of knowledge and truth a way to accommodate the cognitive dimension of art?

There are certainly prima facie reasons to think that Dewey's approach to knowledge has potential for us. First, he rejected the subjectivism of traditional epistemology so that knowledge is no longer to be understood in terms of beliefs held in the mind that then need to be evaluated for their reliability in relation to an external world. Knowledge is no longer a matter of beliefs, except possibly in the more extended Peircean sense. A second and related point is that knowledge is a matter not of what we think but of what we can do in relation to our lived environment. This understanding of knowledge provides much more room for the broader sense of knowledge and cognition to which the arts point. Third, in *Art as Experience* Dewey explicitly acknowledges the possibility that art can be cognitive, specifically in the chapter titled "The Challenge to Philosophy."[14] His concern there, and he is right to have it, is that among the numerous attempts to develop a philosophy of art some have tended to reduce art to a cognitive exercise. He ascribes this view, or at least the danger of this view, to the romantic impulse to understand art as a uniquely powerful entrée into the nature of things. The problem with this approach, he points out, is twofold: (1) There is a tendency to ignore the many other characteristics of art by overemphasizing the cognitive, and (2) without a more careful analysis of knowledge, to say that art is primarily cognitive is to make it more or less equivalent in function to science and other disciplines, but in that case art does not fare well.

The fourth and perhaps the most important reason for hopefulness with respect to Dewey's approach is that both knowledge and art are understood within the broader category of experience. There is what we might call a hermeneutic link between them that may be immensely helpful. It appears to be possible, then, to build into Dewey's sense of logic the cognitive dimension of art in ways that are impossible in contemporary analytic epistemology, naturalist or otherwise.

What, if any, are the obstacles to so doing? There do appear to be potential stumbling blocks. First, Dewey, like the naturalist epistemologists, understood science to be the paradigmatic instance of knowledge. Of course he had a broader understanding of scientific inquiry than the Quinean naturalists have, but still his approach to epistemology, or to logic as he preferred, is undertaken in relation to inquiry. Even if inquiry in his sense is not understood to rely on representations, it is not clear that it can accommodate knowledge that results from query of the sort that characterizes the arts. This points to a second potential problem, which is that in the end, for Dewey knowledge is about propositions and warranted assertability, which as we have seen is likely to be too restrictive to handle cognition in the arts simply because the arts are not for the most part about assertions, warranted or otherwise. Dewey appears to have understood this; in fact, it is the very point he is making in *Art as Experience* when he warns that we do not want to construe knowledge in art in such a way that it imitates knowledge in science. This insight, however, does not appear to have been turned back on his own conception of knowledge such that knowledge can be understood more broadly than as a matter of propositions and assertions, even if their warrant is to be judged in terms of functional success.

It is instructive to note that Dewey, unlike Buchler and Langer, as we shall see, was not disposed to emphasize the differences between knowledge in science and knowledge in art. On the contrary, his inclination was to emphasize their similarities. He does so, however, not by trying to argue that either is simply a form of the other, but rather that both exemplify a more general, creative process. Consider, by way of illustration, the following passages from *Experience and Nature* and "Qualitative Thought":

> If modern tendencies are justified in putting art and creation first. . . . It would then be seen that science is an art, that art is practice, and that the only distinction worth drawing is not between practice and theory, but between those modes of practice that are not intelligent, not inherently and immediately enjoyable, and those which are full of enjoyed meanings.[15]

> Science is an instrumentality of and for art because it is the intelligent factor *in* art.[16]

> Thinking is preeminently an art; knowledge and propositions which are the products of thinking, are works of art, as much so as statuary and symphonies.[17]

> The logic of artistic construction and esthetic appreciation is peculiarly significant because they exemplify in accentuated and purified form the control of selection of detail and of mode of relation, or integration, by a qualitative whole. . . . Artistic thought is not however unique in this respect but only shows an intensification of a characteristic of all thought. In a looser way, it is a characteristic of all nontechnical, non-"scientific" thought. Scientific thought is, in its turn, a specialized form of art, with its own qualitative control.[18]

> The gist of the matter is that the immediate existence of quality, and of dominant and pervasive quality, is the background, the point of departure, and the regulative principle of all thinking. . . . "Scientific" thinking, that expressed in physical science, never gets away from qualitative existence. . . . Construction that is artistic is as much a case of genuine thought as that expressed in scientific and philosophical matters, and so is all genuine esthetic appreciation of art, since the latter must in some way, to be vital, retrace the course of the creative process.[19]

There is a sense in which Dewey in these passages can be read as proposing something like Buchler's point that science and art are both forms of query, which we will develop below. Dewey puts it differently by emphasizing the point that both science and art exemplify a creative process in which, as he describes it, there is invariably a qualitative background in terms of which scientific and artistic products derive their meaning and import. When he says, for example, that both science and art are instances of "the control of selection of detail and of mode of relation, or integration, by a qualitative whole" he seems to be pointing to something similar to what Buchler means by judgment. Thus, there is an important and valuable dimension of Dewey's approach in that he neither radically distinguishes science from art such that neither can do anything that the other does, such as have a cognitive character, nor does he reduce either to the other and thereby limit their distinctive functions. In this respect Dewey appears to enable a more satisfactory understanding of the possibility of cognition in art.

Indeed, as in the case of naturalist epistemology, it may be possible to recast Dewey's logic in such a way that it can accommodate the cognitive dimension of the arts. In fact it seems to be a much more promising project than an attempt to do so for Quinean naturalism. Whether it can be successful, however, is not obvious, and certainly not something we are entitled simply to assume.

Another source of insight into the question of the cognitive dimension of art is Susanne Langer's treatment of the issue. As will be clear from the quotations below, Langer understands art as a symbolic form that has the function of expressing human feeling. Science and other modes of discourse, by contrast, are symbolic forms that have the function of enabling thought and discursive communication. Thus, science and art are both symbolic forms, though they differ in that one enables conceptual thought and discourse while the other enables the expression of the subjective feeling of experience. Each in its own way can generate knowledge.

Langer developed this analysis in *Feeling and Form* and in *Problems of Art*. The latter is a more summary expression of her views and provides a clear entrée into her understanding of the issue. She makes the clear distinction there between discursive and artistic symbolic forms:

> Language is the symbolic form of rational thought. . . . The structure of discourse expresses the forms of rational cognition; that is why we call such thinking "discursive." . . . To express the forms of what we might call "unlogicized" mental life . . . or what is usually called the "life of feeling," requires a different symbolic form. . . . This form, I think, is characteristic of art and is, indeed, the essence and measure of art.[20]

That the expression of the "life of feeling" has or can have a cognitive dimension in Langer's view is clear enough: "Even the discursive pattern has its limits of usefulness. . . . Yet there is a great deal of experience that is knowable . . . yet defies discursive formulation, and therefore verbal expression: this is what we sometimes call the *subjective aspect* of experience, the direct feeling of it."[21] The function of art is the expression of this "direct feeling" of experience, and that expression, in that it brings into focus a dimension of experience "that is knowable," is cognitive.

Thus, the initially necessary ingredients for a suitable analysis of the cognitive dimension of art are to be found in Langer. First, it is clear that for her, art enables us to know something, specifically the subjective aspect of experience. Second, art is distinguished from discursive, propositional knowledge in such a way that both share the critical feature of cognitive activities—i.e., both are symbolic forms, but neither is reduced to the other, which is to say that each retains its distinctive features as cognitive activities. But as for Dewey, it is not clear on the face of it whether her understanding of knowledge in general, and art in particular, is adequate to a fuller understanding of cognition in art. For one thing, it is not clear that it is appropriate to say of art that it has only one function—for example, that it expresses feeling. It is one thing to understand art as a distinctive symbolic form, analogous to Buchler's understanding of it as paradigmatic of exhibitive judgment. But it is quite another thing to attribute one function to art. On the face of it art does many things and has many functions. To express subjective experience or "feeling" may or may not be one of them. But even if it is, there does not appear to be good reason to limit its function in that way.

Buchler was almost certainly aware of Langer's work on art when it appeared in the 1950s, if for no other reason than that they both moved in the same circles in the New York philosophical community. Surprisingly, though, Buchler does not take up her analysis as he developed his theory of judgment and art's character as exhibitive judgment. Dewey's tendency to think of knowledge in terms of inquiry, however, is a shortcoming to which Buchler has directly pointed. Indeed, it is from Buchler's point of view a major shortcoming of Dewey's conception of experience in general.[22] If this criticism has a point, then indeed we need a more adequate understanding of the various ways nature may be questioned and investigated, and by implication of the knowledge that may result. We will propose at this point that Buchler's theory of judgment and his concept of query provide such an improved understanding. Judgments of any kind may yield knowledge. Sometimes they are assertive and propositional, in which case we may achieve knowledge that is susceptible to the evaluative categories appropriate to assertive judgments, such as truth-value. Sometimes they are exhibitive, in which cases we may achieve knowledge that is to be evaluated in other terms—for example, by the deeper understanding and appreciation it enables or by the expanded possibilities it reveals. The former cases are knowledge of the sort that results from the sciences, mathematics, and to a large extent philosophy; the latter are instances of knowledge appropriate to the arts. Neither is reducible to the other, neither is defined in terms of the other, and taken together they enable a broader understanding of knowledge and they reflect the richness of our experience, aesthetic and otherwise.

Judgment and Query

Bear in mind that nature is relational. Moreover, all the complexes of nature, of whatever kind, are constituted relationally. Thus, knowledge, understanding, insight, and any other condition in which some aspect of nature is revealed to us, however that may happen, is the result of a relational process and is a product of a relational situation. People interact with the complexes that constitute their worlds in a wide range of ways. When that interaction takes place through selection of some kind it is an instance of judgment.[23]

To avoid unnecessary confusion let us stipulate from the start that in his use of the term "judgment" Buchler has enabled potential misunderstanding because the meaning of the term in his theory is somewhat idiosyncratic. It is worth keeping in mind that the theory of judgment as we will briefly describe it is a theory of a person's interaction with the complexes of his environment that cumulatively define his life. In this respect the theory of judgment is a component of a broader theory of human being. In order to understand what Buchler means by "judgment," and why he would use that term and not another, one has to have the patience to follow his explication and rationale. Toward this end it may be worthwhile to keep in mind, as we have pointed out, the fact that when he developed the theory in the early 1950s he was explicitly attempting to improve on Dewey's conception of experience and interaction.

Judgment in this sense is not a mental event, conscious or unconscious. It is a selection, a more or less systematic organization or manipulation of complexes toward some end or that produces some result. There are three forms of judgment: assertive, exhibitive, and active. One judges assertively when one issues a statement of some kind. The most characteristic instance of an assertive judgment is a declarative sentence, though assertive judgment need not be linguistic and a judgment rendered in language need not be assertive. A mathematical equation, for example, is an assertive judgment that is not linguistic. Both a poem and a performative utterance are linguistic judgments that are not assertive. The former is exhibitive and the latter is exhibitive and active, about both of which forms of judgment we will say more below. An assertive judgment, as the term suggests, asserts something, and is generally propositional. An assertive judgment as a rule can be said to be true or false, in a conventional way, although one has to be careful here because truth has a broader scope than merely the propositional. One of the reasons there has been confusion about the cognitive dimension of art is that knowledge and truth have unjustifiably been restricted to propositions, and art is a form of judgment that is not propositional and therefore not assertive. To understand that art can be cognitive requires that we expand our sense of truth and knowledge to cover more than simply assertive judgments. The reasonableness of so doing is part of what is at issue here.

The standard instance of an assertive judgment is a sentence or proposition, or a systematic organization of sentences and propositions like a scholarly essay, book, or mathematical proof. An essay, book, or mathematical proof can also have an exhibitive dimension, which we intuitively express when we say, for example, that a mathematical proof is elegant or beautiful. Judgments may take more than one form. The standard instance of an exhibitive judgment is, as the name suggests, a showing of some kind. To define an exhibitive judgment as a showing is accurate but of only limited value, in the same way that defining an assertive judgment as a proposition is accurate but limited. "Showing" and "proposing" in these cases are similar but not identical to "exhibiting" and "asserting." To say that an exhibitive judgment is a showing is misleading if we think of showing as limited to a visual representation. An exhibitive judgment is a manipulation and association of complexes in such a way as to reveal something about them that has not been noticed before, something novel. If a declarative sentence is the clearest example of an assertive judgment, then a painting or sculpture is the clearest illustration of an exhibitive judgment. But the identification of the visual arts and exhibitive judgment should not be drawn too strictly, just as one should not draw too strictly the identification of declarative linguistic statements with assertive judgments. As we have seen, such linguistic judgments as a poem are exhibitive, as are some overtly physical judgments such as a dance. Such judgments are suggestive and evocative, unlike straightforward assertive judgments. They direct our attention to a feature or features of the subject matter, whether it is something formal like color, shape, sound, or movement, or a trait of a represented object or scene that is being brought to light in a new way, or from a new angle of vision, so to speak, a new perspective. Exhibitive judgments show us something, whether visually, aurally, linguistically, or actively, rather than state something. This is not to say that they are devoid of content, only that the content is exhibited rather than asserted.

A relevant point that becomes obvious already is that art has its most direct association with exhibitive judgments. Works of art are in an important sense paradigmatic cases of exhibitive judgment. They may also be assertive, and in the case of dance and in forms of performance art they are active. But in general, the fact that the exhibitive is one of the forms of judgment, and that judgment in general is related to query and knowledge, informs our discussion of knowledge and art.

The third form of judgment is the active. When we manipulate complexes not so much to say or make something but to do something, we are judging actively, even when the results of our judgment are a product. When we chop wood or build a house we are judging actively. Sport and athletic activity are examples of active judgment, as are walking or driving to work. Nothing is proposed or shown per se in these cases, but through our methodic actions we are selecting and manipulating complexes to some effect. As in the cases of assertive and exhibitive judgment, there is overlap with what would otherwise be thought to be ideal cases of the other forms of judgments. As we have said, a performative utterance is an active judgment, and an activity like dance is an exhibitive judgment, as may be an assertion such as a mathematical proof. Our approach to the kinds or modes of judgment must remain flexible for the concepts to retain plausibility and applicability. There is also the fact that a specific judgment may function in more than one mode. A baseball pitcher who is improving his curveball is judging actively, but as the pitch begins to approach perfection it becomes a thing of beauty, and thereby functions in an exhibitive mode; at that point the active judgment that is the pitch is also an exhibitive judgment.

One of the things we do when we judge, though it need not be true of all judgments, is explore our worlds. To understand this dimension of judgment more fully we need to examine the concept of query. In doing so, however, we must keep in mind that the concepts we are examining here—knowledge, judgment, query, and others—are related to one another, and all are related to an understanding of human life and activity. Without going into a detailed discussion of a metaphysics of human being, suffice it to say that human beings, as relationally constituted complexes, are in constant interactive contact with our environing complexes, our worlds.[24] The concept of experience, however it is understood, captures an aspect of this ongoing relational interaction. Our relations with our environing complexes take a variety of forms, from passive undergoing and assimilation to more active manipulation. When we manipulate, which is to say when we order complexes to which we are related, we can be said to judge. Sometimes judgment, in whatever mode, can be episodic or occasional. In other cases we undertake to develop our judgments, to ramify them. When we attempt to develop judgments in one or another methodic or systematic way, we are engaged in query.

The term "query" is selected purposely, in part to draw a distinction with inquiry. This is a distinction that is particularly important for an adequate understanding of knowledge and of the cognitive capacity of art. Query is a genus of which inquiry is a species. When Monet produced his series of paintings of the Thames he was engaged in query, as was Schoenberg in his twelve-tone compositions, and Aristotle in his development of logic, and a baseball pitcher in perfecting his curveball. A painting, a composition, a book, and a pitch are all judgments. When ramified in a methodic way they are instances of query. Though undertaken with different tools and raw materials, all these activities have a certain interrogative character. They are exploring the possibilities and potential of the relevant complexes and of the judgments rendered with respect to those complexes. In each case it is insufficient to be content with what is ready to hand, or on the surface, so to speak. The painter, composer, philosopher, or athlete has to mine his material; he has to reach deeper into the complexes, their relations, and their potential to reveal or expose or create what he can. How he determines when he is finished mining his materials, when his judgments are ramified to his satisfaction, is a function of his intentions, his contexts, and his skill. However that may be, each is a case of the methodic and systematic exploration of the potential of judgment, and each is an instance of query. And insofar as query is in some way interrogative, the results of query are in some way and to some degree revelatory. It is in this sense that the results of query are cognitive and add to our knowledge and understanding. If a work of art queries nature, as it does in any number of ways, it is to that extent cognitive. It not only adds to a "stock of knowledge," to use an inadequate though common formulation, but perhaps more importantly it points to and enables further query; it generates new possibilities for the exploration of nature, as in the example of Malevich's *Black Square*, and to that extent it joins a process of communication carried on by a community of individuals engaged in a common project.

However, a work of art is not, for the most part, an instance of inquiry. Inquiry is a specific form of query, one properly to be associated with assertive judgment. Inquiry occurs when interrogation takes the form of literally asking questions, gathering information and relevant data, and undertaking a rational investigation of the relations among them, the rational inferences that can be drawn from them, and their meaningful implications. In the history of philosophy empirical observation and reason have been taken to be, along with experimentation in science, the sole modes of acquiring knowledge, and as a result epistemological theories have tended to be either empiricist or rationalist. This, however, has been a mistake, and it has sent philosophy and epistemology in directions that have been if not misguided, then unduly restrictive, and the results have been seriously damaging to our understanding of judgment and knowledge. Empirical observation and reason are not the two aspects of the acquisition of knowledge but two forms of the process of inquiry, and empiricism and rationalism are not the two ways of understanding or acquiring knowledge, but at most two aspects of, or ways of understanding, inquiry.

The reason this misunderstanding has been so pernicious is that inquiry is generally and properly associated with assertive judgment, but then knowledge has been associated generally and improperly only with assertive judgment. The result has been that knowledge has been improperly associated only with inquiry. By so doing we have sundered knowledge from other forms of query, and in another instance of the Humpty-Dumpty Fallacy we have created the pseudoproblem of fact and value and have left exhibitive and active judgment in cognitive limbo. To free ourselves from these conundrums we have only to realize that inquiry is not the whole of query and therefore not the whole of knowledge.

Not surprisingly, artists in their own ways have made this point before. John Keats described the writer as "capable of being in uncertainties, Mysteries, doubts, without any irritable reaching after fact and reason."[25] Scientists and philosophers, which is to say those of us who are most at home "reaching after fact and reason" and who make our way in the milieu of assertive judgment and inquiry, do not for the most part find the process either irritating or irritable. Apparently Keats did. But however much he and other artists may stand with fact and reason, they do not shy away from the exploration and interrogation of uncertainties, mysteries (upper and lower case), and doubts. The results of such exploration and interrogation, the ramification of those uncertainties, mysteries, and doubts, had for Keats and great artists generally a cognitive value. Both they and we can come to a better understanding of whatever aspect of nature is being explored as a result, and therein is art's cognitive value. It seems that many people fail to understand this, including a certain species of epistemologist that calls itself "naturalist."[26]

For all but the complete skeptic there is no reason to doubt that through empirical observation and reason we acquire knowledge of nature. Certainly, through these processes, and their sophisticated exercise in the sciences, we acquire knowledge of the material objects and processes of nature. Also through their exercise in mathematics, philosophy, and related disciplines we can extend that knowledge to aspects of nature that are not easily treated as material—for example, to mathematical entities and logical principles. Philosophers have continued to debate whether we can with equal comfort claim to achieve knowledge of other aspects of nonmaterial nature such as ethical and aesthetic principles, as well as of meanings. In all these respects inquiry is the means by which knowledge is achieved. However, if nature is more than material objects and principles, and more than principles of value and meaning; if knowledge is, as we are suggesting, the result of query in its various forms and not simply inquiry; and if knowledge of nature in all its multiplicity is possible, which it appears to be, then we must look beyond inquiry for the other ways in which we have cognitive access to nature. Art is one of those ways.

Art and Truth

It is clear that knowledge as we are using the term here is not limited to propositions that derive from the sciences; indeed, it is not limited to propositions at all. The point we are urging is that there is no good reason to limit our conception of knowledge in such a way. Naturalist epistemologists, those following in the footsteps of Quine at any rate, tend to make the perfectly reasonable assumption that the cognitive sciences are an important source of our understanding of how knowledge happens, of how we acquire knowledge. This point there is no reason to doubt. Their mistake is to infer from the fact that because science results in understandings and insights that we have every reason to count as knowledge, we may therefore regard knowledge generated by science, i.e., propositional knowledge of how various things work and happen, as the paradigmatic instance of knowledge, or even worse as the only sort of knowledge. This mistaken inference has led "naturalist" epistemology to develop its understanding of what knowledge is, how it is to be differentiated from belief and opinion, and how it is related to truth, in ways that result in truncated and distorted conceptions of knowledge, belief, and truth in general. The various ways in which the arts are genuinely cognitive, some of which we have described, all point in this direction. Imagine how differently naturalist epistemology might have developed had it begun with the also perfectly reasonable assumption that because art results in understandings and insights that we have every reason to count as knowledge, we may therefore regard the knowledge generated by art as among the paradigmatic instances of knowledge. That this has not occurred is clear from the fact that one is hard pressed even to find the word "art" in the indexes of major epistemological studies.

If we have no good reason to limit our conception of knowledge to propositional knowledge, then we also have no good reason to conceive of knowledge as consisting of propositions that accurately reflect reality. In this respect we find ourselves in the pragmatist tradition from Peirce through James, Dewey, Mead, and Rorty, and the naturalist tradition from Santayana through Dewey, Langer, and Buchler, all of whom explicitly reject the conception of knowledge as reflection. On the contrary, knowledge is judgment that enables us to move forward. For Peirce it is that which enables us to fix belief; for James it is what works; for Dewey it is what resolves problematic situations, though these simple formulations do not do justice to their far more complex epistemological conceptions. Something similar is true of Santayana, Buchler, and many others in the naturalist tradition. If knowledge is understood as judgment that enables us to move forward, rather than as accurate reflection of reality, then our conceptions of belief and truth, and their relation to knowledge, must be correspondingly revised.

If knowledge is judgment that enables us to move forward, then knowledge is always tentative and provisional. We have all for the most part given up any aspiration for certainty, and we tend to be well aware at least since Wittgenstein, Kuhn, and others, if not much farther back, that knowledge in the best of circumstances is conditional. This fact makes the distinction between knowledge and belief or opinion rather fuzzy. It is not that we are unable to know things. We know quite a lot, including the fact that we are capable of making mistakes, and that what we are sure of at one moment may need revision in the next. If we aspire to achieve certainty then this fuzziness is a problem. But once we realize that knowledge is not a matter of certainty and infallibility, then whether I know that it is snowing outside my window or I am of the opinion that it is snowing outside my window is a distinction without a relevant difference. Subsequent experience will tell me whether I have misjudged or not, and so it is with knowledge in many of its instances.

We do need to be careful here, though, not to dismiss the idea of certainty too quickly, or at least the idea of what we may call operational certainty. For the snow outside my window it may not matter much whether I say that I know it is snowing or I believe it is snowing. But in other circumstances that distinction may make a great deal of practical or operational difference. If the surgeon is about to wield a scalpel in my direction, I want her to know that she should cut at point A rather than point B, and not simply opine that she should do so. Even here, though, the distinction between opinion and knowledge, or between belief and certainty, is not a rigid one. It has to do more with the degree of confidence that *x* or *y* is the case, rather than with a difference in epistemological kinds. Even the surgeon's long-trained and well-experienced judgment that she should cut at point A and not at point B is nevertheless a fallible judgment. Maybe something she had not detected is going on under the surface of my skin, for example. As an operational matter certainty can plausibly be distinguished from opinion, but it is a distinction that points to confidence in action rather than to absolute certainty or to one's infallibility. Knowledge and opinion, then, may not be sharply distinguished.

This is an important point for knowledge and art, and ultimately for truth and art. That I can plausibly claim to have learned something from Kirchner's representation of Berlin street scenes, or Malevich's *Black Square*, or Schoenberg's serialism, does not require that I demonstrate an achievement of knowledge rather than merely opinion. How much I have learned and how reliable that knowledge turns out to be will be determined by other investigations that I undertake, whether in art, history, or politics. How what I have learned fits together with what else I know and learn, and how much of it will be revised or abandoned in the process, will become clear only as the process of query and inquiry unfolds. In this respect the knowledge derived through art and through science differ not at all. Whether my knowledge of the Berlin street during the First World War comes from Kirchner, or historical studies, or an understanding of the power grid that runs the streets' lighting, its depth, accuracy, and meaning always await further study, new information, and creative angles of vision. At any given point the insight and information derived from any one source is no more knowledge or opinion than that derived from the others. Each is conditional and provisional, each takes us as far as it does, and each opens us to further understanding in some way and to some extent. If we think we have a piece of information that goes nowhere, that enables nothing for us, that is incapable of ramification, then in that case we are faced with a hollow judgment, and nothing that we would want to call knowledge. But if our understanding, regardless of its source, enables us to move forward, then there we have knowledge, and it is pointless to wonder whether it is "really" knowledge or "merely" opinion. And as I pointed out in earlier chapters, this does not imply a collapse into ontological relativism.

That our judgments are provisional and conditional, and that they undergo ongoing ramification in experience and query, is a reflection of the general relationality of nature. It does not imply that the complexes of nature with which our judgments engage have their traits relative to our judgments, but merely that our judgments are among their constituent traits, all of which are no less naturally defined for being relational.

This in turn raises the question of truth. In a recently translated collection of essays Gianni Vattimo appeals to Gadamer and Heidegger in support of his claim that "truth happens."[27] He appears to have forgotten about James, who long before either Gadamer or Heidegger, controversially claimed that "truth happens to an idea." What James meant, and presumably Heidegger, Gadamer, and Vattimo have more or less the same idea, should by now be neither startling nor unsettling, especially in light of the general ontology and epistemology we have been unfolding. In nature relationally constituted, in which some of the possibilities of complexes are continuously being actualized and others not, when some traits alesce and others do not, and when throughout their lives people's capacity for judgment is constantly being exercised, with the innumerable implications and consequences that fact implies, there is little sense in regarding truth to mean simply something like "the way things are," or "all that is the case." Of course we still have every reason to use the word "truth" to suggest some sense of objectively determinate or naturally defined states of affairs. We have said that complexes have their traits by natural definition, and it is certainly reasonable to say of propositions, for example, that they are true if they accurately describe the naturally defined traits of the complexes to which they refer. But if we want knowledge and truth to bear a relation to one another, and if knowledge is not restricted to propositional assertions, then truth cannot be restricted to states of affairs. If knowledge is what enables us to move forward, and if knowledge can be or can become truth, then truth has something to do with the moving forward. In a Jamesian spirit, an idea is true to the extent that it moves us forward no less than the extent to which it picks out traits of complexes to which it refers. If there turns out to be an incompatibility between the traits of relevant complexes with which we interact and the directions of our experience and the ramifications of our judgment, that incompatibility will probably sooner or later bring us up short; our desires will collide with the orders of nature in which we function and we will fail to move forward.

Reality, we may want to say, cannot be ignored. We do have to acknowledge, though, that there are many cases in which individuals hold opposing propositions for their entire lives without ever confronting a problem with them. If we accept the reasonableness of the law of excluded middle, which is to say that A and not-A cannot both be true at the same time and in the same respect, at least in certain nonfictional orders, then, for example, the proposition that a creator God exists and the proposition that a creator God does not exist cannot both be true. Nevertheless, there are many people who for their entire lives believe the former, and many others who for their entire lives believe the latter, all of whom are able to integrate their beliefs into their experience to some beneficial extent without ever being forced by circumstances to revise them. If one of them is a false description of things as they are, of the natural definition of the complexes of nature, then it is possible for people to have ideas that move them forward even if those beliefs are false. This means, we may want to say, that truth cannot be understood as that which moves us forward.

We must also acknowledge, however, that truth is not just one thing, and there is no reason that it needs to be understood in only one way. Sometimes it makes the most sense, which is to say it works the best, to say that an idea is true when it accurately depicts its object; in other cases it makes the most sense to regard an idea to be true if it enables us to accomplish something; in still other cases, an idea may reasonably be said to be true if it engenders new possibilities. For the most part we have no trouble negotiating these various senses of truth. In that sense to accept the multiple meanings of "truth" is itself the most workable approach, and to that extent true as far as it goes. We may say that those cases in which we do confront a problem, which is to say the most controversial ideas, insights, understandings, or propositions, are those in which the proper meaning and criteria of truth are themselves up for grabs. This is the point William James was able to put to such brilliant use in "What Pragmatism Means" and "The Will to Believe." Reality may be hard to ignore, but truth is a more plastic matter.

That truth itself has multiple meanings, including truth in the sense in which James and Vattimo mean it, has a particular bearing on the cognitive dimension of art. There is a use of the word "truth" that we find in the writings of mystics that gives us a clue to a more expansive sense of the term. A person who has a mystical experience may say that he has "experienced a profound truth." Those of us not disposed to mystical experiences tend to find such claims puzzling, but one thing that is clear about them is that the mystic in such a case does not mean to say that he has experienced a profound propositional description of a state of affairs. Truth in the sense in which he means it in such cases has to do with the experience of something deeply meaningful and that has a profound impact on him. Vattimo says something like this when he says that "truth changes us." Truth in this sense concerns the consequences of an idea or an experience. There is an "experience of truth," Vattimo says, when a person is truly changed by the experience.[28]

Truth of this kind is tied to the sense of knowledge as that which opens up new possibilities. The truth to be experienced in and through art is or can be of this kind, as is truth in a more conventional sense. Even the standard conception of truth relevant for propositional assertions has this trait as an aspect of what it is for an assertion to be true. It is rather odd to describe even a propositional assertion as true if it leads nowhere, or makes no difference to anyone in any respect. But for the most part art, because it generally does not assert or explicate, is capable of truth in this sense of having more or less important, even profound, consequences, in the sense that it changes us.

The common definition of knowledge in contemporary epistemology is "justified, true belief." The concept of truth in this definition is generally taken to mean some sort of correspondence to or reflection of that to which a proposition refers. Such a conception of truth, however, is, if not quite wrong, far too narrow. There is no better reason always to treat truth as accurate reflection than there is in appropriate circumstances to treat it, following Vattimo and so many others, as what changes us and allows us to move forward. And there is no good reason to restrict truth to propositions or beliefs. We can, as we have seen, quite reasonably and properly say of concepts, experiences, and insights, as well as propositions and beliefs, that they are true. In some cases that truth is a matter of accurate depiction or reflection, in others it is a matter of insightful evocation, and in still others it has to do with having an impact on us. All of these and no doubt other senses of truth have in common the fact that they enable us to carry on, to move on to the next proposition, belief, insight, or experience. Until, that is, we find our way blocked. In that case our understanding or direction requires revision. In that way knowledge and understanding continually unfold, often in unanticipated ways. And in that process art no less than science is a meaningful dimension of our experience.

If we need a single, pithy definition of knowledge then we would do better to turn to Dewey's well-known concept of "warranted assertability." This at least does not require us to beg crucial questions by assuming a concept of truth that is itself questionable. Our assertions may be warranted for a range of reasons, including their efficacy in experience. Even here, though, Dewey's definition in terms of assertions is too narrow in that by implication it restricts us to assertive judgment. If query of any sort is capable of generating knowledge and understanding then we may not reasonably analyze knowledge only in terms of inquiry and the assertive judgments associated with it. Perhaps we should think of knowledge as that idea, proposition, or insight that is pragmatically or operationally plausible, as "warranted actionability," whatever its source and in whatever orders of our experience it is relevant. It is not a graceful definition, but then not everyone can, like Santayana, render philosophy as good art.

Our conception of knowledge must take account of the impact that all forms of judgment have. This is the reason the cognitive dimension of art is relevant to our understanding of knowledge, and it is the reason that epistemology generally would do well to re-examine its principles with the cognitive capacity of art in mind.

PART THREE

SOCIAL EXPERIENCE

Philosophy recovers itself when it ceases to be a device for dealing with the problems of philosophers and becomes a method, cultivated by philosophers, for dealing with the problems of men.

—John Dewey, "The Need for a Recovery of Philosophy"

EIGHT

THE DEMOCRATIC CHALLENGE

If the primary intellectual source of the first several chapters has been Justus Buchler's ordinal ontology and theory of judgment, then the philosophical basis of the remaining chapters devoted to social and political matters is John Dewey's understanding of democracy.[1] It is worthwhile to point out that the two are related in that a relational ontology undergirds Dewey's thinking, and a Deweyan understanding of democracy and all that is implied by it is an expression of a conception of judgment that understands knowledge to be as much about doing and making as it is about asserting. In fact, taken together these two points are a good, short description of what pragmatic naturalism as a philosophic perspective amounts to. In this chapter I will examine a number of issues related to a Deweyan conception of democracy. In the subsequent chapters I will consider some of its potential problems and weaknesses, and the conception of democracy will be applied to several social areas of ongoing philosophic concern.

A word is in order, however, about democracy and its importance. Americans, and many others, like very much to talk about democracy.

That is certainly true of philosophers who work and think in the American vein, and it is perhaps even truer of American social and political leadership. Whether one means simply political democracy in the sense of free and fair elections, or something deeper and richer, we often take for granted the virtue of democracy and proceed as if all that needs to be done is talk about its value and spread it as far around the world as possible. But in fact the situation is far more complicated.

I would like to be able to stipulate without argument that democracy is a desirable way of life. An explicit argument in its favor would easily take a book by itself, as many have. And in any case we may regard the following chapters as an extended argument for democracy, if only by way of example and elaboration of the concept and its problems. So let us assume that whatever its problems, democracy is a desirable form of life and social and political organization. Whether it is the most or only desirable way of life is another question. For one thing, democratic development requires certain conditions. Without them, it may in fact be counter-productive to insist on the form of democracy if to do so is to undermine its substance, and such circumstances do indeed arise. The situation of the media in Russia is an example. For much of the past decade the Russian leadership has been routinely criticized for its domination of the larger and most influential media outlets in the country, the assumption being that the status quo ante was a more desirable alternative. But the situation during the 1990s was one in which the more influential national media outlets were in the control of a small number of owners who used them for their own personal interests while ignoring the interests and needs of the population at large. There was nothing democratic about that despite the fact that there was little public control of the media during that period. What appeared to be democratic form in fact undermined democratic substance. If conditions in the country are such that the only realistic alternatives for the time being are private manipulation of the media for the personal gain of the owners or governmental domination of the media, it is not at all obvious that the latter is not preferable to the former. Though the absence of governmental control of the media may be the more democratic arrangement, it is not necessarily the case that it is to be preferred over all alternatives in any set of circumstances.

Many of us who are inclined to endorse a democratic way of life tend to insist on its superiority to all others on the grounds that it above all is the way of life best suited to human development, but we need to be careful about that. There are nations that are decidedly nondemocratic but we may not necessarily want to say that the development of their citizens is thereby impeded. For example, consider the emirates in the Arab world. Some of them are ruled by sheiks who are in full and authoritative control of the nation, its policy, and its resources. In such an emirate nothing at the macro level, whether economic, social, cultural, or political, happens without the approval of the sheik, and the sheik's word is more or less final. Nonetheless, and even given the significant democratic advances that may result from the Arab Spring in early 2011, it is possible in principle, and in some cases in fact, for the population in such an emirate to live full, rich, and developed lives culturally, socially, and economically. It would be the height of arrogance for any of us to insist that because such a nation is not a democracy its citizens are thereby developmentally stunted. This is not to say that there may not be reasons for people in those societies to struggle for more democratic arrangements. There are in fact such people continuing to do exactly that even after the initial surge of the Spring subsided. The point is simply that we need to be careful not to state the case for democracy in such terms that we do not allow for the possibility that people in nondemocratic societies might lead lives that in their own ways are no less to be valued and respected than the lives of those in democratic societies. We should also acknowledge the fact that in democratic societies there can be and are situations that militate against the full development of people's potential and their freedom. So let us for now be content with the more modest claim that democracy is a desirable way of life that is conducive to the development in all relevant respects of those who live in it, and leave open the possibility that other people may do just as well in other situations.

Furthermore, those of us who do believe that democratic societies are a good need also to accept the fact that many other people, intelligent people of good will, do not. There are various reasons one might not accept democracy as a desirable political and social condition, or at least not desire it for one's own society. Social and political traditions are one such reason. As we have said, there are many societies around the world that are monarchical or aristocratic and are not thereby a danger to their citizens or their neighbors. In fact there can be societies that are nominally democratic that generate far worse conditions than well-run societies that are not. Such a democracy could, for example, be imperialistic to a fault. Or one may simply have a rationale that is at least plausible for supporting a nondemocratic government and social structure. Plato comes to mind.

Finally, many supporters of democracy, and Americans may be the most guilty of this fault, seem to think that it is the responsibility of a democrat to promote the spread of democracy. The main point of contention among such people is whether democracy can reasonably be promoted by force or whether persuasion and example are the most appropriate methods. We will look at this issue more carefully in Chapter 10 in the context of international relations and foreign policy. But it rarely occurs to those who think this way that the responsibility of a democrat is not to promote democracy but to behave democratically. These are two very different things, as my subsequent analysis will attempt to show.

In this chapter we will flesh out the conception of democracy that will inform the remainder of our discussion. Specifically, it is a strain that is in one sense a romantic one, having its roots in Rousseau and Jefferson, and developed in the last century in the work of Dewey and others. It is the sense of democracy in which democracy is to be understood as a way of life, and not simply as a form of government or a mechanism for making political choices. In this sense, democracy, as Dewey might have said, reaches deep into a society and a culture. Its purposes and ideals structure, so to speak, the way people live, the way they interact with one another, their aspirations, and their activities. This is a much richer sense of democracy than the more common political one, but it is therefore also more complex and difficult to realize.

Because Dewey was the most eloquent spokesperson for democracy in the sense in which it is meant here, it is appropriate to indulge in a bit of exposition to clarify the concept, primarily through a discussion of Dewey's essay "Creative Democracy: The Task before Us" and the understanding of democracy he develops in *Democracy and Education.* For those readers who know Dewey well there is likely to be nothing new in this exposition. Nonetheless, there is some advantage in putting one's cards on the table, so to speak. After the exposition we will go on to describe why there is value in this view, and what, under current circumstances, are its prospects for realization. If there are no prospects for its realization, or if they are merely notional, then there is in fact little value in the concept, regardless of the elegance of its expression or the strength of its logic. Subsequent chapters will explore in more detail many of the issues and problems raised here.[2]

Thick Democracy

The best thinking in the American philosophical tradition about democracy as a way of life was done by John Dewey, whose work from the late nineteenth century through the first half of the twentieth was infused with issues having to do with democracy, its nature and its problems. There are two texts in particular that can help us develop a fuller sense of his conception. The earliest is his theoretical account in *Democracy and Education*. We will begin, however, with a later text. In his 1939 article "Creative Democracy: The Task before Us," Dewey gives several definitions of democracy:

> Democracy is a way of life controlled by a working faith in the possibilities of human nature.
>
> Democracy is a way of personal life controlled not merely by faith in human nature in general but by faith in the capacity of human beings for intelligent judgment and action if proper conditions are furnished.
>
> Democracy is the belief in the ability of human experience to generate the aims and methods by which further experience will grow in ordered richness.
>
> Democracy is the faith that the process of experience is more important than any special result attained, so that special results achieved are of ultimate value only as they are used to enrich and order the ongoing process.
>
> Since the process of experience is capable of being educative, faith in democracy is all one with faith in experience and education.[3]

Democracy has everything to do with human nature; in fact, it brings out the best in us, so to speak. It involves a faith in the possibilities of human nature, specifically the possibilities of individual and social development. Our nature is such, or so the democrat believes, that we are able to develop our emotional, perceptual, and intellectual powers to the point that it is possible for us to perceive our situations and our problems, to understand how we might address them, and to care enough to act. That capacity is part of what we are, it is our nature, but the result, the achievement is not. The result or effect of the exercise of this capacity, the achievement of clear perception and understanding, does not happen haphazardly. It is the result of experience of a certain kind, of the exercise of intelligence, of experience that is educative.

This idea of a faith in human nature is critical to democracy. It is in fact the issue that many people from Plato's time to our own day have emphasized in their criticisms of democracy. The idea that the average person is really capable of developing the level of intelligence and understanding necessary to govern his own life and collectively his society is an illusion, many have argued. Dewey found himself in an argument on this score with Walter Lippmann, who argued in the 1920s that the "informed citizen" was a myth, and therefore what democracy there is must have an elitist edge and rely on the knowledge of experts. That Dewey rejected Lippman's view is instructive because it indicates the centrality of the possibility of human development, under the proper and nourishing conditions, to his thought in general and to his understanding of democracy.

Dewey qualifies the first quote with the second, when he says that democracy is not simply faith in human nature, but faith in our capacity for intelligent judgment. The term "intelligence" is an extremely important one for Dewey because in his opinion intelligence is both the means and the end of human experience, both its proper method and its goal.

What then is intelligence? Judgment and experience are intelligent when they are purposeful and more or less self-directed. To say "self-directed" in this context is not to imply that an individual all by himself controls his experience and its direction. The human condition is an inherently social one, and no meaningful experience is in any significant sense "wholly individual." "Self-direction," rather, means that there is some measure of conscious control and purposeful direction to one's experience. It implies a willingness to try new possibilities, to look at things in new ways to see what happens, to test one's own ideas and others, to alter one's own conceptions when experience, query, and inquiry call for it. The interesting thing for our purposes is that in this definition democracy is a way of living predicated on intelligence in experience and in judgment. Democracy, in other words, rests not on blind custom, nor on dogma, nor on rigid ideology, nor on clichés and slogans, but on the exercise of our collective capacity to study ourselves and our world, to perceive its problems, and to apply in our lives a mode of interaction that opens to the possibility of new and creative solutions. That is the exercise of intelligence, and it is a necessary feature of democracy.

This is a future-oriented and creative dimension of experience and democracy, as is the next citation that defines democracy as the context in which experience grows in "ordered richness." This is an obscure and academic formulation of democracy. The critical term, of course, and the most obscure, is "ordered richness." What does it mean here? First, experience is an active process. It is in fact the full scope of the interaction between an individual and his environment, where the environment is to be understood as including social structures and relations. It is the cumulative, developing trajectory of a human life. Understood this way it makes more sense to think of experience as something that grows. The next question, though, is in which directions does experience grow, or better, in which directions would we want experience to grow?

Dewey's answer is that we want it to grow in "ordered richness." The idea is that the most fruitful, the most "rich," and in the end the most satisfying experience is that which most enriches an individual's possibilities. Since we are all basically social in our lived contexts, our possibilities, in a whole range of aspects of our lives, are themselves engendered in social contexts and through social relations. Experience is rich when we as individuals "order" ourselves in our social context such that our individual concerns and interests enhance our social context and that our social relations enrich our individual lives. Experience is rich in that it opens us up, or we open ourselves up, to further enriching experience. Or conversely, we want to avoid so ordering our experience that it closes us off from new and broader contact. When we project our experience, so to speak, when we order it so that it opens to future enriching possibilities, we are living the most human of lives.

The democratic life is one in which the individual and the social are integrated explicitly and consciously, in which individual problems are understood and addressed in their social contexts and social issues are taken personally. This is one of the reasons democracy is or can be so important. The democratic life, with the necessarily related democratic social conditions, constitutes a fully human experience, and is one in which the individual and social space is available to generate the richness of life without which we are in some measure impoverished. With the caveats expressed earlier in mind, this is not to say that people are incapable of "fully human experience" in conditions that are not democratic. It is to say, though, that democracy properly maintained is conducive to such experience.

There is a phrase in this citation that connects it with the next, and that is the reference to the "aims and methods," or means and ends, by which experience will grow. Means and ends are related to one another, and ends are themselves always in some measure tentative. They are, in an expression Dewey frequently used, ends-in-view. Our ends are our goals and purposes in specific contexts, and as such they provide order and direction to our experience. They are always related to the means we employ to reach them, however, in the sense that in an integrated life our methods or means can be expected to reinforce our ends and our ends or goals underscore, or enrich the meaning and import, of our means.

Democracy is a good illustration of this interrelation between means and ends. For example, democratic social structures, say forms of political decision making, are themselves strengthened if the ends or purposes to which they are put contribute to the opening up of experience, to reaching out to broader and more pervasive social relations. They are undermined, however, if they are put to the purpose of restricting experience through authoritarianism or through colonial or imperialistic domination of people in the society or abroad. For example, any society that is aggressive and dominating abroad cannot long remain democratic at home. Similarly, democratic ends are undermined when equally democratic means are not employed to pursue them. Means and ends are mutually constitutive of one another.

The next citation assumes this point of view: The democratic process of experience is more important than any specific predefined result. The reason is that results or ends can be defined only in the context of the process. In the case of democracy, means and ends are basically the same thing; i.e., they enrich and order the ongoing process of experience.

Finally, democracy is defined in terms of education. Experience that grows in ordered richness is experience that is educative. Therefore, a faith in democracy is a commitment to an ordering of human experience that continually educates us, that consistently provides the contexts in which we can develop and grow individually, socially, and I would add internationally. Education in this sense is broader than schooling, but it certainly includes schooling. The schools, in fact, are the place where we can help children develop the habits of mind and the knowledge they need to achieve the kind of open-ended, democratic approach to their own experience that can help them and their experience to grow in ordered richness and to accomplish democracy. The schools are the laboratories of democracy; they are the places where the democratic temper is fostered and achieved. Why think this? There are many aspects of social life that militate against democracy, including well-entrenched social traditions, racial and ethnic tensions, gender inequality, and not least class distinctions. If left untended, each one of these social factors can undermine and even destroy democracy for the simple reason that they tend to close us off from one another rather than open us up. They do not lead to richer experience, but on the contrary they serve to stultify our capacity for growth and development. The schools can and should be the places where a genuinely democratic society can at least partially overcome these debilitating features of the society and allow children the conditions for more fruitful social and intellectual progress. This is done through the structure of the school itself, through the curriculum, and through appropriate pedagogical methods. In other words genuine democracy is educative and education properly conducted is conducive to democracy.

Many of the conditions that define American society today, not to mention other societies around the world, are in fact threats to democracy in the sense in which it has been developed here. The distortion in people's lives and the restrictions of their potential caused by the gross disparities in the distribution of wealth remain fundamental dangers to democracy. American schools are today subject to forces that militate against education and the pursuit of Dewey's "ordered richness." Witness the threats of some years ago to science education at the hands of the Kansas Board of Education. Internationally we continue to speak about democracy while we pursue policies that directly undermine it. American support of the corrupt oligarchy in Russia in the 1990s is a glaring example, but there are many smaller-scale but no less devastating ones around the world. Democracy remains a threatened species today, but that fact constitutes a problem for us to face and to attempt to solve. Dewey's extensive and quite rich treatments of democracy have always been sources of insight and even inspiration, and I expect that they will continue to be.

The second source in Dewey's work of a thick conception of democracy is *Democracy and Education*, in which he describes democracy as a "way of life," which is to say that it is something more than a type of process for organizing political power and selecting people for political office.[4] Political structure and elections are not trivial matters, of course, but if democracy is to be understood as a way of life then they are not sufficient conditions for democracy. In the same book Dewey offered the basis of a definition of democracy. The most significant component of that definition is, to paraphrase a bit, the pursuit of common interests with those outside one's immediate community. In the sense meant here, "community" could be defined in terms of a wide range of criteria. It could be understood as class, or race, or gender, or ethnicity, or neighborhood, or nationality, or any one of a number of other traits. A democratic individual in this sense is someone who is inclined to look beyond his community to seek common ground, common interests, with members of other communities; a democratic society is one that is characterized by public policies and social habits that promote the pursuit of shared interests within and across its many internal boundaries and beyond its national borders.

In order for such an individual and such a society to thrive there must be certain characteristics that predominate. The society, for example, must encourage education and it must encourage communication. With respect to the first, Dewey went to great lengths, as have a number of others such as John McDermott, to develop a conception of education that is likely to help people develop the understanding and the habits that will enable them to live as democratic individuals.[5] It is not an easy ideal to fulfill. A democratic individual is knowledgeable, thoughtful, critical, experimental, and ethically sensitive. As difficult an ideal as this may be, it is what a democracy requires, and education, or the schools, is the one social institution best able to engender the result.

With respect to communication, it is difficult to overstate its importance in a society that aspires to be democratic. The relative absence of communication is to that extent an approximation of fascism. If we think in terms of communication among individuals, groups, and constituencies within a society, a democracy should be expected to promote an interest in and familiarity with one another. Any failure to do so is equivalent to promoting or at least tolerating a degree of isolation that breeds suspicion, distrust, even hatred, which in turn provides the social foundations of fascism. A democratic society simply cannot tolerate such conditions, not if it seriously desires to advance and strengthen its democratic character. Similarly, a democratic society should promote an interest in and familiarity with those beyond national borders. Xenophobia has no more place in a democratic society than do internal hatreds or mutual ignorance of one another. A democratic society is, to put it differently, necessarily internationalist in its orientation. It promotes international understanding, competence in foreign languages, cosmopolitan values, international cooperation, and diplomacy; in short, it pursues common interests with those beyond its borders. This is not easy to do, any more than educating for a democratic society is easy to do, especially in a somewhat hostile environment. Finding common ground with friends is much easier than finding common ground with those one sees as hostile. Nonetheless, this is what is required.

The Democratic Ideal

At this point I would like to turn to the issue of values within a social context. Specifically, my interest is in thinking about the implications of underlying pragmatic naturalist and democratic principles for the development of social and international relations.

As anyone who thinks about questions in social and political philosophy is aware, one of the more sustained debates in recent decades has been between liberalism and communitarianism. It is fair to say that both have important contributions to make, and that both have built-in disadvantages. Liberalism contributes its long-standing emphasis on the moral, social, and political importance of the individual, of individual rights, and of individual freedom. Critics, however, tend to feel that liberalism too easily emphasizes and often overemphasizes the individual, thereby theoretically pulling him out of social and historical context and distorting his nature. In the process our understanding of rights and freedom is similarly distorted.

For its part communitarianism has the advantage of focusing on the fuller social and historical contexts in which we all live, and in so doing provides a rich sense of human individuality and of the relevant issues of responsibility, freedom, and rights. The difficulty with communitarianism stems from the shortcoming of communities themselves. While community is often the source of individuals' self-identification, as well as a source of value, meaning, and comfort, community is, or too easily can be, inward looking to a fault. It is too easy for many people to make the assumption that other communities and the individuals in them are in some way flawed or inferior. In its (usually but not necessarily) innocent forms, this sense of the superiority of one's own community gives rise to rivalries of localities in sports and other pastimes. In its virulent forms it gives rise to nationalism, xenophobia, racism, fascism, and other violent expressions of a sense of one's own community's superiority.

Democracy as we understand it here cuts across the debate between liberalism and communitarianism, and in the end points to a cosmopolitanism that has a good deal to contribute to contemporary social and political issues. The point is made clearly enough in *Democracy and Education*, specifically in Chapter 7, where Dewey offers his definition of democracy. In a wonderful example of the pragmatic method of conceptual development, Dewey derives a description of democracy's most fundamental traits by examining the characteristics of any community or group of people. "We cannot," he says, "set up, out of our heads, something we regard as an ideal society. We must base our conception upon societies that actually exist." However, he quickly points out that in constructing an ideal, it is not enough simply to describe what exists because that will only tell us what is, not what is worth striving for. "The problem," he points out, "is to extract the desirable traits of forms of community life which actually exist, and employ them to criticize undesirable features and suggest improvements."

With that method in mind, Dewey points to two characteristics that appear in "any social group whatever, even in a gang of thieves." The first of them is that within any social group there is some interest held in common, as well as "a certain amount of interaction and cooperative intercourse with other groups. From these two traits we derive our standard," he says. Through a process of conceptual development that we shall skip over for the sake of efficiency, Dewey argues that a healthy community is one that fosters a proliferation of interests held in common, and that promotes ever-expanding and freer communication and interaction among groups or communities. A society characterized by these two traits is the ideal toward which we should strive. It is, Dewey says, the "democratic ideal." It is significant to see why he thinks these two traits are so important. The first of them, a proliferation of common interests, "signifies not only more numerous and more varied points of shared common interest, but greater reliance upon the recognition of mutual interests as a factor in social control." The second, expanding interaction among groups, communities, societies, and, we should add, nations, "means not only freer interaction between social groups . . . but change in social habit—its continuous readjustment through meeting the new situations produced by varied intercourse."

The two traits that define the democratic ideal are also the two principles that we shall develop to describe desirable social and international relations. The same principles also express the sense in which pragmatic naturalism and our conception of democracy cut across the liberalism and communitarianism dichotomy. Insofar as the human individual is in fundamental respects a social creature, a fact indicated if nothing else by the centrality of language to human experience, then the liberal conception of the person is to that extent suspicious. At the same time, one avoids the pitfalls of a potential communitarian overemphasis on a single community, which in practice is one's own community, by an emphasis on the importance of shared interests across community and social boundaries. It is in fact the combination of the two principles, which is to say an emphasis on shared interests across boundaries, that provides both our alternative to liberalism and communitarianism, and at the same time the basic principle on which to develop social and international relations.

The Domestic Dimension

One can fairly say that not long ago the great international divide among peoples was ideological. The primary split was between those who ascribed to some form of socialist principles and those who ascribed to some form of liberalism. The strength of those ideological disputes has dissipated in recent years, even if the source of them, the socialist and liberal ideologies, have not. A longer-standing source of division has been religion. Though religious wars are for the most part not nearly as vicious as they once were, religion remains a point of contestation among peoples, as well as a point of great sensitivity. Pope Benedict's public quotation several years ago from a fourteenth-century Byzantine emperor about the violence that attended the early spread of Islam is a case in point, as is the consequent strong reaction to his remarks in the Muslim world. More recently the Swiss have voted to ban the construction of minarets in any new mosques in the country, another stunning illustration of religious suspicion and distrust.

Though ideology in politics and religion remains a problem from the point of view of the value of human understanding and cooperation, it may well be the case that today even stronger causes of social disunity are nationalism and ethnocentrism. It is not difficult to list examples of both. The problems in the former Yugoslavia had and continue to have these causes, as do many of the tensions throughout Europe; the genocidal wars in Rwanda and Sudan are examples, as are many of the tensions today in Russia; Romania is no stranger to ethnic and national tensions, especially in Transylvania as people of Hungarian and Romanian ethnicities deal with the residue of their respective histories; the extent of hostility and distrust between Armenia and Azerbaijan is stunning in its virulence, from both sides; throughout Europe societies deal with the vexing question of the relation between the majority populations and the

Roma; the Han Chinese continue to come to grips, or fail to do so, with the interests and sensibilities of their Tibetan or Uighur compatriots; and in the United States one of the most pressing social problems in recent years has to do with the strong reaction by many people, including local and national leaders, to Mexican immigration. By most counts, there are now between eleven and twelve million people of Mexican descent in the United States, and those who are concerned about this suspect that one consequence of this massive immigration is that whole regions of the country will become increasingly Latino and less Anglo, thus changing the country in significant ways. Many, if not most of our societies, in other words, are struggling with the disuniting effects of nationalism and ethnocentrism.

Nationalists and ethnocentrists themselves see the problem as one of disunity, though from their point of view the problem is caused by the very existence of diverse nations and ethnicities. If that is the case, then the solution is to separate nations and ethnicities from one another, or in more extreme cases to eliminate one or the other. Leaving aside the point that the consequences of such activities have been and will continue to be disastrous even when not deadly, the fundamental problem with the nationalist and ethnocentric approach is that it serves to separate people, which in turn impoverishes the experience of all involved. Such a situation can never stand as an adequate social condition. We can organize democratic political systems as carefully as possible, but they will amount to very little if our societies continue to be plagued by disharmony based on national and ethnic diversity.

Thus, following Dewey, the "democratic ideal" pushes us in precisely the opposite direction. Notice, however, that the democratic response is not, as some traditional approaches have advocated, to work to absorb minority ethnic, racial, and national groups into the identity of the majority. This approach has been common in American history, in part because American history is replete with waves of immigration—first from Northern Europe, then from China, then from Southern and Eastern Europe, more recently from throughout South and East Asia, and now from Mexico and elsewhere in Latin America. And this is not to mention the forced immigration of the slave trade. There is a strong tradition in the United States of attempts to "Americanize" immigrant populations, to absorb them into the mainstream, dominant culture, a tendency for which Dewey himself was criticized.

The principle we have articulated as central to a healthy, democratic society, however, holds that we are to look for, and when necessary create, common interests among groups and communities within a society. The democratic response to the existence of diverse national, ethnic, racial, and religious groups is not separation, absorption, or even tolerance. The democratic response is to interact with one another in the pursuit of shared, common interests.

This is, to be sure, easier said than done. Dewey understood that it requires very careful attention to education, primarily because we are suggesting that a healthy, democratic society requires different habits from those that are now common in all our societies. These habits do not develop automatically, nor of course do they come into being simply because some number of social philosophers point to their necessity. They will not come into being automatically even if a majority of leaders and policy makers come to see their necessity. The habits of mind and the inclinations necessary for people to pursue common interests rather than disharmony and disunity must be developed in people from an early age.

A reliance on education to advance social ends is nothing new. We need only to remind ourselves that a person's identification with the state, i.e., nationalism in one of its forms, was itself something that had to be purposefully instilled in our populations, and the American case is a clear illustration. For most people the nation state with which we identify is not more than a couple of hundred years old. In all our cases it required something of a struggle before the population as a whole began to think of itself in national, rather than local, racial, ethnic, or religious terms. In the United States—for example, in the mid-nineteenth century before the Civil War, people tended to identify with their state before the nation. That is why when some states seceded from the nation in 1861, many people who were at the time serving in positions of political and military leadership of the nation resigned their positions and joined with the forces of the newly established Confederacy. Robert E. Lee, for example, who became the commander of the Confederate military forces during the war, had been an officer in the Army of the United States before his native state of Virginia seceded from the Union. When Virginia left the Union so did Lee, and the reason was that he was a Virginian before he was an American.

All of us have analogous histories, and in all our cases a sense of national identification had to be developed and the schools were one of the places in which that occurred. The military was another. If we have been able to utilize education and other national institutions to develop nationalist inclinations and habits, it is not unreasonable to look to the same institutions now to do the same in the interests of the habits and inclinations we have identified as central to a healthy, democratic society.

The analogy with the development of nationalism is apt in another way as well. If we are right that our current social problems require something like Dewey's principle of the pursuit of common interests among groups and communities, then one of the implications is that nationalism has outlived its usefulness. And I mean this in both senses of the word "nation," i.e., as an ethnic identifier and as the nation state. Many of our nations, in the latter sense, are multinational in the former sense. While national identity in the former sense is understandable and even valuable, we have been arguing that the current needs of our societies are such that we must look beyond nations and ethnicities, and we must use available social institutions to make that possible. We can turn now to the implications of the democratic ideal for nationalism in the second sense.

The International Dimension

We will look much more closely at the question of international relations in Chapter 10, but it is nevertheless useful at this point to specify how the general conception of democracy has ramifications for international as well as national contexts. The modern nation state was created in the mid-seventeenth century in the aftermath of the Thirty Years' War in Central Europe. The agreement that ended that war, the Treaty of Westphalia, is generally regarded as the historical point at which the nation state as we know it came into existence. At roughly the same time Thomas Hobbes and others were articulating the metaphors and conceptual categories that would frame our conception of the state, and interstate relations, for the next several hundred years. As we all know, Hobbes described the state as the sphere of legal authority of a given ruler. In the absence of such legal authority, people are in a state of nature, which he famously described as a condition in which life is "solitary, poor, nasty, brutish and short." In this general picture, a state of nature exists in two general conditions: in a given land where there is no state authority, and in the "space" between spheres of legal authority, which is to say in the space between nations.

This picture, this metaphor, has framed our conception of the nation state and our understanding of international relations. The point at which nations interact is a state of nature, which, we may assume, is rather like a land without proper state authority, which is to say that it too is nasty and brutish. To this sense of the realm in which nations interact we should add a second metaphor, one common to the Baroque period in general. In this metaphor, as we have already seen in previous chapters, any and all phenomena are understood as ultimately atomistic, as constituted by discrete entities that interact with one another according to describable "laws." This is the picture Newtonian science gave to the physical world, it is the picture Locke gave to the social and political world, and it is the picture Adam Smith gave to the economic world. To see just how pervasive this Baroque metaphor was, one can simply note that the same picture described even music of the period. Baroque music is basically contrapuntal, which is to say that it is characterized by discrete entities, in this case melodic lines, which interact or harmonize with one another according to explicitly articulated laws or rules of counterpoint. Similarly, physical laws describe how the atomic elements of the physical universe interact harmoniously, social law makes possible the harmonic interaction of atomistically understood human individuals, and the laws of economics, Adam Smith's invisible hand, describe the harmonious interaction of economic actors each with their individually determined interests. Common to all of these expressions of the Baroque picture of the world is the assumption that the ultimate entities in any given sphere are essentially unrelated to one another. Each material atom, each human individual, each economic actor, and each melodic line, has its nature, its character, its traits, independently of the others.

The same set of assumptions has been taken for granted in the area of international relations. Thus, three central concepts have been used to frame our understanding of how nation states interact with one another: (1) The sphere of their interaction is a lawless state of nature; (2) nations are discrete entities that interact with one another harmoniously or chaotically, as the case may be, rather like billiard balls bouncing off one another, to use a common Baroque metaphor; and (3) each discrete entity, each nation state, has its character independently of the others, or more to the point, has its own set of interests that are determined independently of one another. Given these three basic assumptions, international relations has been understood as the exercise in which each nation seeks to meet its "national interests" in competition with all the others. Each nation's foreign policy is therefore the framework or set of policies developed for and applied in the pursuit of national interest.

The dominant theoretical approaches to international relations have also tended to make these assumptions. Realism is an overtly Hobbesian theory of international relations, in which it is assumed that each nation crafts its own set of interests and then competes with all other nations in a basically lawless environment to fulfill those interests. Liberalism in international relations theory plays the role of Locke to realism's Hobbes, which is to say that for liberalism the general picture is rather kinder and gentler, but still one in which each nation defines its interests independently of the others and pursues them as best it can. In recent years in American foreign policy neoconservative theory has come to the fore. It differs from the others in that it is less trustful of international agencies and agreements and more inclined to use power, hard and soft, to force nations to bend to the will of the powerful. But underneath such differences, neoconservatism makes the same Baroque assumptions about nation states, national interests, and international relations as do the others.

None of the prevailing theories of international relations, or applied programs of foreign policy, is consistent with what, following Dewey, we have called the democratic ideal, the basic principle of a healthy, democratic society. We have argued that the pursuit or development of common interests among diverse national, ethnic, and religious groups is a necessary condition of a strong democratic society. We have also suggested that the pursuit or development of common interests is equally important, even critically necessary, across the boundaries of nation states. Given the prevailing approaches to international relations theory and foreign policy, however, this is a somewhat radical proposal, or so it appears. To pursue it further we should look first at its theoretical background in the pragmatist tradition, and then to some current thinking in international relations circles.

In the same chapter of *Democracy and Education* in which we saw Dewey develop his definition of democracy and the "democratic ideal," he also considers the international context. His general concern at this point is with education, so he places his remarks in that context:

> Is it possible for an educational system to be conducted by a national state and yet the full social ends of the educative process not be restricted, constrained, and corrupted? . . . Externally, the question is concerned with the reconciliation of national loyalty, or patriotism, with superior devotion to the things which unite men in common ends, irrespective of national political boundaries.

This is of course a rhetorical question for Dewey in that he asks it in order to give an affirmative answer. The important point for our purposes is that he makes it clear that the democratic ideal makes common interests more important than national loyalty and, by implication, independently determined national interests. Whatever value national loyalty and patriotism may have, the democratic ideal requires "superior devotion" to common interests across national boundaries.

If this is the case, then the traditional theories of international relations and approaches to foreign policy are no longer adequate, at least not if we wish to pursue a genuinely democratic international environment. On the contrary, the democratic ideal requires that nation states pursue, and when necessary construct, common interests, and it requires that they coordinate their foreign policies to bring those common interests to fruition. In order to make this conceptual and policy shift it is necessary for nations first to give up the traditional, Baroque metaphor according to which each nation is an independent entity that defines itself without recourse to the nature and interests of others, and second to overcome the traditional assumption of national sovereignty that has been with us since the seventeenth century.

Is this as radical a suggestion as it sounds? First, we should note that the traditional Baroque assumptions about the nation state and the international arena are not the only possible assumptions. We have too readily mistaken a metaphor for the reality in the sense that we have allowed the metaphor to serve as the only possible description of reality. But, as one might expect in this pragmatic naturalist approach, it is important for us to realize that we live in a world that is in many important respects of our own making. In the seventeenth century we made the Hobbesian, Baroque world. In the twenty-first century it is time for us to make a different one. Furthermore, the general relational ontology that we have identified with pragmatic naturalism provides precisely the appropriate general conceptual underpinnings that enable us to understand how a nation state develops its character in relation to others.

Second, even some influential and very mainstream figures in international relations have quite independently come to the conclusion that the traditional assumptions of the preeminence of national sovereignty are too dangerous in the contemporary world to prevail, and that only international collaboration will bring us back from the brink we currently see before us. One such figure is Francis Fukuyama, a onetime champion of neoconservative foreign policy in the United States. Though he does not go as far as we do in that he does not yet recognize the need to determine collaboratively the very interests that drive foreign policy, he does realize that nations, including and perhaps especially the most powerful, must be willing to sacrifice some degree of sovereignty in an effort to address the most pressing international problems.[6]

And third, the fact is that in some places in the world, Europe in particular, the effort to recast international relations is already in process. The European Union, whatever its flaws and difficulties, including a deficit of democratic conditions, is I would submit an example of a process in which nations have sacrificed some degree of sovereignty in the construction and pursuit of common interests and the resolution of common problems. The Deweyan process, in other words, is not only possible, but already underway. Interestingly enough, in the process the EU is facing a rise in the very ethnocentric and nationalistic forces that militate against its success. The result remains unclear.

Insofar as these claims are reasonable and defensible, they offer, as we suggested earlier, an alternative, and a distinctly pragmatist alternative, to the prevalent liberal and communitarian approaches to social and political theory, and to the dominant alternatives in international relations theory. They avoid the inappropriately abstract character of the liberal understanding of the individual, and they avoid the undesirable overemphasis on the importance of one's own community. In their place the principle we have developed points to a kind of cosmopolitanism in which the richness and variety of individuals and communities flourishes only insofar as they interact with one another toward common ends. In practice, this pragmatic naturalist principle, the democratic ideal, offers us a way, I would argue a desirable if not a necessary way, to address our most pressing domestic and international problems. We will look more deeply into several of these issues in later chapters.

The Prospects for a Thick Democracy

Such traits are what a thick democracy is made of. But this is simply a matter of definition, and does not raise the question whether democracy in this sense is desirable. Dewey certainly thought so; in fact he thought that it is the only social arrangement appropriate to free and developing individuals, societies, and nations. This may well overstate the case, as we have suggested, but it is the case that whichever social and political arrangements there are that are conducive to the development of individual and social good, democracy is among them. I would not like to get too far into the question of whether democracy is a desirable condition. As I indicated earlier in the chapter, I would prefer simply to stipulate that it is desirable, on the grounds that an individual who is knowledgeable, thoughtful, critical, experimental, and ethically sensitive is preferable to one who is not, and a society that values public policies and social habits that promote the pursuit of shared interests across internal and external borders is preferable to one that does not.

The relevant question for us at the moment concerns the prospects for and limits of democracy in this sense. As a logical possibility one could say that the prospects for meeting the conditions of such a thick democracy are not bad. There is nothing inherently contradictory about it, and though it is a high ideal, history is full of examples of ideals that at one time seemed absurdly unrealistic but that have come to dominate. The elimination of slavery, the end of absolute monarchy, and even the prevalence of republics are among the more obvious such examples. Slavery, monarchy, and aristocracies were once natural and necessary features of social life, and now they are neither. Individual and social freedoms in the forms represented by the demise of slavery, monarchy, and aristocracy are now the standards against which we measure social and individual life, and there is nothing about thick democracy that precludes it from becoming such a standard in the future.

So as a logical possibility the prospects are good. What about as a realistic possibility? Here things are somewhat trickier, especially in the short run. One reason, the importance of which is not to be underestimated, is that the term "democracy" has been so badly abused in recent years that in some parts of the world it will take a long time for it even to be meaningfully legitimate again. Democracy has meant the free reign of the market and the many predations that has brought about. In Russia in the 1990s it meant the rape of social assets and the impoverishment of millions of people. And in many places around the world, Iraq being only the most obvious, it has meant the political and military domination of the United States, with which even many of America's allies were fed up long before American forces withdrew from direct engagement. Nominally and substantially democracy is in need of rehabilitation before it can serve as a forceful ideal again, never mind become a reality.

There are other problems as well, among them the fact that we do not do very well the things that are necessary for the development of democratic individuals and societies, notably education and communication. There are very few societies in which more than a small number of schools educate in the manner that we have described as appropriate for democratic conditions. Those that do exist, by virtue of their small number and by their tendency to foster academic elitism or to cater to the relatively wealthy, reach very few children and students. In many countries there is also a problem with a sharp differentiation between academic and vocational schooling, a distinction by the way that Dewey deplored and that he discussed to very good effect in *Democracy and Education*. Attending to education remains one of the more important aspects of a social policy that can contribute to the growth of democracy.

The situation with respect to communication is little better. One of the more important forms in which communication occurs in contemporary societies is the traditional publicly accessible print and broadcast media. Just how these media can best serve the interests of communication within a democratic society is not easy to specify. It is easier, though, to indicate some of what they should avoid if they want to play any sort of salutary role in democratic development. For one thing they should avoid passing along information from the powerful to the benighted that they know to be false. Had the *New York Times* and other media outlets followed this simple policy in 2002 and early 2003, there may well not have been an invasion of Iraq. Along similar lines, media outlets, with the exception of editorial pages and journals of opinion, need to avoid overt political partisanship. Both print and broadcast media have a problem in this respect. The problem is in fact bigger than simply political partisanship, and it has to do with the difficulties created by privately, especially corporately, owned media. If media outlets allow or encourage themselves to give voice to the interests of their owners, or to the political forces that represent the interests of their owners, then they are overwhelmingly unlikely to be able to provide the means of communication that a democracy needs. This *Fox News* version of broadcasting is more than a nuisance in contemporary American and other media environments. However we express the ideal media traits in a democratic society, they surely do not include much of the behavior we currently see. It has been suggested that electronic journalism such as blogging is creating new conditions for communication of the sort that will better meet democratic expectations. This may in fact be true, though we have to see how it develops.

There are a number of stumbling blocks, then, to the actualization of individual and social life approaching thick democracy. I mention all this not to create a mood of pessimism, rather simply to clear away the brush, so to speak. We cannot talk about the prospects for democratic development in a naïve, Pollyannaish way if we want to say anything meaningful or useful, so it is necessary to point out the problems. But the problems do not describe the whole situation, or even most of it. For all of the bad education, the miscommunication, the lies, the violence, and the abuse of power let loose in the world, the fact is that there are good reasons to be optimistic about the prospects for democracy.

First, even with respect to those areas that have been identified as problems, i.e., education and communication, there continues to be debate, dispute, and struggle concerning them. In education and schooling, it may turn out to be a surprising virtue that we in fact have little idea what we are doing. I mean to say that for all the scholarship around teaching, educational mission, school organization, evaluation, and educational administration, we really do not know how best to prepare good teachers, how best to organize and fund schools, how to evaluate their success, or for that matter how to determine what they should be doing. I say that this is a virtue because at the very least it keeps the issues alive. For example, there is a periodic outcry in the United States about the failure of our schools to educate properly, and the related failure of our teacher education institutions to prepare great teachers. There is of course controversy about all this, but pretty much everyone agrees that we can do all these things better than we now do them. The result is what appears to be a never-ending experimentation with respect to curriculum, the structure of teacher education programs, the content and format of textbooks, and with the organization of schools and school systems. As is the case with experiments, even of the carefully controlled scientific sort that these are not, the results are often not what we would hope. But that is the nature of experimentation, and it is far better that we keep trying, even if we fail most of the time, than that we rest content with whatever inadequacies we currently have. The ongoing attempt to do it all better, even in a politically charged and often ideological context, is what gives us hope that over time we can approximate an education suitable for democratic conditions. There is no guarantee, of course, and it is not necessarily the case that there will be progress. But the future remains open, or "in the making" as William James would have it, and that is reason enough to be hopeful.

The case with communication is perhaps even more hopeful. There are considerable dangers in the corporate consolidation of media outlets.

But this too is a point of contention and struggle. There are more than a few groups, if we again consider the situation in the United States, that are struggling to keep the airwaves open and available to as wide a range of voices as possible, and to prevent media markets from being dominated by only a handful of corporate owners. It is a political and economic battle to be sure, but the battle is being waged. And here the new electronic media forms and outlets are particularly important. They represent ways that people, individually and collectively, can make their way around the consolidated and compromised traditional media to maintain and strengthen the communicative possibilities that democratic society requires. Of course progress in this situation is no more guaranteed than it is in education, but it is possible, and so there remains more than simply naïve hope.

But what are the prospects with respect to the definitional criterion of democracy that Dewey offered, i.e., the pursuit of common interests across community and national boundaries? Here too there is reason for hope. Let us look first at what are roughly internal matters. We have already mentioned the many serious and too often deadly tensions that remain among various racial or ethnic communities, though the tensions are rarely if ever simply ethnic or racial, i.e., there are generally historical, economic, and political elements as well: Albanian and Serb, Hutu and Tutsi, Jewish and Palestinian, Azeri and Armenian, Han and Tibetan. In the United States before the 2008 election it was thought possible, and by many people likely, that Barack Obama would lose the presidential election largely because he is black. I do not mean to overlook the serious problems that exist. But on the other hand, if the reader will permit me a lapse into overt Hegelianism, the zeitgeist appears to be moving in a hopeful direction. In the United States, though the problem and consequences of racism are real enough, they are no longer nearly as bad as they were in the recent past. The body of law that interferes with personal and institutional racism is growing in bulk and in its effect, and opportunities for people are expanding as well. The fact that the Democratic Party nominated a black man for the presidency, and the fact that a black couple now occupies the White House, has considerable symbolic value, even if it may be too easy to overemphasize. In many respects America is being brought into a more genuine multicultural and bilingual incarnation. It is true that many Americans are being dragged into it kicking and screaming, but it is happening nonetheless. Something similar is going on in the United Kingdom, in France, in Germany, and elsewhere in Europe. Latin America represents another set of processes and in some respects models. New Zealand has embraced Maori traditions and cultures in surprising ways, and for all its problems South Africa remains a hopeful symbol, if not adequately realized. Though it has its own problems with respect to race and ethnicity, the seriousness of which are not to be underestimated, Russia has been for a very long time and remains today a multicultural and multilingual society from which in many respects the rest of us could learn something.

All this bears on the question of the pursuit of common interests across internal boundaries and among communities within individual nations. The examples I have mentioned are all democracies (if we use the term loosely) of one kind or another and to varying degrees, and in each of them processes are underway through which individuals and communities are, either by necessity or design, gradually coming to regard one another as partners in shared hopes and aspirations. The overt repressions and exclusions of the past are much harder to find. If this process continues more or less along these lines then the conditions for more robust and stronger democracies will be expanded. This is not to say that there are not still serious problems of racism and other impediments to the pursuit of common interests across various boundaries, but the movement is for the most part in the direction that thick democracy needs.

The situation is at least equally encouraging with respect to the pursuit of common interests across national borders. In the United States one of the very few happy consequences of the neoconservatives' spectacularly failed penchant for preemptive war has been the rediscovery of the virtues of diplomacy. Even in the latter years of the George W. Bush administration, as we have mentioned, several influential figures in the American foreign policy establishment, among them Richard Haass, Francis Fukuyama, and Zbigniew Brzezinski, published books in which they urged the return to serious diplomacy as the cornerstone of any nation's international relations. As important as this is, however, even the serious exercise of diplomacy is well short of a Deweyan pursuit of common interests.

The reason is that the theoretical underpinning of traditional, realist diplomacy is that the international environment is basically a Hobbesian "state of nature." Again, the root metaphor for Hobbes, and for most of the rest of the theories in every field that arose in the seventeenth and eighteenth centuries, is the mechanical view of nature in which entities distinct in their nature and essence from one another interact mechanically according to a set of natural laws. On this understanding, nations in the international state of nature are distinct in their nature and essence from one another and interact with one another in a "war of all against all." International relations and foreign policy, understood on the basis of this metaphor, is the expression of the laws of the interactions of nations such that violent collisions are kept to a minimum and the essentially distinct interests of each is advanced as much as possible.

Thick democracy of a Deweyan sort, however, rests on an entirely different root metaphor. The reason it makes sense for Dewey to think in terms of common interests is that for him, and for pragmatic naturalism generally, all entities are constituted by their relations with one another. Dewey's metaphor is not atoms in a void but rather an ecosystem. In an ecosystem the systemic interrelations of the constituents determine the nature of the constituents themselves. In this light, the environment in which nation states exist is not a Hobbesian state of nature and war of all against all but, like everything else, a relationally determined state of affairs in which the nature of each is determined by its complex interactions with the others. Understood this way it makes no sense to conceive of national interests as independently determined and then advanced in a competition with other nations. The character and interests of any nation arise in an often dense and shifting complex of relations with one another. If that is the case, then traditional realist diplomacy, as preferable as it is to vicious neoconservative imperial fantasies, is not good enough.

One of the implications of shifting the metaphor on the basis of which we understand international relations is that a profound revision in our conception of national sovereignty is necessary. If the character and interests of nations are understood to arise in their interrelations then a much looser conception of sovereignty is called for. To their credit even some of the traditional realists we have mentioned, Haass and Fukuyama specifically, have called for a "sacrifice" of some degree of national sovereignty in the interest of addressing pressing world problems.[7] But their own realist underpinnings prevent them from going far enough. In the end, the pursuit of common interests across national borders that defines a thick democracy leads to a downgrading of the importance of national borders, and therefore nation states, altogether. In the interest of thick democracy, to put the point more starkly, the era of the nation state needs to be brought to a close.

When put that baldly, thick democracy may seem on the face of it to be either a bad idea or at the very best hopelessly utopian, but neither is true. For one thing, the most serious contemporary problems are not national but international—for example, terrorism and the requirements for security, the environment and global warming, the proliferation of nuclear weapons, the availability of clean water, human rights and energy, and the only way they can be addressed is if nations realize their common interests with respect to them and behave accordingly. This in turn will require treating national sovereignty as a secondary value at best and the collective solutions of the problems as primary. This means that gradually diminishing the importance of nation states in the interest of reaching solutions to our serious problems is not only not a bad thing, it is a necessity.

Nor is the demise of the preeminence of the nation state merely a utopian dream. On a theoretical level, cosmopolitanism of the Kantian and Rawlsian as well as of the pragmatist varieties is receiving sustained attention, and I will explore it in more detail in Chapter 11. More importantly, nations themselves have for nearly a century been in the process, though an admittedly halting one, of coming to terms with the necessity of ever-deeper and more serious forms of international cooperation and indeed integration. The League of Nations, the United Nations, the World Court and International Criminal Court, and such international economic agreements as NAFTA have been responses to the perceived necessity of interweaving our political, economic, and cultural lives.

Each of these efforts has received and continues to receive strong and serious criticism, and one hopes that in their responses to the criticism they will improve. And in fact there is no reason to think that the clock will be turned back to an earlier time, despite ongoing efforts of some to do so.

The most stunning illustration of the fact that we have entered an era in which the nation state will recede in importance is, as we have mentioned, the European Union. By the middle of the twentieth century, Europe had exhausted itself in its murderous and suicidal wars. If there was ever evidence of the ultimately ruinous nature of the nation state's effort to advance its interests at others' expense, it was the condition in which Europe found itself in 1945. From the initial coal and steel agreement through the European Economic Community to the European Union in its current form, European nations have gradually integrated their economies, currencies, higher education through the Bologna Process, and the movement of people in the Schengen Zone, to the point that to a large extent there are few borders left in most of continental Europe. For the first time in history nation states are willingly, in some cases even eagerly, abandoning considerable degrees of national sovereignty in the interests of a more integrated union and the collective solution of common problems. The EU, with all its faults and overbearing bureaucracy, is an example of world-historic importance of the pursuit of common interests across borders, and is therefore an example of a thick, Deweyan democracy in the making. The demise of the nation state is not a utopian dream. It is already a reality, and a process that will most likely continue to develop into the foreseeable future. It is not too outlandish to imagine something like the EU developing in North America, though it would do so against stiff opposition. South American nations may well go in similar directions, and the future of East Asia is itself one of a range of possibilities.

The good news, for those of us who think that a thick, Deweyan democracy is an end worth advancing, is that the process is well underway. It is a flawed process to be sure, with all sorts of setbacks and inadequacies, but it is happening. And all its problems notwithstanding, the prospects for some significant measure of success are rather good. In the following chapters we will look in greater detail at a number of aspects of social and political reality that represent challenges for pragmatic naturalism's understanding of democracy. I have had reason to mention them all in this chapter, but each bears more extensive consideration: social policy, education, international relations, cosmopolitanism, and the necessity of the exercise of intelligence across the spectrum of social life.

NINE

DEMOCRACY AND ITS PROBLEMS

In the previous chapter I explicated a Deweyan conception of democracy and made something of a case for its reasonableness as a social condition to which we might aspire and as an approach to understanding how we might address contemporary social issues.[1] However, even if everything that has so far been said is unobjectionable, which is in any case unlikely, there would remain problems or challenges in practice that it would be wise for a democrat of this sort to consider. In this chapter I will take up two of those potential problems: dissent and education.

First, though, let us remark again on the question of whether pragmatic naturalist democracy has something to offer. There are two ways a useful effect may be felt. The first is in a specific understanding of the role ideas can play in the resolution of social problems and the development of public policy. The second is in a specific set of ideas to be put to use in the treatment of social problems and public policy.

The first possibility is rather more methodological, in that it has to do with treating ideas as tools with which to experiment in the social arena. If pragmatic naturalism can be influential in this respect it will serve as an alternative to the more ideological use of ideas. For example, it is currently taken as a given in much of the world that the market and the more or less unfettered movement of goods and services around the globe is a necessary condition of economic development and a free society. Free market ideologists simply accept this as an unquestionable assumption and proceed to develop policy on its basis. A more pragmatic approach would be to see what happens when this idea is put to work, and to judge its adequacy by its effects. A market economy may well prove to contribute to economic development in important ways, though it may also result in intolerable levels of economic exploitation. Indeed, it has already achieved both. An ideologist who supports the market will assume the truth of the idea and evaluate the results accordingly, typically exaggerating the beneficial results and underestimating the detrimental. If we are already certain that the basis of our policy is true then it must follow that the successes are more important than the failures, or that the failures are unfortunate but unavoidable. Similarly, an ideologist who opposes the market will assume its inadequacy, exaggerate its shortcomings, and underestimate its accomplishments. A pragmatist will treat the idea as a working hypothesis, to be accepted, revised, or abandoned according to the degree to which the results meet the desired ends. These are two very different ways to approach social problems and policy. Currently, and historically, the ideological approach is far more common and influential than is the pragmatic. If pragmatic naturalism in this methodological sense can become more widely accepted and practiced then it will have made a useful contribution, though on its own terms the degree of its value will have to be judged in the results, and the judgments will have to be honestly made.

As a practical matter of course one cannot experiment with social policy the way one can experiment in a laboratory, which may make it seem somewhat pointless to call for experimentation with respect to social problems. But the fact is that a good deal of social policy is as a practical matter experimental. However much we may try to convince ourselves of the virtues of our assumptions, we do not know ahead of time whether this or that policy decision will have the results we hope for. To that extent we are experimenting with social policy all the time. The problem is that we do not treat our policy decisions as experimental. As a matter of practical politics, to say "We will try this because we have reason to believe that it will work but we really are not sure" is likely to be seen as a failure to know what one is doing and thus a political liability. What is worse, even if we were to grant that we are not sure in a particular case whether a certain policy decision will work, we are even less likely to acknowledge that it has not worked. In science, at least in principle, if an experiment does not produce the expected outcome we do not regard this as a failure but as an advance in our knowledge and understanding. In policy, and in the political environment in which policy making is practiced, if an action does not produce the desired outcome it is judged a failure and the people who promoted it are likely to suffer politically.

This suggests that the problem with taking a more pragmatic, experimental approach to policy is not that one cannot experiment with policy. The problem, rather, is in the political culture. To make use of a pragmatic methodology in policy making requires a change in our understanding of the character of public debate and in the way policy makers understand what they already do. Neither of these are simple matters, but it is important to understand where the challenge lies. It is not that policy making cannot be experimental and thereby pragmatic. The problem, or challenge, is in reforming the prevailing character of public debate and political culture.

The second sense in which pragmatic naturalism may be brought to bear concerns its specific conceptual commitments. Especially in its Deweyan version pragmatic naturalism is akin to other forms of twentieth-century liberalism in that it values individual development, free inquiry into and exchange of ideas, and the importance of democratic forms of social organization. It differs somewhat from modern liberalism in its emphasis on community, the critical importance of education as a means to develop experimental and democratic habits of mind, and on its emphasis on the collective approach to and resolution of social problems. Each of these ideas would need to be described in more detail to paint an accurate picture of pragmatic naturalism's commitments, especially since they differ more or less from the ways they are understood in other traditions. The emphasis on education, for example, is shared with many other people who would not describe themselves as pragmatists or naturalists, and the meaning of education is likely to differ among them. For many, education is important as a way to inculcate certain values and views of the world into young people. Its role, in other words, is to raise young people to believe certain things. For pragmatism the role of education is not so much to mold people so that they think this or that; rather it is to accustom people as they grow up to embody certain habits of mind. It is not very important, for example, whether people are liberal or conservative or radical in this or that respect, or whether they are religious or not. It is more important that they approach their own lives, others' lives, and the world in general in an open, thoughtful, and experimental spirit. These are not values built into many contemporary educational methods or school curricula. So education for pragmatic naturalism has its own unique meaning, and the same is true for the other ideas that are central to the tradition, i.e., individual development, free inquiry, democracy, and community. With that caveat in mind, we may say that one of the ways pragmatic naturalism can contribute to the contemporary world is through its central conceptual commitments.

So pragmatism may be relevant and useful in the contemporary world with respect to its methodology and the content of its ideas. We are able now to frame the question in a somewhat different way. Can pragmatism make a contribution to the contemporary world as a political methodology? Such a political methodology would consist of several fundamental commitments: (1) to the conviction that the value of ideas, the ultimate test of their legitimacy, lies in their applicability, in their ability to achieve a desired end, to get a job done; (2) to the paramount value of democracy as a form of life and of social organization, though even here one has to be flexible and experimental; and (3) to the central role of education as the source of the development of the democratic frame of mind and democratic habits.

In one sense the answer to our question is simple enough: In the abstract it is certainly possible for a pragmatic naturalist political methodology to contribute to the resolution of social problems and the development of public policy in the contemporary world. Furthermore, for many of us there is no question but that a social environment in which these commitments drive our approach to social issues and to policy would be far preferable to the condition in which we currently live, in which economic and military power, and its preservation in the hands of those who already hold it, are the driving forces of social policy in many nations, both strong and weak. Of course you will notice that I have answered the question by saying that a pragmatic naturalist political methodology is possible in the abstract. The qualifier is important because in practice it will be difficult to achieve, since it would require, as we have said, an extensive change in the ways we conduct public debate and in the political culture generally. It also requires breaking the power of those who currently make policy in most if not all places. And I am afraid that I have no answer to the question of how that might be accomplished. Revolutions are occasionally tried, but as a cure they can sometimes be worse than the disease. Perhaps the answer is the persistent pursuit and application of a naturalist understanding of the nature of individuals and societies and a pragmatic methodology. Dewey may have been right that the best response to problems in democracy is more democracy.

Pluralism and Dissent

Establishing a pragmatic naturalist, which is to say a Deweyan, political methodology also faces a problem that has been addressed in the recent criticism that Deweyan democracy is intrinsically incompatible with pluralism. We have obliquely alluded to this problem in pointing to the fact that there are many people who hold, and would likely continue to hold, fundamental ideas that differ from those that underpin a Deweyan democracy. In Robert Talisse's expression of the problem, because this substantive version of democracy is characterized by a commitment to the exercise of intelligence in the public pursuit of solutions to social problems, it requires for its success a rough agreement across the population that experimentalism and fallibilism are greater values than any moral or social commitments that individuals may have. Furthermore, because we can always expect that people will have a plurality of views, and a plurality of basic moral and social commitments, which is to say that we have good reason to expect pluralism in the society, pragmatist democracy of the Deweyan sort is an unreasonable expectation. It is in fact defeated as a political theory and, Talisse argues, can and should be replaced by a Peircean theory of democracy.[2]

Talisse has a point, a preferable version of which we will explore in a moment. He has, however, overplayed his hand in drawing the conclusion that Deweyan democracy is untenable. There is only one thing that would render the theory untenable, and that would be its failure in practice. In pointing to a real and serious problem, Talisse makes the common philosopher's mistake of thinking that the question of the plausibility and adequacy of the theory can be resolved dialectically. Philosophy, as we have said repeatedly, is not mathematics, and many of the most important questions that engage philosophers are not to be decided through argument, as surprising as that may sound. This is both a theoretical and practical point. In practice, to give one sort of example, it is rare indeed for an argument for the existence of God to change the mind of an atheist, as it is equally rare for arguments against the existence of God to convert a theist. This is not because the average theist or atheist is an unreasonable person. Rather it is a consequence of the fact that what answers such questions for us is not dialectical argument as much as the success or failure of such intellectual commitments in our lives. This is not to say that careful logical analysis is not important. Its importance, however, and this is the theoretical point, is not in the determination of important questions but in the refinement of our ideas and in the establishment of the plausibility of those ideas. What Talisse has shown is not that Deweyan democracy is untenable but that there is a serious problem with the theory that its proponents need to address. The challenge is due to the fact that the difficulties we can expect in practice have not been adequately anticipated by the theory as it has been expressed. For us to continue to endorse the plausibility of the theory and its applicability in practice we do indeed need to address the problem that Talisse describes in terms of Deweyan democracy's ability to handle the fact of moral and political pluralism.

Let us state the problem not in terms of pluralism but in terms of radical dissent. This is actually a problem that has to do with political methodology in general, that is with the instrumental use of ideas to drive social policy. The twentieth century saw two large-scale applications of a set of conceptual commitments as the basis, the conceptual tools, for social change: fascism and Marxism. Neither of these forms of political practice, in their various versions, turned out well. Contrary to a good deal of mainstream thinking these days, I would say that fascism proved to be far more detrimental than has Marxism, but in the end neither on the whole has served to advance human dignity, freedom, or social development. One of the primary reasons was that in both cases those in authority believed that their ideas were necessary for the development of their respective societies, so much so that dissension, even disagreement, was not to be tolerated. This in turn led to a situation where people who did not endorse the prevailing ideas were forced to flee, fight, and suffer the often-gruesome consequences, comply under duress, or simply acquiesce by exhaustion or fear. Nothing about such a situation speaks well for the ideas at work. More generally, this picture raises the question of whether there might be something unpalatable, unacceptable, about instrumentalism in social life, i.e., about a substantive as opposed to merely procedural political methodology in general.

Of course there is an obvious response to the cases of fascism and Marxism, which is that they are not representative of the full range of ideas that can be employed instrumentally in social life, and that their failings are due not to their role in social construction but to their ideological character. In other words, neither fascism nor Marxism was democratic, and therein lay the problem. This is obviously the case with fascism, but even Marxism, which had and has a greater claim to democratic possibilities, was put to work as an ideological foundation, as a set of truths rather than a set of possibilities to be employed, confirmed, or refuted in experience, revised, or possibly rejected. Nor were the basic ideas formed through the free and creative exercise of individual and community determination of values and ends. Had they been, the pragmatist might argue, i.e., had they been approached pragmatically rather than ideologically, there might have been greater hope of success. But the question we need to consider is whether that is an adequate response to the problem suggested by fascism and Marxism to the whole issue of a substantive political methodology. Is it reasonable to suppose that a more democratic set of ideas can adequately serve as a political methodology, which is to say a means to achieve the desired ends of freedom and development without exhibiting the shortcomings of fascism and Marxism? We might see the problem more clearly by suggesting that for a set of ideas to be efficacious, to be instrumentally valuable in its application to social problems and public policy, there has to be fairly widespread acceptance of those ideas across the population. This is especially true for pragmatic naturalism with its emphasis on the community development of means and ends. What happens when a sizeable portion of the population disagrees or sustains an active opposition? To remain consistent, pragmatic naturalism, with its central emphasis on democratic forms of life and decision making, on collective development of means and ends with respect to social problems and policy, cannot have recourse to the forms of oppression characteristic of other political methodologies. How, then, does it handle dissent, especially large-scale dissent? It appears that pragmatic naturalist values cannot survive large-scale dissent, nor can they repress it. Therein lies the problem.

The literature, with the recent exception of Talisse and the responses his criticism has engendered, has not addressed this question extensively. There have been many fine studies of pragmatist social and political theory, and there have been fewer but no less valuable inquiries into pragmatist methodology and community reconstruction. They all, however, ask the question of how pragmatist principles might work assuming a general agreement among members of a society on the advantages and virtues of an experimental, community-based approach to social issues. And much of the literature about pragmatism and education deals with the question of how such a consensus might be reached. If we accept the idea that education properly organized and executed can achieve a rough consensus of the necessary sort, and that people on the whole can conduct themselves in ways anticipated by pragmatist social theory, then it may well be possible that a pragmatic naturalist political methodology is the best alternative we have. The question is whether it is reasonable to expect that education can succeed in this task and that people can act accordingly. We will return to the question of education shortly.

This is a serious problem for pragmatism, and the issue is not abstractly theoretical. I would not want to argue, for example, that human nature is such that we can never expect this to happen. The concept of human nature, at least with respect to the issue of what people can or cannot be like, is itself too ideologically charged to be of much value in imagining the future. It was once assumed that people are such that some are destined to be masters and others slaves, or that most people require the firm and stable leadership afforded by a monarchy. History has suggested that neither of these views of human possibilities is accurate. On that evidence alone it is far too suspicious to argue against any sort of social organization or approach to social problems by appeal to human nature. The problem for a pragmatic naturalist political methodology is not whether people are capable of acting in ways described by the theory. The problem is more practical than that. It is, simply put, that we can expect people, including or perhaps especially reasonable, well-educated people, to hold a wide range of views regarding the proper role of ideas, democracy, freedom, community, and education. No matter how we organize a pragmatist political methodology, and no matter how careful we are in its execution—for example, in the forms of education it develops and perpetuates, there will inevitably be dissension simply because any large number of people who think for themselves will be more likely than not to come to some number of differing and incompatible conclusions. This is the issue Talisse identifies as the problem of pluralism. We will return to the question of whether pluralism itself is a problem after considering the issue in terms of dissension.

There is a sense in which this is a problem not so much for pragmatism but for democracy. Even contemporary forms of "thin" democracy, by which I mean societies for which democracy means little more than voting in contested elections, can and do face this problem. How, we might ask, do we handle an occasion in which a majority of voters use the polls to elect leaders or endorse policies that are hostile to the very democracy that provides the election? There are those in Turkey, for example, who have been asking this very question for the past several years. The electoral process has brought a moderate Islamic party to power, but many of the more secular Kemalists in the country fear that the ruling party will gradually use its power to enact legislation that will move the country away from democracy and toward theocracy. How does even a thin democracy deal with this? One answer, and not a surprising one given Turkish history, is that the army might step in, as it has in the past, and put a stop to the Islamists, a right or even a responsibility it has according to the Turkish constitution. This might have been effective, but as a problem-solving method there would have been nothing democratic about it. And to offer a different kind of example, in the post–Second World War and early Cold War period in the United States there were many who believed that there was a real possibility that communists would come to power in the United States, and that they would eradicate the democratic system. The government's response to that perceived threat was to undermine the very freedoms of speech, press, and association that define the democratic system. It may or may not have been effective, but like the potential for the intervention of the Turkish army, it was hardly democratic.

If even thin democracies face this problem, without I would add any genuinely democratic way to handle it, a pragmatist political methodology would face it that much more acutely. In a thin democracy like that in the United States, people can simply opt out of many of the social practices that define the society. In most recent elections in the United States, to give an obvious example, more than half the eligible electorate chose not to participate. The system can handle this relatively easily because leaders are chosen simply by adding up the votes of those who do participate (leaving aside the role of the electoral college in presidential elections), and then policy is handled by those who are elected. If people choose, they might pursue possible solutions to specific problems through NGOs, religious organizations, and various other forms of private collaboration that define civil society. But they need not do that either. They can simply not participate in any form of social activity beyond that necessary to meet the needs of their daily lives. In the short run at least, any number of people may so choose, and the system survives as long as there is no active opposition.

In the case of a pragmatist democracy, of a pragmatist political methodology, the picture would be more like the refusal to accept the results of an election than like the choice not to participate or to pursue one's interests through the civil society rather than through the political system. Dewey in the classical literature and others more recently have made the point repeatedly that there is a greater value in collective decision making, so that community interaction is a much more important component of a pragmatist or thick democracy than of a thin one. A community-based democracy of that kind cannot survive if large portions of the population simply refuse to participate. And this is a problem even if there is no sustained opposition or dissension. If there is opposition or dissension then the problem is even more acute.

Consider, for example, the question of education. Pragmatists from John Dewey to John McDermott have argued persuasively that an education appropriate to what I am calling a thick, i.e., Deweyan, democracy must have certain characteristics. It must, for example, instill in young people an appreciation for open-ended inquiry, for a hypothetical approach to problems, for a willingness, even an eagerness, to revise ideas in and through experience, and for the importance of the collective pursuit of solutions to shared problems. But as we are all well aware, there are many people who have very different approaches to education. In the United States today, as we know, it is more common to hear the goals of education described in terms of making people competitive in the marketplace than of developing individual and social capacities to solve problems. And there are many people who believe that the purpose of education is to inculcate in young people one or another set of beliefs, i.e., to raise them as young ideologues. The latter is especially true of fundamentalist religious schools.

The problem suggested by the example of education is that even if we are able to convince many such people of the value of a pragmatic naturalist education, there will always be those who disagree. In fact, I suspect that there will be enough who disagree that they will pose a serious problem for a society that attempts to put to use a pragmatist political methodology. Certainly, there are examples of identifiable communities that would not accept pragmatist education—for example, Amish and Hassidic communities in the United States. These are small enough and sufficiently contained communities not to present a real problem. A problem would be posed, however, by fundamentalist religious schools, in the US case largely Christian. Such schools represent the antithesis of pragmatist education in that they teach young people not to be reflective, experimental, hypothetical, and open-minded, but rather to accept as absolute certain principles and truths and to apply them rigidly. A pragmatist democracy, a pragmatist political methodology, cannot sustain itself if a sizable portion of the population is subjected to that sort of education. A thin democracy can handle it as long as most everyone is willing to accept the results of elections, but a thick democracy cannot.

What are the alternatives available to a pragmatic naturalist methodology in such a situation? Clearly it will not do to employ the methods that are the common resort of ideological political methodologies. No society wanting to call itself democratic can close down fundamentalist religious schools, for example. Nor can it censor or in other respects attempt to control a fundamentalist press, to give another example. As attractive as such methods might be to some, and in certain circumstances, in the end, like many revolutions, they are a cure that is worse than the disease in that they undermine the very principles of democracy itself.

One obvious possibility available to a pragmatist democracy is to hope to prevail by example. Perhaps pragmatist education, especially once it is executed on a fairly large scale, will be so successful that it will attract more and more adherents, and eventually enough to marginalize the non- or antidemocratic alternatives. This would be an extraordinarily risky thing on which to pin one's hopes.

The seriousness of this problem is made clearer when one adds other domains of social life to the example of education. What of the press? Can we really think that the press will behave differently, or very differently, in a pragmatist environment than it does now? If it does not behave differently, then the challenge to a pragmatist political methodology is obvious. And surely in a free political environment political parties will eventually develop that stand not simply in opposition to this or that policy, but to pragmatic naturalist principles in general. It is not hard to imagine a radical Christian party on the model of radical Islamist parties in the Muslim world. This would pose a serious problem even for a thin democracy. Imagine how seriously it would undermine the ability of a pragmatist political methodology to function.

The point is that it is probably not sufficient to expect that the problems of an instrumentalist approach to social issues and policy will be less serious if the political methodology in question is democratically grounded. The problems of political methodology may well be endemic to social instrumentalism itself, regardless of its fundamental values. If so, then as a practical matter the prospects for a thick, pragmatist democracy look bleak. This is not an encouraging situation, especially at a time when even thin democracy is in serious trouble.

On the face of it this is a grim analysis, and one that seems to suggest that Talisse may be right to reject Deweyan democracy in favor of a Peircean or other alternative. But the fact is that most political philosophers who think along Deweyan lines, myself included, are not ready to give up, and that fact bears consideration. It may be that we are simply indulging in what Pierce called tenacity by holding onto our ideas in the face of overwhelming evidence to the contrary. In that case we would be akin to the flat-earthers. But this is probably not the case. For one thing, even if it is true that pluralism and dissent are likely to throw a spanner in the works of pragmatic naturalist democracy, this may mean simply that the methodology is not likely to work perfectly or even near perfectly. It does not follow that it will not work at all. In all likelihood we would have to live with a thinner, imperfect version of pragmatist democracy than the theory describes. The late Michael Eldridge made more or less this point in his appeal to "pragmatism lite."[3] This in itself does not imply the failure of an idea. It means simply that like for every other idea or principle that informs political practice and social policy, there are necessarily compromises to make. But why, we might ask, if there are compromises to make, is it more valuable to pursue this eventually compromised idea rather than another one? The response to this question helps us to understand why there is something important in Deweyan, pragmatic naturalist democracy that makes it valuable even in a less-than-perfect form.

The reason this idea is worth pursuing even if we can expect serious obstacles is that the value commitments of a Deweyan, pragmatic naturalist democracy are themselves worthy values that we would do well to approximate even if we cannot expect to fulfill them. We cannot expect, and probably would not even desire, to eliminate the plurality of ideas, ideals, and commitments that reasonable and responsible people may hold. There is good reason to take to heart Mill's arguments for the value of vigorous debate. But a plurality of ideas and a vigorous debate among their supporters is not inconsistent with a willingness in the course of those debates to pursue common interests and to allow the kind of ongoing experimentation in social policy that pragmatist democracy implies. This is another respect in which Talisse exaggerates the implications of his own useful observations. It is possible for reasonable people to disagree and to live with the disagreements. In fact one might say that any sort of democracy, even a thinner procedural sort, requires a willingness on the part of citizens to live with the outcomes of decisions and policies even if they disagree with them. As long as people are willing to engage in the process, whether it is the electoral procedures of a thin democracy or the public engagement expected in a thicker version, a plurality of views is not necessarily a showstopper.

Again, though, we must turn to the question of dissent. What happens when a significant portion of the population refuses to accept the results of the process? For example, in the months and years following the election of President Obama a very vocal minority of the American population behaved in ways that suggested a flat refusal to accept the results of the election. This was a fairly new development in American political culture, though there was a taste of it in the early 1960s during the Kennedy administration, and it raises a question about whether even a thin, procedural democracy can withstand the active opposition not simply to this or that policy, but to the results of the political system in general. We wondered in the preceding pages whether a pragmatist democracy has a way to respond to such a situation. One is reminded of Dewey's persistent objections to the violent resolution of social problems. To resort to violence, he argued, is to forsake the method of intelligence and thereby to abandon basic social principle. But he was not naïve. He realized that it is possible, and too often happens, that the forces arrayed against a reasonable and democratic resolution to a problem are such that only violence can constitute a solution. Thoreau, despite his pacifism, understood this too.

We seem to be caught on the horns of a dilemma. On the one hand it appears that any form of democracy, including a thick pragmatic naturalist sort, may in the end have no choice but to resort to undemocratic or nondemocratic measures to sustain itself if opposition or dissent threatens it. The greater value of democratic commitments, presumably, justifies this. On the other hand, having recourse to nondemocratic or undemocratic measures in its defense can itself be a threat to democratic procedures either by undermining the system's democratic processes or by distorting its effects. There is no way to avoid this dilemma. It cannot be avoided by rejecting substantive democracy in favor of too "lite" a version because it is a condition any form of democracy finds itself in.

The only recourse the democrat has is to acknowledge the dilemma, which implies two significant points. First, the democrat grants that there may be occasions in which nondemocratic measures are called for. Thoreau knew it, Dewey knew it, and so did Lincoln, so it turns out that there is nothing novel in this realization. The second point becomes then the more critical. The fact that a democratic system may have to resort to nondemocratic measures under extreme conditions is a sustained warning to the democrat that he must do whatever possible, consistent with democratic values, to avoid such extreme conditions. Such nondemocratic measures as, for example, violations of individuals' civil liberties, invasion of privacy, and economic or military actions abroad are for the serious democrat a last resort, and never to be undertaken lightly. Democracy, thin or thick, is a fragile thing, a system and a set of values that require sustained attention. That is the only way to deal with democracy's dilemma.[4]

But if it is true that any democracy faces such a dilemma, then we have even more reason to prefer the thick to the thin variety. We have said that the values of a thick, Deweyan democracy are worth pursuing. As important as the procedural practices of a thin democracy are, and they are indeed important and valuable, people need and deserve more. Being able freely to participate through elections in the decisions about who shall represent us in the political bodies of a society, and being able to hold those people to account through re-election, are values not to be dismissed. But by themselves they do not suffice to engender the kind of free and developed life of which we are capable. For many people the opportunity to pursue their interests through a free market is also important, and such people deserve that opportunity. But this too is not enough. Human beings are intelligent and creative creatures, and we deserve the opportunity to develop our intelligence and creativity throughout our lives. Such development requires an education appropriate to our capacities, and it requires social conditions through which we may exercise them. Thin, procedural democracy alone does not provide those conditions. In fact it can militate against them if we accept the idea that it is sufficient. By emphasizing democratic procedures, even with a more or less free market economy, as the highest achievement to which we can aspire we can easily, and often do, derail attempts to develop the material and social conditions necessary for human development. When we let the market determine the principles and ends of education we deprive ourselves, and our children, of the kind of experiences we in fact need to develop more fully. When we allow even democratic political processes and a market environment to forestall opportunities to meet the material and social conditions we require to develop and exercise our intelligence and creativity, then we are likely to fail to achieve both the means and the ends of which we are capable and to which we are entitled if we are entitled to anything.

This means that we do ourselves a disservice by settling for anything less than a full substantive democracy. We may have to settle for less in practice given the problems inherent in any form of democracy, but we are better served to strive for more rather than resign ourselves ahead of time to less. For reasons such as these, a Deweyan democracy is an ideal and a set of possibilities that are worthy of our aspirations, the problem of pluralism or dissent notwithstanding.

Education and Democracy

Some years ago Riccardo Petrella, then a councilor to the European Commission and professor at the Catholic University of Louvain, wrote that there are five "traps" (*pièges*) that confront education today.[5] They arise, he said, from the political, social, and economic changes of the past thirty years and more. These "traps" serve to legitimate current inegalitarian social divisions, and importantly they indicate that we have forgotten that "the school is above all a place where we construct our social world, where we should elaborate the 'democracy of life.'" The five traps, challenges, or problems nicely summarize the issues that a Deweyan democracy would need to address, which is to say the problems it would face.

The five traps are

1. the belief that education serves to produce a "human resource," no different in function from other "resources" in the economy;

2. the shift of education from the "nonmarket" sphere to that of the market, where the purpose of education is to produce resources for the economy;
3. the presentation of education as the sphere through which the individual and the nation can compete in the world economy;
4. the subordination of education to technology, on the assumption that technology is the driving force of social change, and therefore education must conform to technological change; and
5. the use of the educational system to legitimate new forms of social division—for example, between those who have access to information and technology and those who do not. These divisions tend to conform to the older divisions between developed and undeveloped or underdeveloped societies.

Petrella chooses an appropriate word to describe the dangers that these approaches to education pose to a thick, pragmatic naturalist democracy. They are "traps" precisely because they seem to emerge so naturally from contemporary democratic commitments, yet they threaten democratic education. Petrella's point in fact nicely indicates the difference between a thin and a thick conception of democracy. Thin democracy, one that in current circumstances associates itself with the market, quite naturally leads to the application of market principles and values to nearly all aspects of the society. Marx made something like this point in his criticism of the nearly totalitarian influence of capitalist principles. If the "free" market is taken to be a fundamental condition of a free society and a free life, then it is an easy move to want to apply its principles and values to the society as a whole. Furthermore, if the market, precisely because it appears to be a condition of a free society, is taken to be a necessary condition of democracy, then a democratic society can easily find it appropriate to organize its institutions in accord with market values. When this is done in the case of education, we have the traps of contemporary liberal democratic society's commoditization of education. They are traps rather than adequate expressions of democracy because they militate against both the means and ends of education that a thick, pragmatic naturalist understanding of democracy requires.

It is interesting to note that these points are made by a European. That Petrella is a European is not in itself of note since Europeans are concerned about education no less than anyone else. What is interesting is that these remarks so neatly encapsulate an understanding of education that has permeated American thinking since Jefferson. Jefferson argued that in a democracy leaders can emerge from the population in general, from anywhere in the society, a point that was radical in its time and that informed his educational thinking and policies from the promotion of local schooling to the creation of the University of Virginia. In principle this is still assumed to be true, but in practice several factors interfere. They include the disparate and unequal distribution of wealth, social status, and traditions, not to mention racism, xenophobia, radical nationalism, and other similar individual and institutional impediments to access to equal education. It is instructive to notice that all of these social traits are consistent with the educational values of a market-driven education, the values that Petrella identifies as the traps that we face. If Jefferson was right, and experience indicates that he was, then one implication is that it is in the interests of society, particularly a democratic society, that the highest-quality education be available to all its citizens.

This in turn means that there is no room in a democracy for education construed to conform to market values or for market principles in determining access to a high-quality education, and to the highest levels of education. Without such access there is the danger that some segments of the society will be dominated by others, and this undermines the principles of even a thin democracy. Furthermore, because democracy is characterized by the ongoing pursuit of common interests, a democratic society requires that its citizens interact with one another in a spirit of mutual cooperation and a collaborative pursuit of common ends. Therefore the goal of a democratic education cannot be primarily about besting others in a competitive market.

For our purposes the critical point to notice about these characteristics of contemporary education is that they threaten both the democratic character of education and the requirements a democratic society must place on its educational system. Why this is so is to be found in libraries full of literature devoted to the subject, from Dewey's early writings to the present. There is little that we can add in this context to that extensive literature. There has been less said about these issues in relation to the contemporary university, and it is to that topic that I would like to turn.

The University

Every social institution must grapple with the fact that it exists at the intersection, so to speak, of some set of distinct values. A hospital, for example, must juggle economic and health concerns, and in some cases political issues. It has a responsibility to meet the health needs of its patients, to survive and if possible to prosper in its economic environment, and in cases of state hospitals to navigate the political waters as well. An art museum is in a similar position, with the difference that rather than health values it must handle aesthetic interests and commitments, which a hospital need not. Similarly a church must negotiate not only economic and to one degree or another political concerns, but it must also address spiritual values. A bank is in a similar position. Its primary concern is economic and broadly corporate, but even it, like all corporate entities, must also take account of the broader political context in which its regulatory expectations are determined and enforced. Sometimes the general situation changes to such an extent that the specific character of the commitments changes. For example, in the recent financial crisis one of the policies of the US government was to provide funds to large banks to keep them solvent. In some cases in order to receive such funds, the banks were compelled to turn over control of a significant proportion of their stock to the government, thus in effect being partially nationalized. Such a situation places a bank in a whole new set of political concerns and issues. Journalistic institutions are another interesting example. In the US, print journalism in particular represents a striking illustration of a case in which one set of values has nearly completely dominated the others. Even major newspapers are regularly criticized for sacrificing journalistic for commercial, and sometimes political, values. All the more striking is the fact that in so doing they have not been able to prosper as journalistic institutions and are closing down in alarming numbers.

National differences can also be relevant. Institutions in all nations have political and economic sets of values with which they must function, but they may differ quite a bit. For example, the economic and political environments in which a major museum must function are different, for example, in Russia and in the United States, at least in many respects, and therefore the specific details of the commitments and responsibilities of the museums differ. Russian museums, like those in many countries, rely to a greater extent on state funding while American museums tend to rely for their survival on philanthropy, and in recent years decreasing governmental support. In general, though, whatever the differences in details, the general situation is comparable in any nation and for any social institution. They all must deal with the intersection of a set of values.

Higher education is not an exception to this generalization. In fact, we may define higher education as that social institution that resides at the confluence of academic, social, and economic values. By "academic" values I mean here expectations of advanced teaching, scholarship, and research, and whatever those activities require, where the emphasis on its advanced mission distinguishes higher education from lower-level schooling. We may understand social values as those expectations and their resulting commitments that arise from the political arena, which is to say the application and exercise of state power, and from the broader cultural and social contexts generally. And we may understand economic values as referring to principles and practices, both organizational and fiscal, which characterize corporations and the commercial world as a whole.

Many academic people, primarily teaching and research staff, or what in English we call the professoriate, assume that the university is an academic institution and that the other pressures on it, primarily the political and the economic, represent alien forces that should be avoided whenever possible. Such a view of the university is, however, a mistake. In making a case for that claim I would like to make three points: (1) Social and economic values are not extrinsic to the university; (2) the three sets of values need not but often do come into conflict, and special care is required when handling such conflicts; and (3) the overall health of the university as an academic institution requires that a balance be maintained among the intersecting values that characterize it. In the end the capacity of the university to play the role it should in a thick democratic social environment depends on an accurate recognition of the character of the institution in relation to the factors of its environment that constitute it.

We may go as far as to say that the university, like other social institutions, has a trinitarian character. This phrase has an odd theological ring to it, given the place of this discussion in the larger context of a consideration of pragmatic naturalism, but it makes an important point. I have said that the professoriate is mistaken to think of the university as consisting of or committed to academic values alone. The reason it is a mistake to think this way is that the three kinds of values—academic, social, and economic—are so much intertwined that they are mutually constitutive. The character of the social values is itself determined by the relation in which those values stand to the economic, and vice versa. The same is true for the university's academic values. Each of these sets of values is determined by its relations with the others so that it is impossible to untangle them without each being changed considerably. The prevailing political principles and practices would be quite different, for example, if they were not related to a specific set of economic conditions, histories, and practices. This point is expressed when people say that a free society is one that requires a free market, or when other people say that a free society requires protection from the depredations inflicted on us by the free market. Whichever side of this debate one is most comfortable with, both sides recognize that the social and the economic determine one another. That complex relationship is only multiplied when one adds academic values to the mix. In contemporary universities the academic values, while not reducible to the social or economic, are nevertheless conditioned by them such that they are determined by their relations to them. Thus, we have, for example, the "marketplace of ideas," a phrase that would never have been used in a feudal economic environment. The same is true for "academic freedom," a concept that would not resonate at all in a medieval university or in any environment in which a church or a totalitarian government exercises political power. If the social and economic values were other than what they are, so too would be the academic. This means that those values that we regard as definitive of the university are conditioned by our political and economic environment.

If that is the case, then it makes little sense to understand the university as solely an academic institution that must struggle with extrinsic and alien social and economic forces in order to survive. The university is an academic institution not because it is characterized only or primarily by academic values, but because of the unique set of values that constitutes it. In a similar way a hospital is not solely a health institution and an art museum is not purely an aesthetic institution. The university is an academic institution because academic values are one of the values that intersect where the university resides. The set of values as a whole differs from all others, thus rendering the university a distinct kind of social institution.

Thus, it is a mistake to think, as many academic people in the United States do, of the university as an ivory tower, an institution that resides at some remove from the rest of society. The rest of society is not and cannot be held at a distance from the university because the rest of society is part of what constitutes it. When I say that "academic people" make this mistake I am thinking primarily about teaching and research staff. University administrators in the United States tend to make a very different mistake. They too often not only think that universities are social/political and economic institutions, but they go further in thinking that the academic dimension of the university is reducible to the economic. In this spirit many administrators bring to bear on the university financial and managerial practices from the corporate sector. They will, for example, apply cost-benefit analyses of academic programs to determine their value, or make use of corporate motivational mechanisms for academic staff, or insist on efficiency as the key factor in determining class size, teaching load, etc., or put into use corporate language and categories when referring to a university's constituency, so that students become customers and the university becomes a purveyor of a product or a service.

Such practices and tendencies are a mistake because they fail to take account of the fact that because academic values are a distinct strand in the broader set of values with which the university must operate, the university is therefore a distinctive type of institution that cannot be treated as if it were a corporation any more than a hospital, museum, or church can be treated as if they were simply or primarily corporations. If one fails to understand this fact, then among other problems one faces the likelihood that when the academic needs and values of the university do not sit comfortably with the others, the problem will not be properly understood. This introduces for us the second general point, which concerns what happens when values collide.

Conflicts of Values

We have said that the three strands of values that intersect in the contemporary university generally live comfortably with one another. If this were not true then universities would be unmanageable and would not survive. Not only have they survived, but they are among the most important institutions in any developed society. So clearly they can be managed. But there are occasions in which, either because of general changes in a society or because of a specific event, the values collide, and in those cases one must be very careful.

We can look to the case already mentioned of the galloping "corporatization" of the university, especially in the United States, as an example of a conflict generated by broader social changes. As our societies have commercialized themselves more and more over the last several centuries we have reached a point where we begin to think of virtually everything in market terms. That process has finally reached the university as students and their families are described as customers, as staff members are urged to provide better "customer service," as programs and academic departments are increasingly judged on their capacity to generate income, and as the defining characteristics of a university are referred to as its "brand." The problem is that commercialization to such a great extent conflicts with the academic values of the university. For example, there is a wide difference between a student and a customer. A customer in a department store pays for a product and receives it. The store and the customer have no responsibilities toward one another except to interact honestly and in compliance with relevant laws. The store must not misrepresent its product or secretly replace it with something inferior, and the customer must not use a stolen credit card or pay with counterfeit currency. Beyond that, the store has no responsibility to the customer to offer a specific product and the customer has no responsibility to the store to do anything in particular with the product.

A university's relation to a student is quite different. First, in most cases a student must compete even to enroll. Once enrolled, having paid tuition or accepted the terms of a scholarship, the student does not receive a product or even a service. The student receives an opportunity and assumes certain responsibilities. The university also assumes responsibilities. For example, if the university's mission includes providing a broad liberal education, which includes, to select one example, an education in geology, then it has a responsibility to provide instruction in geology suitable to the level and expectations of the students and the society. Similarly, if a university has as its mission to provide a liberal education, then it has a responsibility to make available the academic programs and other conditions that enable a strong liberal education. If we weigh the interaction of students and their instructors, or the importance of certain academic disciplines, against these standards, we can easily get a far different picture than if we weigh them against consumer-oriented commercial standards. An advanced course in geology may enroll few students and therefore be unprofitable, but necessary nevertheless because of the academic values that inform the university. Or it may be inefficient for an instructor to spend an hour or two with one student, but it may be exactly what the student needs academically at that point. Because the university must take seriously its academic values, and because a student is not a customer, it may be that the instructor has a responsibility to do the least efficient thing in such a case. Examples of this sort can be multiplied many times.

Universities elsewhere in the world are not in quite the same situation as American universities, but the general condition is the same. For the most part European universities, for example, have for centuries taken for granted that the state will support them and their students to whatever extent is necessary. That understanding is cracking and has been cracking for some years. One of the reasons for the Bologna Process has been to rein in the costs of university education and reduce the burden on the participating states. As state funding becomes harder to get, choices must be made, and one of the choices made in the context of Bologna is to offer a shorter, usually three-year, initial degree. One can argue, and many have, that the economically motivated decision to limit bachelor's programs to three years is inconsistent with academic values, and even with the needs of the broader society. To narrow the example, the choice made in Russian universities to confront insufficient funding has been to increase the number of programs funded not by the state budget but by the tuition-paying students who enroll in them. Furthermore, faculties and deans in many Russian universities have become increasingly entrepreneurial in their efforts to locate funding to renovate their buildings, provide adequate salaries, offer services to students, and so forth. In some cases, no doubt, the entrepreneurship of clever deans can far outstrip the academic needs for which it was originally sanctioned, and in such cases universities run into new conflicts between their economic and academic values.

It is easy simply to say that there are cases in which the university must honor its academic values even if they conflict with the economic, but doing so can be difficult. Smaller classes and smaller faculty-student ratios are academically desirable, but often economically impossible. If the funding is not there then something else must be done. The important thing for an academic administrator and policy maker to understand at that point is that in order to minimize the damage done in such cases it is critical to be aware of the values that are at stake. If an administrator eliminates a French language department in order to save money, even if in fact he did what needed to be done, he ought not to be proud of it, because such a decision comes at a great academic cost. Unfortunately, many administrators are proud of themselves when they make such decisions, and in such cases they are simply making it clear that they do not understand the character of the institutions for which they have responsibility.

Conflicts are not always over money. Some of the tensest difficulties that arise in American universities are over conflicts between academic and political values. During the late 1940s and 1950s, for example, some universities in the United States fired teaching staff who were suspected of being involved in some way with communism, or who refused to cooperate with morally and legally questionable investigations into such things by a congressional committee. Similar things, and worse, have happened and continue to happen in other countries, each for their own reasons. Another sort of example common in the United States concerns the presence at many universities of Reserve Officers' Training Corps

(ROTC) programs, which are military programs oriented to university students. Many American universities refuse to allow them on the grounds that military policies, and often-broader political policies that the military is obliged to implement, are inconsistent with the academic values to which universities should be committed.

In some times and places the examples can be complex and fascinating. Contemporary Turkey is such a case. The universities are supervised by a Higher Education Board (YÖK) that until recently was staunchly secular and Kemalist in its orientation, and that insisted that universities enforce that secularism. Thus, for example, women were not permitted to wear headscarves in classes and in some cases on university grounds. In recent years, the Islamist AK Party has gained power, entirely legitimately, and it is now slowly trying to undo some, perhaps all, of the secular commitments of the universities. In the course of this process many secular academic leaders have been arrested and charged with treason. This is such a complex conflict that it raises the question of the very definition of academic values for Turkish higher education.

In 2005 the American scholar Ward Churchill, then a professor of ethnic studies at the University of Colorado, gave a talk at a conference in a small college in New York State in which he made remarks that drew public attention to an article he had written the day after the events of September 11, 2001. In that article, "On the Justice of Roosting Chickens," Churchill referred to the people who were killed that day as "little Eichmanns."[6] That remark caused a firestorm of very public protest. Eventually, after investigation of Churchill by the university and amid a range of charges of fraud against him, he was fired by the University of Colorado in 2007. Many people, primarily outside of academia, were so offended by Churchill's comment, in most cases without understanding what he meant, that the university determined it simply could not tolerate him or what he had said. Here is a striking case of a conflict between academic freedom and broader public sensibilities, political and social.

This is the kind of situation about which university administrators have nightmares: whether to acquiesce to public and political pressure to punish a person who enrages the community, or to defend even extremely offensive remarks as an exercise of the academic freedom that all academic people know is crucial to a thriving university. A university does of course have a responsibility to defend academic freedom as a central component of its basic academic values; but it also has a responsibility to the community of which it is a part to function within the general parameters that the community embraces. There is a good deal of flexibility in that respect, but the flexibility is not infinite. A public or private university cannot, because it is a social and political institution, simply thumb its nose at the public. At the same time a university cannot be content to silence its scholars because they say unpopular things. No university can sustain its academic reputation and responsibility to its students if it creates a climate in which scholars are afraid to criticize received opinion. This is one of the most serious sorts of conflicts of values that a university can face.

There is of course no simple solution. If there were it would not be a difficult problem. One of the reasons problems like this arise is that the public does not fully understand that scholarship requires an environment in which scholars and teachers do not have to worry about public opinion. The same can be said about art, and in the United States artists occasionally run into the same kind of problem that Professor Churchill encountered, though usually outside of a university setting. One of the lessons to take from experiences like these is that universities, and arts organizations, need to do a better job helping their political and other public constituencies understand the importance of being able to express ideas, even if they are criticized and rejected by the academic or the general community, and even if that same community is paying for them.

To offer one more example, there was recently a controversy in the US state of Georgia. Several socially conservative members of the generally socially conservative state legislature tried to force the state-funded university to eliminate its programs and courses in queer theory and gay studies. Those of us in the university world understand the value and legitimacy of the sociological study of homosexuality and the critical study of literature by gay writers and about gay experience. Some legislators, though, take the rather myopic view that taxpayer money, money paid in taxes by a socially conservative populace, is being used to teach about a subject matter that is abhorred by that same populace. Why, they ask, should taxpayers support such a thing? The view may be myopic, but it is understandable that the public and its representatives might ask such a question. It does little good to say in response to the legislature simply that academic freedom justifies the scholarly study of homosexuality, even if academic freedom does in fact justify it. It also does little good to say to the university community that we must do what the legislature says because it pays the bills, even though it does pay the bills, or at least some of them. The first response ignores the social and political dimension of the university and the second response ignores the academic. And in the end, in any case, neither response will solve the problem.

A Balance of Values

We are not justified in offering a simple formula to solve such problems as these. It will not do simply to insist that in the name of academic freedom the university is justified in ignoring the public, nor will it do to insist that the public is justified in determining directly what does or does not go on in a university, nor will it do to insist that corporate policies and practices strengthen universities, and it is of course impossible to ignore the economic factors and conditions in which a university must function. None of these approaches take into account the complex intersection of values that defines a university. The most we can say in general by way of advice is that university administrators must be mindful of the fact that they preside over a social as well as an economic and academic institution, and all its values must be taken into account in handling difficult conflicts.

In the end a balance among the three sets of values must be maintained, even if the emphasis may shift from one day to the next or from one problem to the next.[7] A balance among the three sets of values can certainly be maintained because in fact they are in balance most of the time. When conflicts such as those we have mentioned arise, they indicate not that alien forces are trying to corrupt the university but rather that the appropriate balance has been lost. The task of an academic leader is to bring the values back into balance. That task can be more or less difficult, depending on how far out of balance things have become in any given case. When a legislature dictates to a university what its curriculum should be, or when corporate forces pressure a university to behave like a commercial enterprise, or when the professoriate thinks that it can ignore the community of which it is a part and which in some cases provides its funding, then things have became rather far out of balance, and the academic leader's task is that much more difficult than it has to be.

This fact does suggest that administrators would be wise to cultivate among their academic, economic, and social constituencies, long before any particular problems arise, an understanding of the genuinely complex nature of the institution and an awareness of the differing forces at work on it. To do so, however, administrators must first understand it themselves. I should like to think that analyzing the contemporary university as the intersection of academic, economic, and political values will help in that regard, wherever in the world one finds oneself. And in any case, understanding the constitutive relations of the university with its academic, social, and economic environments is necessary if the institution is to fulfill its functions. The problems to which Petrella refers can be understood as consequences of failing to understand both the proper role of the university and its complex relational context. To solve those problems, and to avoid those traps, requires that we keep in mind both the character of the democracy to which we would wish the university to contribute and the set of values that constitute the university's substance.

TEN

INTERNATIONAL RELATIONS AND FOREIGN POLICY

Borders of all kinds are both a blessing and a curse.[1] On the one hand they are a blessing in that they allow us to distinguish between this and that. Importantly for philosophical purposes they allow us to individuate one complex from others, whether that complex is an individual human being, or an ethnic group, or a society, or a biological species, or indeed anything whatsoever. With respect to social groups they allow us to conceptualize the differences we encounter in experience—between genders, or ethnicities, or classes—thereby allowing us to categorize individuals. With respect to nation states they make it possible to fix the extent of the writ of national law, national policies, and treaties of all kinds, and to formalize the meaning and implications of an individual's citizenship.

On the other hand, they are a curse in many of the same respects. Philosophers, and I dare say many political theorists and practitioners, have made something of a fetish of borders and have, in their minds at least, fixed them so inflexibly that they have become a hindrance to both understanding and policy making. For example, philosophers for centuries have assumed that in order to individuate human beings there must be rigid borders between them, an assumption that has led to detrimental conceptions of mind, self, and consciousness. Even at the level of physiology philosophers have failed to realize that the border between an individual's body and his environment is so porous that it is impossible to fix the identity of an individual independently of that environment, and this is no less true with respect to psychology and personality than to physiology. Much the same is true for the distinctions we draw and the boundaries we establish among social groups. The category of race is a good example. In social and political theory for a long time it was assumed that race is a clearly delineated category and that policy and other decisions may plausibly be made on the basis of the borders we establish to distinguish one race from another. In recent decades that assumption has fallen out of favor, and now that we are less confident that racial borders can be clearly or even coherently drawn, we are far less comfortable than we used to be in making racially grounded policy.

The borders between nation states present a distinct illustration of the general problem. The impact of Hegel and Marx notwithstanding, the residual influence of Platonism and Aristotelianism in European intellectual culture (and when I say "European" here, I mean to include those intellectual cultures such as the North American and the Turkish that are heirs to the European) inclines far too many of us to understand nation states and their borders ahistorically. To repeat a point made earlier, we have retained a decidedly Baroque conception of the nation state, which we can easily see in the example of international relations and foreign policy. Whether realist or liberal, we tend to assume a conception of the nation state that derives from the seventeenth and eighteenth centuries. Nation states are, we seem to think, discrete entities clearly delineated from one another, each with its own internally defined and determined characteristics and interests; these distinct entities, rather like billiard balls on a table, to use again an eighteenth-century metaphor, move about in a void, or a "state of nature," to use another Baroque metaphor, with sometimes benign and sometimes detrimental effects. In this, and I am afraid all-too-common, understanding of international relations, the role of foreign policy is to manage the collision of nation states to minimize the damage and to advance as much as possible the interests of one's own. As we have pointed out several times already, this point of view is more or less the same as, or at least analogous to, the approach to the physics of the period, wherein the objects that constitute the material dimension of nature are discrete atoms interacting with one another in a void and governed by Newtonian laws of thermodynamics. Something similar may be said of the economics of the time, wherein economic actors each have their own interests and interact with one another in a state of nature to pursue their interests. Smith's invisible hand may have been thought to manage this process automatically, but economic policy was also based on this assumption, and its desired effect was to maximize the economic advantage of some actors in the economic sphere. That this way of understanding nature in all its variety permeated the period can be seen when we realize that roughly the same assumptions underlay even musical composition at the time, wherein distinct individual melodic lines were woven together to produce a harmonious result. To this day students of musical composition continue to study the principles of Baroque counterpoint. Whether in music, physics, economics, or international relations, the assumptions of the Baroque have defined our understanding of the nature of the subject matter. Physics and music have gone their own ways over the past four hundred years, as has economics to a certain extent. The Baroque understanding of the nation state has proven to be more durable, to our collective detriment.

What might happen, I would like to ask, if we abandon the Baroque conception of the nation state and replace it with a conceptual perspective in which borders are differently understood? And further, what might be the implications for a democratic understanding of international relations?

If the nation state is not to be taken by analogy with a Newtonian atom in a void or a ball on a billiard table, what is a plausible alternative? The answer to this question has already been suggested when I mentioned the alternative conception of human identity and in a previous chapter the international implications of the democratic ideal, and indeed as a consequence of the pragmatic naturalist ontology of constitutive relations. At the most general level, the alternative to an atomistic understanding of any entity is to conceive it relationally, which is to say that any entity whatsoever, any complex, is constituted by the relational interactions in which it participates. Thus, a human being is not a discrete mind, or spirit, or even body, but a complex entity that has the character that it does by virtue of the many relational interactions that it undergoes and undertakes. Any individual's physiology is to some extent a function of the relations it has with its environment. Some of those relations are more relevant than others to his nature and identity, but all are constitutive. Similarly, an individual is also constituted by the social relations in which he stands—a son or daughter, a father or mother, an employee or employer, a scholar or football player, a citizen, a Russian, Serb, Turk, or American, to mention only a few of the many relational contexts in which each of us stands. We are, each of us, not discrete entities that merely happen to stand in each of these relations. On the contrary, we are the individuals we are by virtue of these relations. They are, in other words, all constitutive of us. We are not atoms in a void; we are relationally constituted complexes.

If we are to take the general ontology of constitutive relations seriously, then we must understand nation states in the same way. A nation state is not a discrete entity, with its nature and interests internally determined and that just happens to interact with other nation states in a web of political, economic, social, and military relations. On the contrary, a nation state is the state that it is by virtue of the political, economic, social, military, and many other relations in which it participates. Some of those relations are more relevant than others in the case of any particular nation state, but for any state all of its relations are constitutive, which is to say that taken together its relations *are* the state. Louis XIV was wrong. Even an absolute ruler is not the state, though the more absolute his power, the more relevant a constituent relation is his interaction with the other complexes that together constitute the state.

What happens to our conception of borders when we construe the state in this sort of diffuse, relational way? First, it enables us to acknowledge at the most general conceptual level something of which we are all aware in our experience: Borders are loose, flexible, porous, and shifting. Our political borders change from time to time, usually creating all sorts of problems; most of our nations are faced with the more or less difficult problems that result from the fact that the porous nature of our borders enables only limited control over immigration and emigration; our borders are also porous, perhaps even irrelevant, in relation to communication, particularly contemporary forms of electronic communication; borders are often obstacles in the face of contemporary processes such as economic globalization; and perhaps most importantly, the most serious of our contemporary problems, from terrorism and security to financial stability to the environment, are impervious to the divisions among us that our nation states and their borders have established.

This is not to say that borders are or should be treated as irrelevant, but it is to say that they are not to be understood as firm and inflexible barriers between or among our respective nations. They are, if we need a new metaphor, not walls between us but more like permeable membranes that help to set off one entity from another. And like cellular membranes, they are as much the condition that enables our interaction in the sense that they can help to provide mechanisms through which we may draw on one another's resources and support. If we understand nation states to be entities constituted by their relations with one another, and with other factors such as their own respective citizenries, then borders help to establish the terms in which nations interact purposefully with one another, rather as membranes help to enable cellular interaction and growth.

The biological metaphor is not accidental, and it is instructive to notice that as a science biology developed little until the older Newtonian assumptions about the nature of material entities, and the conception of the fixed universe in which those assumptions resided more comfortably, were superseded by the evolutionary and then genetic revolutions in biological thought. The metaphorical picture of the Newtonian universe is no more suited to international relations than it is to biology, and we are served well to shift our conception of nation states and their interaction to a more biological, indeed environmental metaphor. Nations are not atoms in a void; they are elements of an ecosystem, to put the point directly. With this shift in metaphor we are able to see more clearly how we might understand not only national borders, but also the related notions of national interest and the character of a democratic interaction among nations.

Our understanding of national interests has for too long been a captive of the Baroque understanding of the nation. We have assumed that as self-determined entities nations can develop their understanding of their interests internally, and then complete with those interests they enter the arena of international relations with a foreign policy designed to achieve them. But if nations are to be understood as complex entities the nature and character of which are defined by the relations in which they stand to other nations, and to the many other factors such as historical traditions, cultural forces, ethnic relations, economic development, legal principles and structures, and the ethical expectations that constitute them, then it makes little sense to think that a nation's interests can be defined or determined independently of its ongoing interactions with its environing conditions. We may well say that it is when a nation insists on defining its interests without due regard for its relations with its political, social, and economic environment that it gets itself, and others, into trouble. The American inclination in recent years to allow its bankers to run wild is an example, as is the Israeli insistence on maintaining its settlement policy. Another is the pursuit by Iran and other countries of a nuclear capacity, indeed the insistence on the part of all nuclear-enabled nations that they are entitled to maintain their arsenals, no matter how large or small. It is precisely because nation states are not atoms in a void that it is entirely misguided to understand national interest as we traditionally have. On the contrary, given the proposed understanding of nations as one among many factors in a political, social, economic, and moral ecosystem, it is far more sensible to realize that even national interests are to be understood and constructed only by bearing in mind the relations with other nations and global forces that constitute the state itself. If this is the case, then the traditional realist and liberal approaches to foreign policy also need to be rethought, and with them even our traditional understanding of national sovereignty.

We shall consider each of these issues in greater detail, and do so by asking a specific question: What would a reasonably thoughtful and consistent pragmatic naturalist do if in a position to make foreign policy? The possibility of a "practicing" pragmatist being in such a position may seem remote, and it may in fact be remote. With respect to the pragmatic naturalist philosophical tradition, however, the question is apt, as the well-known quote from Dewey that philosophy ought to address the problems of people indicates. With respect to political reality, the prospect of the legacy of an important philosopher or philosophical tradition being brought to bear on national policy is not in fact so remote. Much had been made in the early years of the George W. Bush administration in the United States of the influence among prominent American policy makers of the work of Leo Strauss.[2] Whether Strauss can be fairly tarred with the policy decisions of many of those who appealed to his legacy, or to whom his influence was attributed by others, is another question. The fact is that at the time there were many people in influential policy-making positions in the American government who regarded themselves and each other as thinking in the Straussian tradition. If Strauss and those who identify themselves with him can have that kind of influence, there is no reason that Dewey, other pragmatists, and those who identify themselves with the pragmatic naturalist tradition could not.

The conclusions to which we come, some of which I have already suggested in earlier chapters, may also seem far-fetched or unrealistic to some. Among the principles that drive a pragmatist's thinking on foreign policy questions is that the fundamental values of a democratic way of life are more important than national interest or national sovereignty. For those whose understanding of international relations is rooted in the realist tradition, such a view may suffer from naïveté at best and is possibly delusional and dangerous at worst. But Timothy Garton Ash has suggested that "Americans were Wilsonian long before Wilson."[3] He is right to say that American foreign policy (and my concern here is with American policy, though I think that the pragmatic naturalist perspective can be generalized) has always been rooted, for better or worse, in values of some sort, i.e., social or moral commitments beyond simply national interest and sovereignty. This, I take it, is what he means. If he is right, and I suspect that he is, the point applies to the foreign policies of many other nations as well. There is nothing inherently naïve for any nation to ground its foreign policy on principle that stands outside or above the moment's understanding of the nation's interests. In fact there is nothing inherently naïve about holding that a nation's general and long-term interest is to ground its policies, foreign and domestic, on principles that stand outside or above narrowly defined interests.

Furthermore, there are influential, and very mainstream, figures in international relations and foreign policy circles in the United States who have come to realize, though perhaps they knew it all along, that acceptable foreign policy requires the sacrifice of the preeminence of national sovereignty. In his 2005 book *The Opportunity*, for example, Richard N. Haass, a former ambassador and subsequently president of the Council on Foreign Relations, makes just this point, if somewhat reluctantly.[4] Francis Fukuyama in *America at the Crossroads* also argues that whatever value national sovereignty has had historically, and whatever value it may retain, it is now something of an anachronism and is in fact a dangerous component of contemporary international affairs.[5] The pragmatic naturalist, as we will see, is more unabashed about the secondary nature of sovereignty than either Haass or Fukuyama, and urges the point more forcefully and thoroughly than the others might. Nonetheless, there is every reason to believe that a foreign policy built on pragmatic naturalist principles is neither naïve nor dangerous. In fact, it is very much what both the United States and the world are currently in need of.[6]

Pragmatist Principles

At the risk of some repetition, it is worthwhile to lay out the traits of pragmatic naturalism that are most relevant for an exploration of the problems of foreign policy. The tradition, following Dewey and others, tends to avoid dichotomies that are drawn too sharply—for example, between being and action, or between means and ends. With that caveat in mind, we will list several relevant characteristics of the philosophical tradition, distinguishing among ontological traits, means, and ends. All have a bearing on the implications of pragmatic naturalism for an understanding of international affairs and the development of foreign policy.

Pragmatic naturalists, and even less naturalistically oriented pragmatists such as Peirce, avoid the more atomistic view of reality that characterized the empiricist and rationalist traditions that stem from the eighteenth century. In its place we tend to view things as constituted by their relations. Ours is not a billiard ball, or Newtonian, conception of nature, but one in which things can only be understood in the contexts in which they reside. The shift from an atomistic to a relational understanding of nature was made at least a century ago, and probably more, in physics, at least since Darwin in biology, and it is well understood in the arts. Philosophers other than pragmatic naturalists and some postmodernists have been slower to catch on, as have many social scientists. The same is true in international relations theory in general, a point we return to below. Pragmatic naturalists, furthermore, are also likely to understand the traits of nature as contingent rather than fixed, which point of view contributes to the fact that pragmatic naturalism is a constructivist philosophical tradition, a point that has been developed in an earlier chapter. The world, again in a Jamesian phrase, is "in the making."

Pragmatic naturalism, like any philosophical tradition, places enormous emphasis on the methods of query and inquiry, as we have seen. It is, in Dewey's language, an instrumentalism, in that the very role of ideas is to serve as instruments, tools, which we bring to bear in the resolution of problems. In that process we are empiricists in the sense that we take experience seriously. We seek to develop a critical intelligence that enables us to approach experience and generate ideas carefully, but in the process we are thoroughgoing fallibilists. We do not insist with ideologically driven certainty that any set of truths is unquestionable; rather we take it as a given that any of our ideas, in the face of experience and the ongoing development of problems and their solutions, may require revision or even abandonment. This much, at least, we have learned from the methodology, ideally conceived, of the natural sciences. In the analysis of problems and in their solution we think that communication is a permanent necessity. Working together, we believe in the need and have a faith in the possibility to act individually and collectively to bring about desirable ends. Such individual and collective action requires education, and education of certain kinds, to develop the appropriate skills and habits of mind.[7]

Desirable ends are always to be developed within the contexts given by specific problems. With respect to the social world, which is the relevant context for our interest in foreign policy, we nevertheless approach problems with the assumption that certain ends are likely to be most desirable. We assume, for example, that our social world is always in need of improvement, of reconstruction. The past and present, whatever virtues they may exhibit, are never good enough. Most fundamentally, and most importantly for foreign policy, pragmatic naturalists bring to the social problems with which we engage a commitment to democracy as a social structure and way of life well suited to the human condition, as a desirable state of social affairs. The pragmatic naturalist commitment to democracy is both the most fundamental and the most problematic of its social commitments, as the two previous chapters have suggested, especially when discussing foreign policy. In the American context everyone favors democracy and wants to see it spread, including those with whom pragmatists have the deepest disagreements. The specific meaning of democracy in the pragmatic naturalist sense, and its place in international relations and foreign policy, are at the heart of our considerations.

Democracy and Imperialism

We have claimed that pragmatic naturalism's approach to democracy is central to the issue of foreign policy, so it is best to begin there by returning to a discussion of basic democratic principles. We have seen that in Chapter 7 of *Democracy and Education* Dewey defines democracy through its two most fundamental traits. The first is that a democratic society is one that is characterized by the ongoing pursuit of common interests among its members; the second is the encouragement, and the implied changes of habit, of "interaction and cooperative intercourse" with members of other "groups," i.e., the pursuit of common interests with those beyond the borders of one's own group, which is to say beyond one's own immediate community, class, race, gender, and, what will be most important for our purposes, beyond one's nation.[8]

Two points to note about this definition are, first, that it is consonant with the better-known and -developed trait of Dewey's conception of democracy that it is more than a form of government or a process of political decision making; rather it is a way of life, "a mode of associated living, of conjoint communicated experience." Second, it describes not political institutions, though those are of course important, but habits of mind and forms of behavior. A democracy is a society in which its members are inclined to pursue common interests with one another, and to assume an expansive rather than a restricted sense of the relevant other. This is the reason that a democratic society can tolerate no forms of racism, sexism, or any other attitudes or behavior that exclude rather than include people or groups. Similarly, there is no place for xenophobic nationalism in a democracy. This, of course, is the very feature of democracy that raises the problem of pluralism and dissent that was discussed in the previous chapter.

The inclusive nature of democratic behavior points further to the fact that democracy understood in these terms is by its nature outward looking. To pursue common interests with those beyond the boundaries of one's group, regardless of the kind of group on which we might focus our attention, is to say that the democratic individual regards boundaries and borders as at best of limited meaning and value. In this respect pragmatic naturalist democracy cuts across the standard distinctions between liberalism and communitarianism. Democracy, and social and individual good, is not grounded primarily in either individual or community values or goods. The fundamental trait, rather, is the restless search for, which should be taken to include creation of, interests held in common with others, i.e., with any and if possible with all others.

This point raises a curious problem. To say that a democratic society is one in which its members pursue and construct common interests with others is to say that it seeks to bring others within its orbit. I suggested in a previous chapter that it is more important for a democrat to behave democratically than to spread democracy. Here, though, we encounter the fact that to behave democratically is to engage in something that looks like spreading democracy. To pursue common interests with others, and to open and maintain the lines of communication that common interests imply, is to some extent to seek to attract others to one's own habits of mind and behavior. The pursuit of common interests is in the end possible only if the other comes to recognize the same common interests, and is eager or at least willing to engage in the communication necessary to pursue and develop them further. Without such reciprocal interaction the initial pursuit is soon aborted. But such reciprocity of interests and communication in this case amounts to a shared set of values, means, and ends. To draw the other into communicative interaction in the pursuit and maintenance of shared interests is to draw the other into the habits of democratic living. Pragmatic naturalist democracy, in other words, seeks by definition to spread itself beyond its own borders.

In its commitment to democracy as a desirable form of social organization or form of life, and in the fact that democracy is understood as, we might say, the spreading of the democratic form of life beyond one's borders, pragmatism shares two of the basic conceptions of neoconservatism. The latter, as it developed in the United States from the 1970s, insists on democracy as the highest form of social life and on the importance of liberal democracy being spread as widely as possible throughout the world. In this respect neoconservatism has at its core an imperialistic impulse. The recent American regime in the administration of President Bush, to the extent that it embraced these neoconservative principles, took this imperialistic impulse seriously, and sought to implement it militarily.

These features of a pragmatic naturalist conception of democracy raise two questions. First, we must ask ourselves whether we really want to hold, as many do, that democracy is the only form of social or political organization suitable to the fuller development of our human capacities and thus of a fully human life. I argued in Chapter 8 that democracy is a desirable way of life, but that in conditions of certain kinds it may not necessarily be the most desirable. And we also suggested that it requires an unflattering degree of arrogance to hold that it is the only form of social organization, or way of life, appropriate for genuine human development. It is possible for people living in societies that are not democratic to develop in ways and to degrees that are suitable for human beings. If that is the case, and it certainly appears to be, then we must be careful not to overstate the case for the desirability and value of democracy.

We turn, then, to the second problem. Does pragmatic naturalist democracy, which by virtue of its pursuit of common interests across borders seeks to expand the range of the democratic way of life around the world, amount to a brand of imperialism? If we wish to say that it does not, then we must ask the question of how we can differentiate the outward orientation of pragmatic naturalist democracy from the aggressive imposition of democracy characteristic of most neoconservative writings and policies. One possibility is to distinguish between liberal democratic imperialism and (what shall we call it?) the liberal democratic reach of pragmatic naturalism.

One way to approach this question is to consider the argument for a more aggressive, imperialistic brand of liberal democracy. In his 2004 book *Colossus: The Rise and Fall of the American Empire*, British economic historian Niall Ferguson provides just such an argument, to which we now turn.[9]

Ferguson argues that the United States, taking up the mantle of the British Empire before it, has been on an imperialistic course for a century, and that all things considered this has been for the good. The latter claim is rather a startling one, in that there are relatively few people who actually want to be considered, or consider themselves, imperialists.

Ferguson is undeterred. In his opinion, there are several features of American imperialism that have overall been of value:

It brings liberal democratic institutions, political and economic, to its imperial subjects;
It provides protection from forces hostile to liberal democracy;
It brings investment and material development;
It creates educational opportunities: higher education at least for an elite, and broader access to basic education for the general population;

and, though Ferguson does not say this, one might add the neoconservative point:

It expands an integrated set of liberal democratic nation states.

This set of presumed virtues of imperialism requires, of course, that a liberal democratic empire be managed properly. Ferguson argues clearly and forcefully that Americans have failed in this regard, and are likely to continue to fail, even if the best intentions are ascribed to their efforts. But this is an issue we must leave aside.

What, now, do we make of the claim that if properly structured and managed, a liberal democratic imperialism, which is to say an imposed democracy, is a good thing? The claim is often made that it is self-contradictory to impose democracy. But is it? The answer must depend on the defining traits of democracy, its distinctive characteristics. If we look at Ferguson's list of the virtues of imperialism we can see the traits that he thinks define democracy: electoral political institutions, the rule of law, more or less open markets, flexible labor markets, fiscal restraint, capital investment opportunities, political and economic stability, and transparent and corruption-free public administration. This list of the defining characteristics of liberal democracy defines what had for some years been called the "Washington consensus," and they would probably align well with the views of the national leaders of the United States and those of many other leaders and citizens throughout the liberal democratic world, despite the fact that there is far less consensus today than there once was. And it is significant to note that there is nothing in this list of traits that could not be imposed without contradiction. In other words, each of these traits could be generated by an imposing force that had the knowledge and commitment to do it. If this is what democracy means, and if we leave aside the question of whether in fact an imperial situation is capable of sinking the roots of such characteristics deeply enough into a subject culture and society, then surely it can be imposed without contradiction.

But still, there are those of us who are troubled by the imposition of democracy, by liberal democratic imperialism, because we continue to suspect a lurking contradiction. The only legitimate reason, however, to be troubled by the imposition of democracy is if one does not accept the list of defining traits just described as sufficient. Or to put it a better way, one may be troubled by the imposition of democracy only if one accepts this list of defining traits of democracy as *at most* a necessary but definitely not a sufficient account of the characteristics of a democratic society. Even granting this is almost surely to give away too much, in that certain of these traits are likely to conflict directly with pragmatic naturalist democratic principles. The most obvious of these is the commonly articulated interest in "flexible labor markets," which is itself a code term for crushing the capacity of labor to defend its interests. Nonetheless, for the sake of argument let us grant even the outlandish.

If the list of standard traits of liberal democracy is insufficient, what other characteristics might we say are important for a more robust democracy? Precisely here is the relevance of the pragmatic naturalist understanding of democracy.

First, as we have said, democracy is a way of life, a set of habits, and the democratic way of life has a number of features not present in what we might call the standard model of liberal democracy. It requires on the part of its citizens that we be reflective with regard to our lives, our society, its problems, our policies, and the directions in which our society is moving at any given time; it requires that we be experiential in the sense that we rely more on our experience than on a set of ideological principles, even when that experience is troubling for one reason or another; it expects of us that we be willing, even eager, to take an experimental approach to policies designed to deal with specific problems; and it demands of us a desire to be genuinely communicative with one another.

Second, democracy is a form of life and of social relations that is conducive to people's development, i.e., to the development of people's potential. This feature points to one of the most critical weaknesses of the standard model of liberal democracy, which is that it emphasizes form over content. Even if it is true, for example, that relatively open markets, opportunities for capital investment, and flexible labor markets are conducive to a fairly fluid movement of people, goods, and even ideas, it is never acceptable to ignore the actual consequences of such structures, or to attend to them only selectively. There is no doubt that over the past century liberal democracies have created unprecedented wealth in their societies, and that in many respects that wealth and the opportunities it has created have spread to a larger proportion of the population than ever before. This, along with the relative freedom of citizens in liberal democracies in political and cultural matters, is the outstanding achievement of liberal democratic principles, policies, and traditions. But it is also the case that in practice, especially when its principles, policies, and traditions have been imposed on developing nations, the results have often been far from desirable in economic and other respects. Even in some of the stronger liberal democracies like the United States, poverty, infant mortality rates, underemployment, illiteracy, and other markers of economic insufficiency are much greater than we should tolerate, and they are generally growing worse rather than improving. If the democratic form of life is one that is conducive to the development of people's potential, and to the creation of material and cultural opportunities for all citizens, then the standard model, judged on its record to date, is inadequate.

Third, pragmatic naturalist democracy is both individualist and communitarian in the sense that the development of each requires the development of the other. It was mentioned above that pragmatist democracy cuts across traditional liberal and communitarian points of view, and in so doing it draws from both. The development of the community cannot be ignored in favor of the development of the individual, nor can the significance of individual development be buried in an emphasis on community values or social development. The standard models of liberal democracy and traditional socialism have both made this mistake, though in opposite directions. The failure of traditional liberal theory to appreciate the fact that individuals and communities, or societies, are relationally constituted is one of its most serious flaws. It is here that we see the insidious effects of the Baroque metaphor mentioned several times earlier. Societies are not the aggregate of the mechanical interactions of individuals, nor are individuals atoms in a void. If the development of both individuals and their communities and societies is an important aspect of a democratic society, then its principles of behavior and policies must take into account the many factors relevant to the development of both. In its reliance on the development of individuals and their opportunities, the standard model of liberal democracy simply assumes that social development will follow automatically, much as Newton held that order in the physical universe follows from the laws of the interaction of bodies, and in this it is mistaken. The failure of socialist policy has been to assume that if social and economic structures are adjusted to exclude the exploitation characteristic of more or less unregulated capitalism, then individual development will result automatically from social harmony. But it does not work this way either.

Fourth, pragmatic naturalist democracy is egalitarian in that it values an equality of opportunity for all people insofar as that can be achieved, a principle that follows from the third. The standard model is satisfied in creating conditions of which any number of people can take advantage, and it reduces traditional class advantages to individual and social development. But it is content to allow whatever new class advantages emerge, and justifies them as the unavoidable outcome of an otherwise desirable set of conditions and policies. On pragmatist principles, however, no democracy worthy of the name can be content with this. If policies and practices throw up even inadvertent obstacles to people's opportunities, obstacles that are through other policies and practices unnecessary, then they are inadequate to a democratic polity and way of life.

These are four defining traits of a pragmatic naturalist democracy and way of life, yet they are absent from the standard model. If we augment the standard model with them, i.e., if we conceive of democracy in a pragmatic naturalist rather than standard way, then an imposition of democracy is much more difficult to justify. This is not necessarily to say that it is a logical inconsistency, but surely it rings false to impose on individuals or whole societies reflective, communicative, and experimental sensibilities. If these are central traits of democracy, then democracy must be nurtured; it cannot be imposed. Pragmatic naturalist democracy is inherently internationalist, as is Ferguson's imperialist liberal democracy. The difference is that pragmatist internationalism can only be exercised in ways consistent with its other democratic traits, which rule out imposition. Pragmatic naturalist democracy is not and cannot be imperialistic. In whatever ways its outward-looking, international reach is expressed, it cannot be imposed. Thus, its international character is consistent with the importance of behaving democratically over spreading democracy.

It is significant to note that for the most part, the traits of pragmatic naturalism that we have been exploring throughout these chapters do not provide the assumptions or conceptual tools on which the foreign policy of any contemporary state rests, though some are coming close. Nor do they figure prominently in the discipline of international relations theory. The possible exception is the reliance on experience, though even fairly clear lessons of experience can be and often are dismissed in favor of ideological commitments. Thus, two critical questions emerge: (1) How can pragmatic naturalism's internationalism be expressed, or how is pragmatic naturalist democracy nurtured in an international environment, and (2) how might democratic foreign policy embody and reflect pragmatic naturalist principles?

Foreign Policy

We have suggested that a nation state's interests are to be understood fully within the relational context in which it finds itself. We may just as well have said that given a relational understanding, i.e., on the metaphor of an ecosystem, a nation state's interests are to be constructed democratically, and the reason we can put it this way is that to develop interests knowingly and honestly in a relational context is to pursue common interests, and the pursuit of common interests is a defining characteristic of a democracy, or so we have been arguing. Domestically, democratic societies function on the assumption that all citizens have equal and legitimate interests in pursuing their individual interests in consort with their compatriots. This implies that individuals pursue and when necessary construct their interests in common with those within the many communities they inhabit, and with those across the borders of their own communities. Thus, I may most appropriately pursue my own interests only by seeking and supporting decisions and policies that accord with the interests of those beyond my own relatively narrow circumstances. Not only do my own democratic impulses push me in this direction, but the health of the entire society, which is to say the political, social, and economic "ecosystem" of which I am a part, requires it. This is the sense in which the relationality of the state and the democratic condition converge. Thus, domestically the pursuit of common interests across the borders of one's own communities is the democratic expectation.

The situation is the same in the international arena. Any nation state that takes seriously its commitment to democracy has as an obligation the pursuit of common interests with those beyond its borders. In some cases such common interests are easily identifiable. In other cases they require more creative policy making. In fact in some cases the democratic obligation is not so much to pursue common interests as it is to construct them. The more difficult cases of foreign policy fall into this category. For example, there are many respects in which the United States and the Russian Federation have obvious interests in common—the defense against terrorism, financial stability, the solution of environmental problems, to name just a few of the more obvious. But there are other respects in which common interests need to be consciously developed—for example, with respect to American and Russian relations with former Soviet republics, or in the geopolitics related to the oil and natural gas markets. Examples such as this can be multiplied indefinitely across the globe.

Francis Fukuyama suggests that there are four major theoretical alternatives in contemporary American foreign policy. The first is traditional realism, with its assumption of distinct states interacting on the basis of their internally determined interests, and the realpolitik that accompanies it. Realism of this sort tends to regard the domestic characteristics of states as their own business, to be accepted as describing the conditions that define the international situation and the pursuit of one's own nation's power. The second is liberalism, with its interest in advancing certain goods internationally—for example, human rights and democracy—and its inclination to employ international organizations of states in pursuit of those ends. The third is neoconservatism, which insists that the nature of other states' regimes is of paramount importance and where possible can be defensibly interfered with in the pursuit of the expansion of liberal democracy. Neoconservatism tends to distrust international organizations as toothless, and as too prone to require the sacrifice of national sovereignty. The fourth is isolationism, more or less strict and usually with a dose of xenophobia, that regards national interest as best served by avoiding interaction with other nations to the extent possible.[10]

In general this is a fair account of the most influential alternatives currently available, though it does not take into account recent innovations and suggestions. One of them is a rethinking of realism that looks to take into account relational conceptions of nation states.[11] Another is the effort in recent years to explore the implications of pragmatism for international theory, foreign policy, and the ethics of foreign policy.[12] With the exception of the latter, however, none of the alternatives currently available take adequate account of pragmatic naturalist democracy in the crafting of foreign policy.

In the development of the traits of pragmatic naturalist democracy we had recourse to Dewey, and it is both consistent and useful to turn to him again to develop an appropriate approach to international affairs and foreign policy. In *Democracy and Education*, later in the same chapter in which Dewey defines democracy, he raises questions that point us in the right direction. We had recourse to this passage in our earlier development of the concept of democracy, but it is prudent to look at it again. Couching his remarks in the context of education, he asks,

> Is it possible for an educational system to be conducted by a national state and yet the full social ends of the educational process not be restricted, constrained, and corrupted? . . . Externally, the question is concerned with the reconciliation of national loyalty, or patriotism, with superior devotion to the things which unite men in common ends, irrespective of national political boundaries. . . . The secondary and provisional character of national sovereignty in respect to the fuller, freer, and more fruitful association and intercourse of all human beings with one another must be instilled as a working disposition of mind.[13]

Dewey here is assuming the necessity of the principles, habits of mind, and behavior of pragmatic naturalist democracy as we have described them. He goes on to indicate the relation of democracy so conceived to national loyalty and national sovereignty. With respect to both, the democratic traits take precedence: The "devotion to the things which unite men in common" is "superior" to "national loyalty, or patriotism," and national sovereignty is "secondary and provisional . . . in respect to the fuller, freer, and more fruitful association and intercourse of all human beings." This is the crux of the matter as far as foreign policy is concerned, and the greatest challenge to those who would like to frame contemporary foreign policy on pragmatic naturalist principles.

Though it sees the value of the expansion of democratic societies around the world, pragmatic naturalism's commitment to democracy does not imply that installing democracies is a necessary goal of foreign policy. The commitment to democracy rather means that foreign policy must embody the traits of the democratic form of life. Democracy is relevant to foreign policy insofar as it bears on means more than on ends. We may say, in fact we have already said, that the responsibility of the democrat is not to spread democracy but to behave democratically, and the same applies to any nation that would consider itself to be democratic. The details of a foreign policy flow from this basic principle.

Consider the question of international cooperation. It has been a given for American governments since Woodrow Wilson and the creation of the League of Nations, at least until the strong strain of unilateralism of the Bush administration, that international collaboration is a key component of any successful foreign policy. The difficulties with the United Nations and much of Europe in the months preceding the Iraq War, however, led the Bush administration to forego traditional alliances in favor of what it called a "coalition of the willing." To generalize this approach, it had become more or less official policy to assume that national interests will best be served not by building strong and sustained international partnerships but by crafting coalitions that can be expected to shift with each new international problem or crisis.

The difficulties that were faced in Iraq since the beginning of the war in 2003 have, however, generated a renewed interest in international collaboration among foreign policy specialists. Richard Haass in *The Opportunity* defends a fairly traditional realism. He argues against making the promotion of democracy the centerpiece of foreign policy, and he develops a sustained argument for what he calls the principle of integration, by which he means collaboration among states for any successful handling of international problems. His rationale for the necessity of integration among national foreign policies, if not among states themselves, is first that the process of globalization in economies, technology, the flow of information, and so forth has produced a de facto integration already; second, contemporary problems have an international dimension—for example, terrorism, environmental problems, economic dislocations, and disease; and third, integration is more effective because though it is always possible for a powerful nation to act alone, it is rarely possible for it to succeed alone. For these reasons, the United States and other nations must be prepared to cede some degree of sovereignty and integrate the pursuit of their interests.

Fukuyama, though approaching the question from a different set of conceptual assumptions than does Haass, comes to a similar conclusion. He argues for what he calls a *realistic* Wilsonianism. By this he means first, unlike Haass though somewhat consistently with his earlier neoconservative principles, that the United States should continue to care about the internal character of other nations, i.e., it should continue to promote the spread of liberal democracies. However, to do so requires that to a large extent it demilitarize its foreign policy: "The most important way that American power can be exercised at this juncture is not through the exercise of military power but through the ability of the

United States to shape international institutions."[14] Breaking with the traditional hostility of neoconservatism to international organizations, one of its previously most prominent representatives is here calling for the United States not simply to tolerate them but in fact to promote them and to structure its foreign policy around them. Thus, Fukuyama endorses to no less an extent what Haass calls integration. He makes an additional interesting point by urging what he calls "multi-multilateralism," by which he means that we should expect and encourage not a single overarching international institution such as the United Nations as the most workable forum through which to act, but a multiplicity of international institutions that can be expected to arise and develop around various different issues and problems.[15] In this respect he manages to combine the more liberal interest in multilateralism with the neoconservative penchant for coalitions of the willing.

There is a degree to which these are the sorts of things a pragmatic naturalist might say too, though there are weaknesses in both Haass's and Fukuyama's views that point up important differences. The basic difference is that if pragmatic naturalism is committed to a robust, Deweyan democracy in its foreign policy, Haass's integration and Fukuyama's realistic Wilsonianism are halfheartedly democratic at best. At several points Haass speaks as if the important foreign policy goal of the United States is that it must make every effort to convince other nations to cooperate with it.[16] The significant inadequacy of this approach is that it assumes that the United States, presumably like every other country, should and would determine its foreign policy unilaterally, and only then seek international cooperation. To assume a unilateral determination of national interest and policy, however, is to ignore one of the defining traits of democracy as we have been developing it, i.e., the pursuit and construction of common interests across borders. An adequate foreign policy cannot understand integration and collaboration merely as an effort to convince others to do as we do or as we want. Rather, integration and collaboration mean to work with others, in this case other nations, in the very determination of what we should be doing, individually and collectively, and in the most appropriate means of doing it. This is the stronger, and most appropriate, sense in which nations should be prepared to cede some degree of sovereignty. Haass thinks it is enough to concede that the United States in any case should agree that whenever possible it will not act alone. The pragmatic naturalist democrat, however, insists on the much stronger point that what is required is collaboration and communication in the very process of foreign policy formulation.

Fukuyama has a similar problem. As we saw in the short quotation above, he calls on the United States to promote, actually he says to "shape," international institutions, and to work through them in the handling of international problems. One cannot object in principle to the "shaping" of international institutions. After all, if institutions are to be developed they must be shaped. But it sounds as if Fukuyama advocates that the shaping be done primarily by the United States, rather than collaboratively by all parties involved. Like Haass, he suggests a certain ceding of sovereignty only to reinsert it at another level. It is also interesting to note that in a footnote he nods in the direction of Haass's more traditional realism. In the context of a discussion of promoting democracy and economic development in the Middle East, he says that "it might be possible to argue for an authoritarian transition in the Middle East if one could find any truly modernizing autocrats in the region, *comparable to Park Chung-Hee of South Korea or Lee Kuan Yew of Singapore*" (my emphasis).[17] In the end, and notwithstanding our point that democracy is a desirable if not a necessary social condition for human life and development, it appears that Fukuyama is willing to forego democracy in both means and ends.

The critical point is that for the pragmatic naturalist democrat the pursuit and construction of common interests across borders is the fundamental principle, and it is so because the pragmatic naturalist is committed to democracy so defined. Furthermore, democracy in just this sense takes precedence over national interest unilaterally defined, national sovereignty, and national allegiance.

This is likely to be a bitter pill for many people, or many Americans at any rate, to swallow, but it *is* the pragmatic naturalist position. If Haass is right that contemporary problems pay no heed to borders—terrorism, a deteriorating environment, disease, the economic and social problems generated by a globalizing economy—then the foreign policies at least of influential states must themselves be reconceived to look beyond borders in their determination. If our problems are international, then conditions are ripe for us to live out the very definition of pragmatic naturalist democracy: the pursuit and construction of common interests across borders. If even the timid versions of this view that we find in Haass and Fukuyama indicate the need to cede some degree of sovereignty, then the stronger, pragmatic naturalist commitment is to overcome sovereignty in much more thoroughgoing ways.

This may seem difficult if not impossible to realize, at least in the United States, given the strength of appeals to national sovereignty and national loyalty. But that difficulty is due in part to the fact that the alternatives have been mistakenly construed. Many government and policy figures tend to think and to speak as if the alternative is between a rigid sovereignty and surrender. The point that needs to be insisted upon, however, is that it is in the interest of the citizens of the country, and it is in the interest of democracy itself, for national policy to be designed and defined through communication and collaboration with international partners, as many as can be induced to participate in the process. We may in fact speak, as Larry Hickman has, of the importance of "global citizenship," even if we may do so only loosely.[18]

That this is not simply an abstract and utopian ideal can be seen in the fact, or so we have suggested earlier, that this process is precisely what is currently underway in the ongoing formation of the European Union. For all its difficulties and setbacks, the EU is a case, the first in history, where nations have voluntarily constructed institutions through which they agree to determine policy. To date the policies have dealt more with domestic issues, though they are domestic with respect to the EU as a whole, not simply with respect to each of its constituent member nations. The common formulation of international interests and policies has proven to be more difficult, but the process is underway and all things considered is moving in the direction of a collaborative pursuit of common international interests. That the EU, in both principle and practice, is more a success than a failure to date can be seen in the fact that many neighboring nations are clamoring to join. It is a model whose time has come, and it is in many respects an illustration, even if not consciously, of the desirable means and ends of a pragmatic naturalist democracy.

The Problem of Power

If communication and collaboration are among the defining traits of democratic behavior, then it is obvious that institutions to enable them will be a necessary component of an adequate foreign policy. This much the pragmatic naturalist shares with most other foreign policy makers. And like most others, the pragmatic naturalist will not simply take as a given whatever institutions are handed to us, but will seek to reform existing institutions and create new ones that will best fit democratic principles and their application in the international arena.

Unlike most others, however, the pragmatic naturalist will seek to craft institutions, existing and new, in a genuine partnership with other nations. Furthermore, if he is an American he will employ those institutions not as forums in which to urge US policy or to bend other nations' policies to US will. On the contrary, the pragmatic naturalist will work through the institutions to develop policies that are likely to lead to the recognition and the construction of common interests among participating states. In this respect it will bring to bear the Deweyan commitment to "interaction and cooperative intercourse" with those beyond our national borders.

Precisely which such institutions will be the most viable is impossible to say ahead of time. Perhaps the United Nations can be reformed in such a way as to provide an appropriate forum for this purpose, but perhaps not. The UN was founded and is organized on different principles, and it may or may not ever be equal to the task. It is likely that Fukuyama's proposal for a multi-multilateralism is something pragmatic naturalists should take seriously. It is quite possible that differing problems require collaborations of different nations to address them most effectively. Nuclear proliferation, the environment, disease, terrorism, relations with the Democratic People's Republic of Korea, the unfolding consequences of the Arab Spring, to name only a few current problems of foreign policy, most centrally involve differing sets of nations and can be addressed most fruitfully through differing sets of coalitions and related institutions.

Nonetheless, there is a current need for the United States and other liberal democracies to take seriously their common characteristics and to build on their basis the possibility for a sustained pursuit and construction of common interests and policies. In their recent books both Garton Ash and Fukuyama mention an organization called the Community of Democracies, an organization that was founded in Warsaw in 2000, with the support of the Clinton administration.[19] It still exists, but it has no effective structure, staff, or budget. It is, however, the right idea in that it is just the sort of institution that could provide a forum for pragmatic naturalists to pursue democratic policy, as we understand it.

In addition to the development of appropriate international institutions, the pragmatist will also take seriously what is called public diplomacy. Though public diplomacy has waxed and waned in recent decades as an instrument of US foreign policy, it is without doubt an important element of a pragmatic naturalist internationalism. Public diplomacy is, basically, the effort to expose others, which is to say other nations and their people, to the best of one's own public, nongovernmental institutions and achievements. It generally takes the form of exposure to one's highest intellectual and cultural achievements.

Public diplomacy is, in a sense, what has come to be called "soft power," though that term must be used circumspectly. Some years ago Joseph Nye, dean of the John F. Kennedy School of Government at Harvard and an occasional figure in the US State Department and National Intelligence Council, introduced the concept of soft power, as opposed, not surprisingly, to "hard power."[20] The latter, as Nye defines it, is the means at a nation's disposal to compel other nations to do what it wants. Hard power is generally military, though there are also economic weapons that may fall into this category. Soft power, by contrast, is the means at a nation's disposal to induce other nations, as Nye puts it, "to want what we want." A nation's cultural, intellectual, and educational institutions are among its most obvious mechanisms for the exercise of soft power.

Even a casual reflection on Nye's formulation of the definition of soft power reveals the same sort of simultaneous progress and regress that we have seen in Haass and Fukuyama. If we are to induce others to "want what we want," then presumably we will already have determined what we want independently of our interaction with others. In that case, soft power turns out to be at best a kinder and gentler form of manipulation than armed force, but something far short of the kind of democratic policy tool the pragmatic naturalist would want. In one sense Nye's soft power is the right idea, but only if we reconceive and reformulate its definition. Soft power is a valuable tool for the pragmatic naturalist in the international arena not because it is a way of inducing other nations to want what we want, but because its instruments are among the best we have available to us to exercise across borders the communication and collaboration necessary for an international pursuit and construction of common interests. It is probably best to give up the term "soft power" because of the inadequacies of Nye's initial definition, though with an acknowledged debt to Nye for having made the relevant distinction in the first place. We may better speak, as we already have, of public diplomacy.

The instruments in question are a nation's cultural, scholarly, educational, and in some cases and to some extent its political institutions. American film, musical, and arts institutions, and those who work in these fields, are among the strongest representatives of what is best of American society, in both their popular and "high" forms. The same can be said of American universities, and the people who work in them. There have been for years programs through which Americans in these fields and institutions bring their work abroad and have the opportunity to work with their colleagues from other countries. Typically, however, these programs have been the neglected stepchildren of foreign policy. A pragmatist would put them front and center, not simply because a pragmatist is likely to be an intellectual and most at home with them, but because they are aspects and dimensions of the society that lend themselves to the expression and development of the common interests we so desperately need.

It should also be noted that whatever their flaws, many of the political institutions that democratic governments have evolved over the centuries are an important foreign policy resource. The parliaments and legislatures of advanced liberal democracies, for example, represent a rich source of political and institutional experience. It would be narrow minded and foolish to think that such institutions could or should simply be transplanted anywhere, but it would be equally foolish to think that there is nothing important to be learned from them. The experience and lessons learned from years of working on and through such institutions, and the expertise of many people who know them well, should be put to the service of a pragmatic naturalist democratic foreign policy.

We have yet to discuss the most difficult challenge that would face the pragmatic naturalist in the pursuit of a democratic foreign policy, which is the role and proper use of Nye's "hard power." In the Obama administration in the United States there has been increasing talk of "smart power," though this is not in fact a third type of power; it simply indicates the sensible and intelligently governed use of soft and hard power. We have discussed how one might make use of soft power properly understood and defined. But what of its often seductive and frequently more persuasive cousin, particularly in its military form? What if any are the appropriate purposes, forms, and occasions for the use of military force?

One possible answer is pacifism, which is to say that there are no legitimate purposes, forms, or occasions for the use of military power. The pragmatic naturalist is predisposed against the use of military power as a means to achieve one's ends. As a method it is antithetical to the pursuit of common interests across borders. And, following Dewey, the use of military power even as a last resort is an admission of the failure of the application of intelligence in the solution of a problem. If militarism and pacifism were the only two alternative approaches, then our own methods and goals would require that we forswear the use of military force in pursuit of national interests.

In principle, however, the choice is not that sharply drawn. There is a fairly wide range of theoretical possibilities between the poles of pacifism and militarism. Though our principles predispose us to resist the use of military force, there is nothing that compels us to hold that it is never legitimate. It is far wiser, for the reasons we have been developing, to conduct foreign policy through the development of a diplomacy that assumes the value of the pursuit of common interests. In practice, however, this may well fail, and it may be necessary for self-defense or possibly other reasons to resort to the coercive methods of hard power, military or economic. At least there is nothing in our principles that rules out this possibility. The question remains, then: Under what circumstances and to what ends is the use of hard power legitimate?

The initial answer has to be that the use of hard power is legitimate only in those cases in which our goals are justifiable and all other more reasonable methods of achieving them have been exhausted and all have proven unsuccessful. This view is not unique to pragmatic naturalism. Other than fascists, no one holds that military action is a good in itself. A fascist will claim that war has the virtue of strengthening the character of those who participate in it and thereby strengthening the society and the nation itself. This of course is entirely inconsistent with an emphasis on the pursuit of common interests and the virtues of diplomacy. Others, who would not likely consider themselves to be fascists, occasionally and perhaps frequently will say that war has the virtue of strengthening the economy of a nation that wages war, if it does not destroy the nation's capacity to produce or otherwise drive it into bankruptcy. Or they may say that war can under certain circumstances have the virtue of making new resources, natural or human, available to the nation that undertakes it. Clearly, though, from the point of view of the democratic principles that we have been urging, war for these reasons is not acceptable, at least not for these reasons alone. It is also clear that war under false pretenses—for example, that a supposed enemy is alleged to have attacked one's ships in the Gulf of Tonkin, or that a presumed enemy is harboring weapons of mass destruction—is always unjustifiable. To wage war in any of these circumstances, from economic gain to false pretenses, so fundamentally violates democratic principles that it can and should be considered an egregious abrogation of the leaders' responsibilities.

Clausewitz famously said that war is politics by other means. Unfortunately, the way foreign policy is often conducted in the common realist, liberal, and neoconservative versions, politics amounts to war by other means. The reason is that both war and traditional foreign policy, which is to say both hard and soft power of the standard sorts, amount to coercion, and it is coercion itself that is inconsistent with democratic principle. So to put the question another way, if coercion is not consistent with our democratic principles, and if war as hard power is a form of coercion, then how can it ever be an acceptable means of interaction with another nation? The answer is that we must distinguish between aggressive and defensive coercion. To wage war on another nation for the purpose of forcing it to bend to one's will—for example, for economic reasons or for the purpose of regime change—is to engage in aggressive coercion and is therefore inconsistent with democratic principles. To defend oneself militarily in order to prevent another nation from exercising aggressive coercion against one is itself a form of coercion, but it is defensive coercion. There is nothing inconsistent with democratic principles in defending oneself militarily, and if there is also nothing in democratic principle that implies pacifism, then defensive military action is acceptable on democratic grounds.

This is a theoretical point that people who would not consider themselves to be thinking in pragmatic naturalist terms also endorse. That is all to the good. There is no necessary virtue in having a position that is unique in all respects. In practice, pragmatic naturalists may also not be unique, by which I mean that if we were in a position to craft foreign policy any of us might, like so many others, be tempted to use military force or other forms of aggressive coercion in indefensible ways. One can only say in the face of such possibilities in practice that wisdom would require of us that we keep our principles in mind, and understand them well enough to be able to see when and how we are in danger of overstepping them. We have, it turns out, developed here not simply a conception of international relations but also a democratic ethics of foreign policy. Dewey once wondered why it is that international affairs is one area in which it is regularly presumed that ethics is irrelevant, especially when on the face of it, it is a field clearly in need of ethical underpinning.[21] The traditional assumption of the prominence of national interest and sovereignty most likely helps to explain the paucity of ethical judgment in foreign affairs. Pragmatic naturalism, however, insofar as it elevates its conception of democracy above national interest, loyalty, and sovereignty, provides an occasion to revisit the question of ethics in foreign policy to more satisfactory effect.

A number of questions remain to be explored on another occasion. For example, a more thorough inquiry would also need to address the question of economic and political development, and the national and international institutions that have evolved to deal with it. What, for example, would a pragmatic naturalist in the United States have USAID do, and would it be different from its current mission? How do we handle the International Monetary Fund, the World Bank, and the World

Trade Organization? Another area to which precious little attention has been paid in the current phenomenon of globalization is the internationalization of higher education. Most nations have developed in recent years policies to advance the internationalization of their universities, but the United States has lagged far behind in this respect.[22] Because higher education is such an important dimension in any serious effort at public diplomacy, a pragmatic naturalist foreign policy would without question pay it close attention. And there is the phenomenon of NGOs and their increasingly important role around the world. It is commonplace to say that they need to be taken seriously, but it is another matter to consider how one might do that as a component of an adequately democratic foreign policy. There are, then, serious and difficult issues to be worked out.

It is clear that because of its commitment to a deep and thorough form of democracy, a pragmatic naturalist foreign policy would not be easy to implement, especially in the United States in the current political environment. Many things would no doubt have to change before it would become possible. Nonetheless, there are many reasons to think that pragmatic naturalism has a good deal to bring to foreign policy, and that a nation would be well served by a foreign policy conceived on its principles. It is to be sure a cosmopolitan conception, and to that extent runs contrary to the nationalism now so strong in many societies. Nonetheless, it is the approach that both nature and democratic principle suggest.[23]

ELEVEN

COSMOPOLITANISM AND HUMANISM

Despite the triumphalism in the West at the end of the Cold War, the past two decades have for the most part not been a good time for democracy.[1] As a practical goal for political development, it has been used too readily to justify foreign and military policies and practices that are so questionable in their wisdom as to render the very term "democracy" undesirable in many places and contexts. Many people around the world are now suspicious that an appeal to democracy is a veiled attempt by those making the appeal to dominate, to manipulate, or in other ways to advance their own interests at others' expense. The most glaring example is the use of democracy as an ideal by the United States, the United Kingdom, and their allies in Europe and elsewhere in the world to justify the war in Iraq. In Russia, to give another example, the appeal to democracy to justify the economic, political, and social perversities of the Yeltsin era has seriously damaged the ability to appeal to democracy as a guiding principle or an end in view. Along similar lines, there are political scientists and other theorists who have simply given up on democracy as a valuable component of policy analysis or political theory.[2] In its place some have decided that human rights are a far-less-polluted ideal on which to base international political goals. Unfortunately, human rights have so frequently been used as a political bludgeon that they too have lost a good deal of their normative force.

What does this mean for those of us who think about social and political issues in terms that draw on Dewey and other figures in the American pragmatic naturalist tradition? First, democracy as a social and political ideal is far too important to surrender to those who would misunderstand or abuse it for their own ends. Second, there is more than one way to understand democracy, and the meaning Dewey and others have given it differs considerably from the versions advanced by Mr. Bush, Mr. Blair, Mr. Yeltsin, and the countless others who make them possible. For that reason alone it is important to continue to develop Dewey's line of thought to the greatest extent possible.

Cosmopolitanism

The idea I would like to explore is, in addition to the problems we have considered in previous chapters, yet another reason for continuing to draw on Dewey and the pragmatic naturalist tradition in the exploration of appropriate approaches to contemporary social issues. Dewey's understanding of democracy was outward looking. As we have seen, nearly a century ago, in *Democracy and Education*, he defined democracy in part in terms of the value of pursuing shared interests with those beyond the boundaries that define one's own experience. Dewey meant boundaries of all kinds, including national boundaries. This means that democracy for Dewey is inherently and necessarily internationalist, not in the sense that a democratic society should or may export democracy as it pleases, but in the sense that a democratic society and people are expected to make every effort to identify, or if need be to create, common interests across international borders. Democracy in this sense is cosmopolitan, and it is this cosmopolitanism that I would like to develop.

Cosmopolitanism is for us a guiding principle, the discussion of which can be framed by two questions, the first methodological and the second substantial: (1) How does the principle of cosmopolitanism function? and (2) what is its content? We shall consider the two questions in order.

There are two ways in which much of the relevant contemporary philosophical literature treats cosmopolitanism. One of them is as an abstract principle from which we can deduce moral commitments—for example, about human rights.[3] In this sense cosmopolitanism is the principle that moral obligations apply to all people regardless of their national identity or citizenship. This is the principle of cosmopolitanism that is rooted in Kant. Recently analytically oriented philosophers have gone to considerable lengths to explore the justification and implications of this principle, frequently to valuable effect. The point I want to make here does not concern the details of the arguments in this literature. Rather, I wish simply to make the methodological point that the philosophical exploration of cosmopolitanism as a guiding principle, and as a crucial component of a pragmatic naturalist understanding of democracy, does not proceed this way.

The broader point has to do with the nature of meaning, justification, and valuation within such a philosophical inquiry. Following both Dewey and before him Peirce, the meaning of a concept is to be found in the effects it produces when applied in relevant ways. In this sense, the meaning of cosmopolitanism depends on what difference it makes or would make if it were taken to heart, for example, in public policy or for individual behavior. Substantially, this point bears on the content of the concept, to which we will turn below. Methodologically, however, it points to an important distinction between pragmatic naturalist and analytic philosophy. The analytic philosopher tends to be interested in the implications of a concept, specifically those that are revealed through logical analysis. The pragmatic naturalist philosopher, by contrast, is interested in what happens when a concept is put to work. In the end the distinction may be less stark than it appears because in practice it is often more a matter of emphasis than a sharp distinction. Nonetheless, it does point to an important difference in approach to philosophical inquiry, a difference that will distinguish this more or less Deweyan analysis of cosmopolitanism from the bulk of the related philosophical literature currently in print.

The understanding of meaning is one of the important distinguishing traits of Dewey's and other pragmatists' methodology. Another concerns justification and valuation. In this respect William James, and to a lesser extent Richard Rorty, provide the model: An idea is justified to the extent that it works for us. When put this baldly, the point seems controversial at best and foolish or even dangerous at worst. James and Rorty both spent a good deal of their energy responding to objections to this understanding of the value of an idea, and I will not rehearse their points here. For our purposes, suffice it to say that we will assess the value of cosmopolitanism as a guiding principle by determining whether when applied, again in policy or personal respects, it contributes to outcomes that we have adequate reasons to desire. As in the case of meaning, this methodological trait of pragmatic naturalist inquiry distinguishes it from more analytically oriented approaches. As a result our evaluation of the significance of cosmopolitanism will differ from the examinations of the concept in much of the philosophical literature. To this end our interest is not in the deductively inferred implications of cosmopolitanism but in its practical effects and their value.

To continue the methodological theme, a second way in which the principle of cosmopolitanism appears in much of the recent literature is as a deductively drawn conclusion from other principles—for example, from a principle of justice. A good deal of the work based on John Rawls has this character. Another obvious example of such a principle would be human equality, so that if we accept the proposition that all human beings are morally equal then eventually it follows that the distribution of goods, in particular such moral goods as human rights, cannot justifiably be based on citizenship or nationality or ethnicity; hence cosmopolitanism. Arguments like this, though much more fully developed and articulated, are extensively discussed in the literature. And not surprisingly there is a good deal of disagreement about them. As in the previous case, though, I am not interested here in discussing the details. I simply want to point out that whatever interest and value there may be in considering the question of whether cosmopolitanism follows from any other moral or political principles we might hold, it is at least as important, and maybe more so, to consider whether cosmopolitanism as a guiding principle does the work we want it to do. This kind of inquiry, and it is the distinctively pragmatist approach, will in the end do us more social and individual good than any other. More specifically, cosmopolitanism will be justified because it is a wise way for us to understand ourselves in the current political and international environment. It may in fact be wiser than the alternatives.

Let us move now from the methodological to the substantial question: What do we mean by cosmopolitanism? Though the fuller meaning of the principle can emerge only as we develop its effects in application, it is possible to begin with a working definition, and in this case it is a definition that is tied directly to Dewey's general account of democracy. The principle of cosmopolitanism calls on us to take to heart, that is to take seriously, the interests we share with those beyond our own ethnic, national, and cultural borders. It is an internationalism, though it is more than that. If internationalism means to value international interaction and cooperation, then cosmopolitanism goes further and asks of us that we interact with others in ways that allow us to identify, and where necessary to create, common interests that enable us to work together in their pursuit.

This is an important point because it helps us to distinguish our sense of cosmopolitanism from another fairly common way of understanding the term. For some, cosmopolitanism means to be at home in the world, or at least to be able to feel more or less at home wherever one is. There is a virtue in this, in that those who are able to feel more or less at home wherever they are can be open to a fairly broad range of experiences, and that itself is a good. The problem with cosmopolitanism in this sense is that it is severely limited. For one thing, in practice it is an unduly elitist principle because it applies only to a small segment of the population. It is a tiny minority of the world's population that has the opportunity to spend enough time abroad to develop the sense of comfort that this sense of cosmopolitanism is describing. The only segment of the population to which this principle can apply consists of those people who have the wealth and the opportunity to travel a good deal or to work abroad. While feeling at home wherever they are may be a virtue for them, it is a virtue for such a small number of people that it can never rise to the level of an important guiding principle.

A second and more important limitation of cosmopolitanism in this sense is that it also does not rise to the level of a foundation for public policy. It is a principle of personal value, which is not a bad thing but is nonetheless limited. If cosmopolitanism is, as I am suggesting, tied to the very nature of democracy itself, then it must have to do with more than personal satisfaction and the richness of an individual life.

Another sense of cosmopolitanism that we should distinguish from ours, this time having to do with institutions rather than individuals, is that cosmopolitanism means world government. There is a great deal of disagreement about whether world government is an ideal worth pursuing, and one can easily imagine the arguments that may be advanced on either side of the issue. On the one hand, world government can provide consistency and continuity of policy, a value in a globally integrated environment. On the other hand, a single world government presents a danger in that there is no other comparable power that can serve as a counterweight if and when it goes bad. However the ideal of a world government might fare in the debate, it is virtually certain that for the near future it is a thoroughly unrealistic ideal. Simply consider the objections made in the United States to the United Nations and the World Court. It is not difficult to imagine how deep would be the resistance to world government in the United States and elsewhere. It is important to understand, though, that cosmopolitanism in the sense in which we are developing and defending it here neither requires nor expects world government. It would not necessarily be opposed to it, but that is another matter. Cosmopolitanism in our sense is not a form of political organization, but an ideal that has policy and behavioral implications.

So cosmopolitanism is something other than world government, and something more than an individual interest in other nations and cultures and an ability to function to some comfortable extent in them. It is rather something of an obligation of democratic societies and democratically minded individuals. The cosmopolitan obligation, if we may put it this way, is to use our public and where appropriate individual resources to develop common cause with individuals, institutions, and governments abroad. Let us be clear about this. To develop common cause, that is to pursue common interests, with those beyond our own national boundaries is on this view not merely something that is nice, or desirable, or admirable, or interesting. It is a democratic responsibility, an obligation on those of us who would claim to be democrats or to value democratic institutions and societies. It includes the necessity for respect for other peoples, nations, histories, and cultures; a desire to move beyond one's own history and categories to attempt to understand others; a readiness to work collaboratively with others to advance shared interests and solve shared problems; and a willingness at least and better an eagerness on the part of national governments, if we are to think about policy-oriented cosmopolitanism, to suspend to some degree national interest as traditionally understood in favor of the promotion of common interests among nations, their governments, and their people.[4]

The case for cosmopolitanism runs straight up against the question of how to interact with cultures we have reason to oppose. We have just said that among the traits of the democratic responsibility is a respect for other peoples and cultures. But how far, we may reasonably ask, can this obligation be expected to extend? After all, there are cultures that have characteristics that we cannot plausibly be expected to respect, if only because there are cultural characteristics that directly conflict with the democratic expectation to pursue common interests. There are many cultures, perhaps all of them, that include some traits and practices that are deeply nondemocratic or antidemocratic. What, for example, about cultures that sanction slavery? Or to select a more pervasive phenomenon in our times, how can we be expected to maintain a respect for cultures that overtly oppress women? There is a wide range of cultural characteristics that might be seen as oppressive of women, from the compulsory veil, to the denial to women of social goods from driver's licenses to education, to forced teenage marriages, to genital mutilation, to wife beating and even murder.

This is an important question because it goes to the heart of what it means to respect cultures and therefore to what it means to behave democratically. The first point to be made is that respect for a culture does not imply the acceptance, never mind endorsement, of every practice of that culture. There are no grounds on which those of us at home in Western liberal democracies can be expected to condone the stoning to death of a woman for unfaithfulness to her husband, for example, or the murder of a young woman by her family members because she has dishonored them by being raped or abducted. Our abhorrence of such practices does not, however, mean that we have a reason to reject the culture as a whole. The same is true with respect to cultural practices that are less egregious but nonetheless still oppressive, like denying to girls the opportunity to go to school. We may rightly oppose the practice but not the culture that practices it. Other examples make the point even more clearly. Denying women the opportunity to drive is clearly a form of male domination and to that extent unacceptable from a Western liberal point of view. Forcing men and women to segregate themselves during religious services, as is the case in Orthodox Jewish and Muslim communities, also has the look of unacceptable male domination from a Western liberal point of view. Even if we oppose such practices, however, we would not, and should not, dismiss as generally improper the Orthodox Jewish and Muslim cultures in general. Presumably, Orthodox Jews and Muslims may find equally objectionable the practice in liberal societies of some men encouraging women to participate in beauty pageants and assisting them in the contests. Many in liberal societies also object, but it would make little sense, and it would not be appropriate, to dismiss Western liberal culture in general as unacceptable. The range of practices directed against women in many, perhaps all, cultures is a useful example because such practices are extensive in our own time, and they provide a useful illustration of the point that it is plausible to object to specific culturally bound practices while still respecting a culture as a whole. Beyond that, though, there is nothing special about practices that oppress women, in the sense that we might have chosen other kinds of objectionable practices—for example, concerning race or ethnicity or sexual orientation—to make the same point.

It is certainly possible that there might be a culture that requires for its existence and identity a practice that we cannot accept, in which case we may want to say that the culture in general is intolerable. There are many who might still say, for example, that antebellum American culture in the southern states was so dependent on slavery that the culture itself was corrupted beyond redemption. However, even in such a case it would not follow that all aspects, practices, and products of that culture were or are condemnable. That is the reason that we can condemn slavery, and a political economy and culture predicated on it, while still admiring a literature, architecture, and even political theory that emerged from it.

So it is clear that it is possible to have good reason to object to a cultural practice, even to object in the strongest terms, but still not reject overall the culture that includes it. Furthermore, it is possible to reject as unworthy or unacceptable a culture that requires for its existence a practice that itself cannot be accepted while still respecting aspects of that culture, or indeed the culture as a whole. These two points combined help us to understand what it means to say that a component of a democratic responsibility is to respect other cultures, even those with which we may have the strongest disagreements. Of course not to reject a culture as a whole, or aspects of it, is not equivalent to maintaining respect for it. To claim as we do that respect is in order, there must be additional motivation. That additional motivation, or rationale, is the value, indeed the necessity, of fruitful interaction. On the grounds that it is inappropriate for men to patronize women, we might object to the pervasive Ukrainian custom that at virtually any gathering the second toast should be to the women present—to their beauty, wisdom, and general virtue and value. But if we wish to communicate to any good effect with Ukrainians, it is necessary to interact with respect, notwithstanding any customs we may regard as patronizing. It is also worthwhile to recognize that Ukrainian women will, for the most part, not take this custom to be patronizing, any more than Russian women will regard receiving flowers and special attention on March 8, which is International Women's Day, to be patronizing. There is a danger on the part of some of us, too frequently indulged in, to engage in a certain degree of imposition of our own sense of propriety when interacting with people from other places, cultures, and practices. Far too often such imposition is, regardless of the sense of moral virtue that motivates it, an expression of an arrogance and self-superiority that others find insulting and that can have the unintended effect of inhibiting rather than enabling communication.

Examples like toasting women, or following common practices on International Women's Day, are trivial compared with oppressive and deadly cultural practices of the kind we have mentioned. Even in the latter cases, though, the value of fruitful communication suggests that we interact with people out of respect and with a recognition of their dignity regardless of what we may think of their customs and commitments. The alternative is to act out of a sense of one's own moral superiority, and no one responds well to that. If, as we have been urging, the democratic responsibility is to pursue and where necessary seek to create common and shared interests, then a necessary condition of such interaction is to deal with people out of respect for them as individuals and for the cultures they represent, reflect, or embody. Such behavior is relatively easy when interacting with those whom we might be able to regard as friends. It is much more difficult when interacting with those whom we regard as enemies, or who engage in or defend practices we find abhorrent. Easy or difficult, it remains the democratic expectation and obligation for the simple reason that the alternative impedes communication and fruitful interaction.

Dewey was clear that democracy as he understood it, and as we understand it here, has its roots in community. In *Democracy and Education* he derives the basic characteristics of democracy from the basic traits of communities, and they are, fundamentally, the collaborative pursuit of common interests. This is the reason that Dewey in effect identifies democracy with community. He extends the observation, however, to say that a community cannot remain self-enclosed and isolated from those around it. The same processes and habits of mind that bind a community together must, if the community itself is to prosper, be extended beyond the confines of the community, beyond its boundaries. Because among the boundaries that circumscribe our various forms of communities are national boundaries, democracy means in its core the pursuit by members of a democratic society of common interests with the people of other nations and their institutions. This is the sense in which cosmopolitanism is part and parcel of democracy, and if democracy can be identified, as Dewey does, with community, then it can equally well be identified with cosmopolitanism.

So we have identified three aspects of cosmopolitanism: (1) It is a central trait of democracy; (2) it is therefore a democratic responsibility; and (3) it means the sustained attempt to develop and pursue common interests across national borders. In the exercise of this democratic responsibility we can expect to embody other distinctive traits of a democratic society and way of life. There are two that are especially important: fallibilism and experimentalism.

I began this chapter by pointing out that recent military and political adventures by a few of the leading liberal democracies have placed democracy itself in a precarious position in the contemporary world. One of the reasons this has happened is that the leadership in the United States and elsewhere has allowed ideological rather than democratic principles to drive its policy decisions. Ideology, by which I mean the tenacious commitment to a set of principles in the face of experience and evidence that may suggest otherwise, is in fact one of the most profound dangers for a democratic society. In the twentieth century it strangled whatever democratic potential socialism may have had, and now it threatens the viability even of liberal democracy. A rigid commitment to and insistence on the adequacy of one's ideas, principles, and policies make it unlikely that one will revise them when events do not go as predicted or expected, and they make it less likely that new problems will be adequately understood and that solutions to them will be found.

The democratic alternative to ideological commitment and tenacity is fallibilism and experimentalism. Fallibilism means simply the assumption that even our most cherished ideas and values may be mistaken, or at least that they may need revision in the face of change in our individual and social environments. Our ideas and principles are not rock-solid foundations on which we stand; they are tools with which we make our way through our lives. And any tool can become dull and lose its effectiveness if and when the material on which it is put to work changes its characteristics. If new material appears that is harder or more resistant than that with which we are accustomed to deal, our tools need to be sharpened, improved, or even replaced with something more appropriate to the changed nature of the task we face. To understand ideas through this metaphor of course raises a set of epistemological questions and problems, with which pragmatist philosophers have engaged themselves for more than a century. We do not need to rehearse all of that here, so let us take it as an operative assumption that a plausible instrumentalist understanding of ideas and principles can be reasonably sustained.

If we embrace such an instrumentalist conception of ideas and principles, then fallibilism is a natural approach for us to take. That it is also an important aspect of democracy results from the fact that a democratic society is one in which its members individually and collectively engage the problems they face with an eye toward their resolution and the maintenance of conditions that are conducive to individual and social development. To achieve this end in any sort of sustainable way we must be willing and able to examine our ideas, principles, and habits and revise them as needed. The cosmopolitan principle embodies this same understanding and approach. To pursue common interests with people and nations beyond our own requires that we at least be willing to examine critically the principles and commitments that we bring to the process. It also requires that we be willing, and even eager, to try to understand the world and whatever problems we face from the point or points of view that our partners bring to the process. And it requires, in the process of identifying and developing common interests with others, that we be willing and able to revise those with which we began. These predispositions that the pursuit of common interests requires are precisely what it would mean to take fallibilism seriously. To attempt to interact with others toward any kind of common end, or with a common purpose, without such fallibilist predispositions would doom the process to failure. This is the reason that the government in the United States has as much difficulty as it does in its foreign policy. It too often operates with ideological and very much undemocratic and noncosmopolitan purposes. Even when there is an inclination to change course, as the Obama administration has said it has, it is very difficult to do. One of the primary reasons it is so difficult is that in its political culture the United States, and I suspect most other nations as well, is generally not prepared to act as if prior decisions might have been mistaken or at least are no longer operable. We have not, in other words, learned the lesson of fallibilism in our politics and public policy.

If the cosmopolitan principle embodies a democratic fallibilism, then it equally well embodies a democratic experimentalism. To the extent that it means exploring new forms of interaction with international partners, cosmopolitanism is itself an experiment. If we consider foreign policy to illustrate the point, there are painfully few examples of cases in which nation states have set aside their internally developed interests to seek common ground with other states. The most outstanding case in which this has been done is the European Union, in which a growing number of nations have willingly and in some cases eagerly set aside internally determined interests in pursuit of common interests and common ends with their neighbors. And whatever else it is, the European Union is a grand experiment, the outcome of which remains uncertain.

However it turns out, the European instinct is the right one. Despite being bogged down in its own bureaucracy, it is experimenting; it is trying policies that have not been attempted before in an effort to develop new solutions to new problems. Sometimes the experiments fail—consider the fate of the proposed constitution, not to mention the current problems in the Eurozone—but they are succeeding more than they are failing, and that so far is the EU's great achievement. Such an experimental frame of mind is the sort of mood that the cosmopolitan principle calls for, and as should be clear by now, it is also an appropriate trait of a vibrant democracy. It may be thought that experimentalism in social policy and practice is impossible, and there are obvious reasons for this suspicion. One can experiment in the laboratory, or in the context of psychological and other social studies, because it is possible in those cases to frame the context of the experiment carefully. One can, for example, set up control groups, structure the experiment to address only the hypotheses in question, and so forth. The situation in social policy is never this clean, and therefore the methodological principles of experimentation cannot be applied. This is true enough, but it is also true that in practice our social policies are experiments regardless of the complexity of the situations in which they are applied, as I have argued in an earlier chapter. They are not "cleanly" experimental, as they can be in a laboratory or in a psychological study, but they are undertaken without any certainty that they will succeed. We may have good reasons in any particular case to believe that a specific policy will produce the desired outcome, but we are frequently mistaken; policy experiments often enough fail. This then becomes a problem not only because the initial problem has not been solved, but also because we have not developed the social habits that allow us to acknowledge failure and try something new. If we were to do so, as difficult as that would no doubt be, we would be far better off.

We may still ask at this point what we can expect cosmopolitanism to help us achieve. The obvious first item on the list, because it is built into the definition of cosmopolitanism, would be common interests. It may be obvious, but its significance should not be underestimated, particularly given certain features of the contemporary world. As the processes of globalization transform nearly every feature of our lives, from the economy to medicine to art, science, and education, the significance of the traditional nation state is fairly rapidly decreasing. Unfortunately, the relations among nation states have not yet caught up with this transformation. In a world as interrelated as ours is it is potentially catastrophic for nations to continue to interact with one another as they have throughout the roughly 400 years since they developed. The member states of the European Union appear to understand this, but other states are slower to catch on. In the area of foreign policy the world will be a safer place for all of us to the extent that governments adopt the cosmopolitan principle and begin to work with one another in the pursuit of shared interests and their realization.

In order for the pursuit of shared interests to produce fruitful results in commerce, education, research, foreign policy, and other fields, there must be other changes in our habits and practices. The cosmopolitanism we are defending here is conducive, for example, to increased and more refined communication. This is a good in itself, but it is also a condition of the ongoing development of democratic social relations both within any community and among communities. In turn, putting into practice the cosmopolitan principle will lead to democratic development overall. Democracy is not a fixed and stable condition. It is quite capable of being eroded, degraded, and of turning into something else. Even currently democratic societies will benefit from practices and policies that exercise the crucial characteristics of democratic communities. Furthermore, with respect to international relations, democracies behave best when they lead by example. A serious cosmopolitanism is the best example we can provide, and the way most likely to attract other peoples to democratic social and political structures that are conducive to their own individual and social development. To the extent that they embody the traits of democracy and cosmopolitanism that we have been describing—common interests, experimentalism, fallibilism, communication, and so forth—such structures carry with them a deeper respect for human integrity and human rights, however we might define them. And in the end, as the model of the European Union suggests to us, democratic development and the pursuit of shared interests across borders, and a foreign policy that exemplifies these values, are more conducive than any alternative to the prospects for peace.

To put to work the cosmopolitan principle is no easy matter. We have talked about it in general terms, pointing out its centrality to democracy, its meaning, and its pragmatic justification. But we have not considered the obstacles to policy development along cosmopolitan lines, and there are many. There is, first, the fact that the principle itself is little understood by many people, including national leaders, especially its democratic importance. Second, in many nations, including and perhaps especially the United States, it is difficult for policy makers and influential thinkers to accept the prospect of setting aside national interests in pursuit of common interests with other nations. Third, and perhaps most seriously, there is the fact that the world includes both nations and nonnational forces that have other agendas than the development of shared interests with us. How we are to interact with them presents a distinct challenge to cosmopolitanism. But as serious as this challenge is, it does not count against cosmopolitanism as a critical democratic value. It simply points out that in its application we must grapple with the world as it is, and not as we would like it to be in theory.

Notwithstanding such difficulties, the fact remains, or so I have argued, that the cosmopolitan principle, grounded in an instrumental, Deweyan understanding of democracy, is a crucial component of our interactions with one another and of democratic development in general.

Humanism

Pragmatic naturalist democratic principles suggest cosmopolitanism. They also suggest humanism. It would be highly inappropriate to claim that there is a single philosophical basis or underpinning of humanism. Humanism is a rather large tent, and there are in fact many ways into it. There is a religious or theologically based humanism, roughly on the grounds that life and its material conditions are a gift to people and we have a religious responsibility to care for the conditions and make the most of our lives. There is also agnostic and secular forms of humanism. And of course there are theological, agnostic, and secular ways of living and thinking that are anything but humanistic. The point is that there is not a neat correlation between a particular underlying philosophical perspective and humanism. We would not want to say that pragmatic naturalism and humanism imply one another, for example, so it is probably fair to say that I would like to speak not about "the" philosophical background of humanism but about "one possible" such background.

Basically, humanism is the view, in part, that our problems, whether they be personal, social, political, environmental, or any other sort, are of our own making, or are simply consequences of the circumstances we find ourselves in, and that the problems are ours to solve. Furthermore, the principles on which we act, or on which we say we should act, are themselves of our own making. There is room to differ on this point given the possibility of a theological humanism, but the humanism I am discussing here includes this point. There is a great deal of room for interpretation and disagreement in a conception of this breadth. For one thing, there is disagreement about what counts as a problem. For some people the mere existence of dire poverty is a problem, but for others it is only a problem if it directly affects them. Sensibilities in this respect can be quite different. And even if it is a problem, whose problem is it? To say, as we have, that it is "ours" is simply a way of saying that from a humanistic point of view we cannot expect the solutions to come from anything other than a human source. But that does not help us to decide, for example, whether the responsibility to solve the problem is individual or social. Do we address poverty by making individual donations to relief agencies, or is our responsibility on something of a broader, more social scale, wherein we should be seeking to bring about social, political, and economic policies, national or international, that we have reason to believe will address the problem? And even if the latter is accepted, there is wide disagreement about which policies would produce that end and therefore about which policies it would be appropriate to pursue.

So the defining characteristics of humanism in terms of the natural source of our circumstances, the natural source of our solutions, and indeed the natural source of the principles on which we act, generate at least as many questions as they answer. But we do find ourselves pointed in a conceptual direction here, and that is to the "natural" context of our lives, and it is this "naturalness" that I would like to focus on as a philosophical basis of a coherent humanism.

The natural context of human being has produced a rather paradoxical situation in contemporary philosophical life. On the one hand a naturalistic weltanschauung is out of fashion as a point of departure for technical philosophical thinking. The most common use of the term "naturalism" in philosophy, as we have noted at several points, refers to the view that all genuine knowledge derives in one way or another from the natural sciences, or at least that "naturalism" means an identification of nature with the material world and its access through science, an idea that has its roots in Quine and others. This, however, is an overly narrow conception of knowledge and rests on a grossly truncated understanding of nature, as we have been at pains to illustrate throughout. The paradox is that philosophers and scientists on the whole assume a kind of naturalism despite the fact that as a general philosophical perspective naturalism in a broad sense is out of fashion, given the general acceptance of the methods of science, both natural and social. Though probably most of us, that is to say most philosophers and Western liberal intellectuals, are naturalists by instinct, very few of us actually do philosophy in the context of an explicitly articulated conception of nature and its implications. This is the paradox. Its relevance for humanism, or so I want to suggest, is that if we were to think more explicitly in naturalist terms, or more precisely pragmatic naturalist terms, we would as a result be able to develop, express, and justify a robust humanism.

It would perhaps not be too repetitive to indicate again that the key concept, or conceptual point of departure, is the idea of nature itself. There is a fair bit one can say about nature, though as it turns out it appears impossible to give it an adequate definition. The reason for this is that part of the role of a definition is to distinguish the thing being defined from other related terms or objects. In the case of nature, though, we are driven to say that nature is "whatever there is," i.e., that nature consists of everything. In that case, the only contrast to nature is something that the conception already relegates to the imaginary, i.e., a non- or supernatural. If nature is everything, then there is nothing by contrast with which it can be defined.

But this is not as hollow as it may sound. If the only contrast to nature is the non- or supernatural, and if we have said that the non- or supernatural does not exist anyway, other than in imagination, then whatever we encounter in experience is fully natural. And because we encounter far more in experience than simply physical objects, we can say of nature that it is not limited to the physical. Dreams, fictions, mathematical entities, principles of logic, ideals, ethical principles, individuals, societies, histories, space, time, objects big and small, what we encounter and what we produce—all are constituents of nature. The previous chapters provide an illustration of the meaning and usefulness of this point. This implies not only that nature consists of far more than simply the material world, but also that the means and methods by which we come to know and understand nature are not limited to the methods and procedures of the sciences. This is the reason that the more common contemporary philosophical, scientistic naturalism is insufficient.

To illustrate the point, if photons and molecules are no more constituents of nature than color, sound, and language, then physics and chemistry are no more encounters with nature than are painting, music, and poetry. All of them are ways in which we interact with constituents of our natural environments. In fact they are not only interactions, but they are judgments on those environments in the sense that we methodically select and manipulate aspects of our environments toward specific ends. In some cases those ends are experimental, in some cases they are deductive, in others they reveal traits and relations otherwise unnoticed—for example, the way light at different times of the day affects the cathedral at Rouen, or the consequence of certain harmonic and rhythmic juxtapositions. All these forms of interaction and manipulation bring to light, in some cases create, meaningful traits of nature of which we heretofore were not aware. In this sense the arts no less than the sciences are meaningful and cognitive activities. If understood this way, then nature must be available to us in far more ways than the sciences allow.

So to understand nature in the all-encompassing sense we have suggested turns out to have extensive implications. At this point the relevant question is what those implications are for a practically valuable humanism. I say "practically valuable" because we need to be dealing in the realm of the practical ramifications of our ideas and not simply the theoretical. This turns out to sit comfortably with philosophical naturalism because naturalism of the sort we have been explicating is a pragmatic enterprise. In the end, naturalism, or more properly pragmatic naturalism, is justifiable only on pragmatic grounds. There are no valid arguments, deductive or inductive, that end with the proposition "therefore naturalism is true." One of the reasons for this is that there are no valid arguments, deductive or inductive, that lead to the proposition that any particular philosophical point of view or framework is true. Philosophical perspectives, as paradoxical as it may sound, do not rest on valid argument. They make use of argument as a method of inquiry to be sure, but they are not themselves justified by argument. This is the reason that there exist so many different philosophical points of view and methods of philosophical inquiry. If deciding among differing philosophical approaches were simply a matter of argument we would have resolved the debates among them by now, and philosophy would look a lot like mathematics. But the debates are not resolved, and philosophy, no matter how hard some of its practitioners try, is not mathematics.

If a philosophical point of view is not justifiable by argument then its valuation, if it is to be anything but arbitrary, has to be pragmatic. A philosophical point of view is as good as its results, and this applies to naturalism no less than to any other. The difference is that pragmatic naturalism understands this point and does not operate under any illusions about it. For our purposes, if humanism is to be an aspect of pragmatic naturalism, then it too must be a matter of practice in some meaningful sense, and its value is to be determined by its practical implications. What might those be?

On the face of it, there is some evidence that to approach our world and its problems in a humanistic way is well worth a serious try. The evidence is that the alternative has failed miserably. A supernaturalistic theistic approach to ethics and to action has over the millennia brought us some of the most dreadful individual and collective behavior in all our historical experience. This is not evidence against theism, I should point out, any more than the disastrous consequences of French imperialism in the Napoleonic period are an argument against the republicanism that led to it. But it is evidence that the widely held belief that without a divine source of its values, human life and action are condemned to be unprincipled, is questionable. Our experience suggests that the opposite is at least as likely to be true, i.e., that a belief in the divine source of one's principles and actions contributes to the unprincipled character of our behavior. This may be a bit surprising to many, but the reason is not hard to see. If one believes that one is in possession of the ultimate truth, then any behavior no matter how outrageous is or can be justified in its defense and advancement. We have enough evidence that this is precisely how people have thought and behaved on countless occasions over the centuries, to be more than suspicious about divine sources of inspiration, principles, and truths.

And if our experience in the past is not sufficient evidence of a practical failure of religiously based ethics and action, our current experience provides still more. Fundamentalist Islam is making a hash out of a good part of the world, and fundamentalist Christianity seems more than happy to go along. Fundamentalist Judaism contributes to the simmering and frequently explosive set of problems in and around Israel that feed into the general difficulties in the Middle East, and fundamentalist Hinduism fans the flames of violence in India and Kashmir. Each of these groups of people has God on its side, each is absolutely certain of the righteousness of its cause and action, and each is plunging the rest of us headlong into disaster. In any other case such disastrous outcomes would make us question whether a revision in approach might not be in order.

One could certainly point out that religious fundamentalism has not been the only source of outrageous behavior in recent and current experience. Political ideologies, even secular ones, have brought about similar results, as have deeply rooted nationalist and ethnic identifications and commitments. One would be quite right to point this out, and the comparisons would be instructive. American imperialism brought us the genocidal wars on the Native American populations; Stalin's Soviet Union brought us the Ukrainian famine, wholesale murder and assassinations, and millions disappearing into the labor camps; Pol Pot's "socialism" brought us Cambodia's tragedy; and then there are Rwanda and Darfur. But all of these examples have something in common with fundamentalist theocratic behavior, and that is absolute certainty on the part of the primary actors in the rightness of their cause and their methods, and this is the problem.

One of the traits that humanism absorbs from its pragmatic naturalist source is fallibilism and experimentalism, as we have noted in the previous section. As every scientist knows, in any particular case we might be wrong, and we must therefore be prepared to revise our ideas, our principles, and our actions according to the adequacy of their consequences. In practice we do not always follow this principle as carefully as we ought to, but at least our underlying conceptual commitments encourage, indeed require, us to do so. Political ideologies such as Stalin's socialism or America's imperialism did not incorporate such a fallibilism; neither does fundamentalist religion.

Not all religion is fundamentalist, of course, and one might suggest that a more humanistic approach to religion would not embody this problem. Perhaps not, and in fact just such a point is what allows for a religiously based humanism. But it is worth noticing that no religious belief, at least among the major monotheistic religions that ground themselves in what they believe to be divine revelation, can be fallibilist on pain of self-contradiction. I will leave it to the theologians to work out this problem.

So a case for a humanist approach to our contemporary world is that it would allow us to apply creative and experimental methods to the problems we face. This is no small matter, particularly because at least some of the problems we face are new in our historical experience and therefore require creativity and experimentalism. The problem of the availability of energy is profoundly important and profoundly difficult. It is also one that has no precedent in our experience. The same is true of the problem of global warming and the distinct possibility that we are in the process of making the planet itself uninhabitable regardless of what energy sources we might find and secure. The crisis in the availability of clean drinking water is another. It has been estimated that half the hospital beds in the world would be empty if there were adequate drinking water available. In none of these cases will our traditional habits of insisting on preconceived ideas, and ignoring whatever is not convenient to see, allow us to approach the problems with any hope of resolving them. Only a willingness to apply and test creative approaches will give us any chance of solving these and other serious problems.

This is the pragmatic argument for humanism and for the naturalism that underscores it. The point of course is not that pragmatic naturalism and humanism have built into them ready-made solutions to anything. They do not. The point is that if we are willing to think and act on the assumption that we are responsible for the problems and for their solutions, and only in this case, we will have a fighting chance of dealing with them. Otherwise we will likely see just more of the same, and that we cannot afford to do.

At a philosophical level there is always more to do and to say. As was pointed out earlier, many people believe that without a divine source there is no adequate ground for ethical principle. It is incumbent upon naturalist and humanist ethicists to demonstrate that this is not true, and that in fact a secular ethics is possible. Fortunately, this process has been underway for a long time, and there is a rich body of literature attesting not only to the possibility of a naturalist ethics but to its substance as well. There are also epistemological issues that continue to invite our attention. We have passed lightly over the point that valuation is and must be pragmatic, but in fact there are more than a few conceptual problems with this view. How, for example, are we to determine what is to count as verification? When do we know whether an idea or an action "works"? Is the criterion individual or social? Is it psychological or material? These are issues that pragmatic naturalist and humanist philosophers have been working on since Peirce and James, and they continue to do so. Pragmatic naturalism is not a finished set of ideas that one can simply pull from one's pocket and put to work.

Neither is humanism. In this sense humanism is not, as its detractors like to claim, simply a "secular religion." It is not a set of beliefs and principles to be applied. If anything it is a set of beliefs and principles that need to be examined, refined, in some cases rejected, and above all to be applied carefully and with eyes wide open. I confess to a certain degree of pessimism in this respect, only because absolutist assumptions and conceptions are so deeply rooted in our habits. Consider how easily the neoconservative ideology pushed a nation to war in the face of all evidence as to its likely outcome. At the time too many Americans believed what they wanted to believe. A serious commitment to humanism, as I have described it here, makes such behavior less likely, or at least its fallibilism and experimentalism should make it less likely. And that is the strongest argument in its favor.

CONCLUSION

Pragmatic Naturalism and the Big Narrative

Hamlet reproached Horatio for failing to account for ghosts in his philosophy. We of course should not be too hard on Horatio because most of the rest of us would until now not have been able to account for ghosts either, not to mention any number of other features of many people's experience.

In fact in this respect Horatio finds himself in the same position as most other thinkers in the history of philosophy, East and West. Plato had trouble with the natural world, and had to reduce it metaphorically to shadows and caves; Aristotle like Plato had trouble with change, and so froze all natural kinds into eternal forms; the Christian philosophers and theologians did not know what to make of the natural world, metaphysically or morally, so they reduced it to a vaguely understood realm of lesser being, whatever that means; and similar conceptions pervaded the rest of philosophy, particularly in the Islamic world, India, and China, with the possible exception of Confucianism.

And lest we think that these confusions have been cleared up in the modern world of science and mathematics, keep in mind that the seventeenth- and eighteenth-century philosophers so atomized the natural world that something as simple as the fact that eating ice cream makes me happy became a fundamental philosophical problem, and various approaches have been adopted to deal with it. Some despaired of the possibility of explaining how the ice cream and I can be so related; others denied the ice cream and replaced it with the idea of ice cream; others reduced the ice cream to a set of sense perceptions and my happy self to a bundle of perceptions; still others declared my inability to know what ice cream is, but only to know how ice cream appears to me; later the tables are turned, and ice cream becomes knowable while my pleasure is reduced to brain events; and most recently, some have thrown up their hands in a final gesture of frustration and declared it pointless even to care to inquire into the philosophical character of ice cream, of me, and of the relation between us!

Ideally it is clear by now that none of these distortions or frustrations, and many others like them in the history of philosophy, is necessary. The ghost that so surprised Horatio is no more of an ontological problem for us than the monster in the child's closet or Santa Claus. The same may and should be said of Hamlet and Horatio themselves, the world of experience, change and stability, matter and mind, individuals and societies, complexity and simplicity, the multiple avenues of knowledge, objectivity and creativity, faith, nation states, democratic policy, and all the rest of the innumerable phenomena, whatever they may be, with which we interact in ordinary or intellectualized experience.

Despite the rhetorical tenor of these remarks, though, they are not to be taken as an appeal to "common sense." That is to say, we should not expect to resolve philosophical questions or problems of social action and policy through common sense any more than we can expect to resolve scientific questions simply through direct experience. Common sense is not a method of inquiry or query, though it can well serve as a barometer when our thinking begins to go off the rails. What is needed in the approach to philosophical questions and social issues is not so much common sense but a sensible philosophy, one that is able to handle tricky philosophical matters without forcing us into experientially absurd propositions and points of view. This is why we cannot simply insist on the unreality of the monster in the closet in the face of a child's terror, nor can we think away the importance of religious experience as wish fulfillment or the need for a father figure. Our common experience has an integrity that our philosophical conceptions have not sufficiently appreciated.

We are in need of a set of philosophical ideas and directions that enable us to offer plausible conceptions of things that allow us to integrate the things in heaven and earth in all their integrity. We have made the case that pragmatic naturalism as described and developed here is such a set of ideas and directions. It may not be the only such set of ideas and directions, but it is at least one of them. More specifically, an ontology of constitutive relations and a rich theory of judgment allow us to meet the demands of philosophical rigor and experiential fidelity. Furthermore, this general philosophic conception commits us to pragmatic valuation. Beyond needing to demonstrate a sufficient degree of plausibility and reasonableness, the adequacy of pragmatic naturalism turns on its acceptability in practice, which is to say the usefulness of the work it does in application. Thus, we have gone to considerable trouble to explore what happens when we think through more specific dimensions of experience with these ideas in mind—religion and faith, art, democracy, education, the nation state, foreign policy and international relations, and the moral character of the humanism and cosmopolitanism that pragmatic naturalism suggests. If our treatment of these matters recommends itself then we have to that extent justified the philosophical value of pragmatic naturalism. The reader may now be in a better position to judge whether this project is a success.

Of course there remain many questions, theoretical and practical, that philosophers may and should profitably address. Some of them were mentioned earlier in reference to the work being done by others in the pragmatic naturalist tradition. One question we have not addressed but should has to do with the "Americanism" of pragmatic naturalism and what bearing that may have on its value. It is clear enough that in the current globalized world, no philosophical conception that is bound too closely to a single place will have much value in a larger context, and the "things in heaven and earth" certainly counts as a large context. So we have the obvious question: Is there something American about pragmatic naturalism that renders it unsuitable elsewhere in the world?

There is more than one way to approach this question. For one thing, there is the fact that many cultures have intellectual traditions that are more or less indigenous and that are properly identified with their national places of origin. We can speak of the French philosophy of existentialism, structuralism, and more recently of deconstruction and the several versions of postmodernism. We may also speak of German and Austrian philosophy, and include Kantianism, Hegelianism, neo-Kantianism, positivism, and phenomenology. There are British empiricism and Russian religious thought. Confucianism is certainly Chinese, and Vedantic thought is clearly enough Indian. Some of these traditions have exported quite easily. Much philosophy in America, Canada, and Australia, not to mention Latin America, including pragmatic naturalism, is influenced by British, German, and French traditions, and early twentieth-century Japanese philosophy is overtly neo-Kantian and phenomenological. Indian Vedantism and Russian religious philosophy, more or less orthodox, have traveled less well, largely I imagine due to their close ties to the religious traditions of their homes. Confucianism has not traveled well either, probably because of its close ties to historical Chinese social structure. It is clear, though, that under some circumstances it is easy enough for philosophical perspectives indigenous to one culture to be appropriated by others. Pragmatic naturalism, by virtue at least of its roots in broader European traditions, appears to be more like the British, German, and French cases than the Russian, Indian, or Chinese.

We should also note that pragmatic naturalism has been for some years attracting increased attention by scholars outside the United States. Of course, even in the early twentieth century there were several prominent European philosophers within the pragmatist school, and Dewey's influence in China is well known. It is also well known that Dewey himself was invited around the world by scholars and governments, including to the Soviet Union, Japan, China, and Turkey, and his work in those countries is remembered today. There was a strong tradition during the Cold War years in the Soviet Union of studies in American philosophy, primarily pragmatism.[1] In the past decade alone the study of pragmatism and naturalism in Europe has sparked a number of organizations and regular conferences dedicated to enabling American and European scholars to explore the history and applicability of these traditions. The

Central European Pragmatist Forum is one such organization, and similar groups have developed in Italy, Spain, the Netherlands, Hungary, and Scandinavia. Annual or biannual conferences devoted to American philosophy in the pragmatic naturalist tradition have become commonplace in Romania and Poland, and these organizations and conferences are publishing their work in journals and books. If scholarly interest is a criterion, then the question of whether American pragmatic naturalism can travel is answered.[2]

It is an interesting question why this is happening. One possible answer, at least with respect to Central Europe, is that the demise of the ancien régime created both the intellectual space and the practical need for new ideas, and in such conditions it is natural to look to established traditions for possibilities. Another possible answer has to do with the nature of the European Union. If it is, as we have suggested, an experiment in the kind of international behavior to which pragmatic naturalism points, then it would be natural that those dealing with issues and problems within it would find congenial a philosophic perspective that accords with their circumstances.

I suspect that there is, though, an additional reason for the current interest in pragmatic naturalism in the United States and abroad, and that has to do with the demise of ideology. That is not to say that ideology is no longer a force. Religious ideology is alive and strong in many parts of the world, the United States included. But at the same time, for an increasing number of people, scholars and policy makers alike, the grand narratives, to use Lyotard's term with which we are all familiar, have lost their appeal. The late Tony Judt makes this point in his study of Europe after the Second World War.[3] Given the state Europe found itself in after 1945, it is little wonder that some of the narratives that had driven it to near suicide were discredited. Forty years later, the other grand narrative that fed European life underwent its own demise, and it will not recover in anything like its previous form, if it recovers at all. Lyotard's insightful term, and his point that it is largely behind us, applies to far more than philosophy and intellectual life.

Ironically, an exception to this general observation is the United States itself. A potentially tragic American political mistake is to continue to present itself as the last "big narrative" standing; as the end of history; as the expression of the final hopes of humankind. Fortunately, there are few people outside the United States who accept this particular narrative. Ironically, though its origins and development are decidedly American, pragmatic naturalism is an intellectual, philosophical framework that belongs in and to a world without big narratives. In this sense it is not revolutionary, i.e., it does not overthrow an old narrative to replace it with a new one. If we must, it is "postrevolutionary," in that its place is a world in which the period of revolutions is over, in which we no longer seek to replace one big narrative with another. In its social and political ramifications, for example, it is not "the" philosophy of democracy, which would be just another big narrative. It is an alternative to ideology, one that can profitably be put to use in any cultural situation. It will be different in differing cultural circumstances. A Chinese pragmatic naturalism will have to weave into itself strains of Confucianism, not because it must do so to survive in a Chinese context but because the Chinese context is Confucian. In an American context pragmatic naturalism is for similar reasons necessarily liberal.

The place of pragmatic naturalism is anywhere in the world that has broken free of the bonds of religious or political ideology and that has problems to be solved. If the United States continues to understand itself within a "big narrative" framework—for example, as the missionary of democracy—then pragmatic naturalism will have no comfortable home there, despite its origins. Pragmatic naturalism has its place wherever there are intellectuals and policy makers honestly confronting their worlds and their experience, without insisting a priori what must be there and what story it must be made to tell; it has a home wherever there are problems to be solved, with a desire to do so reflectively, experimentally, and honestly.

Of course, in order to be of value pragmatic naturalism must be a reasonable and conceptually plausible point of view and angle of vision. This book has been an effort to make the case that it is, and to consider how it might be put to good use.

Notes

INTRODUCTION

1. Richard J. Bernstein, *The Pragmatic Turn* (Cambridge, U.K.: Polity Press, 2010); Joseph Margolis, *Pragmatism's Advantage* (Stanford, Ca.: Stanford University Press, 2010); Larry A. Hickman, *Pragmatism as Post-Postmodernism: Lessons from John Dewey* (New York: Fordham University Press, 2007). One might also point to the work of the late Peter H. Hare, and the "pragmatic realism" that he championed. In his development of pragmatism, Hare also drew explicitly on the Columbia Naturalist tradition, among other sources, which as the reader will see is a prominent source for this volume. For an interesting look at Hare's work through others' commentary, see A Symposium in Memory of Peter H. Hare, which occupies the entirety of *Transactions of the Charles S. Peirce Society* 46, no. 1 (Winter 2010).

2. Richard J. Bernstein, *Beyond Objectivism and Relativism: Science, Hermeneutics, and Praxis* (Philadelphia: University of Pennsylvania Press, 1983).

3. See letter from Justus Buchler to Beth Singer, reproduced in Victorino Tejera, *American Modern: The Path Not Taken* (London: Rowman and Littlefield Publishers, Inc., 1996), 153–54.

4. For example, Jennifer Welchman, *Dewey's Ethical Thought* (Ithaca, N.Y.: Cornell University Press, 1997); Paul Kurtz, *Living without Religion: Eupraxophy* (Amherst, N.Y.: Prometheus Books, 1994); Emil Višňovský, "Social Control, Self Control, and Norms: A Pragmatist Approach," in *Self and Society*, ed. Alexander Kremer and John Ryder, Central European Pragmatist Forum, vol. 4 (Amsterdam: Rodopi, 2009), 161–72; Kathleen Wallace, "Common Morality and Moral Reform," *Theoretical Medicine & Bioethics* 30, no. 17 (2009): 55–68; Gregory Fernando Pappas, *John Dewey's Ethics: Democracy as Experience* (Bloomington: Indiana University Press, 2008).

5. One may look to almost any of McDermott's works as examples. For the most recent collection, see John J. McDermott, *The Drama of Possibility: Experience as Philosophy of Culture*, ed. Douglas R. Anderson (New York: Fordham University Press, 2007). One may also look to nearly any of John Lachs's works,

including *In Love with Life: Reflections on the Joy of Living and Why We Hate to Die* (Nashville, Tenn.: Vanderbilt University Press, 2008).

6. Representative examples include John O'Neill, Alan Holland, and Andrew Light, *Environmental Values* (New York: Routledge, 2007); Paul Thompson, *The Spirit of the Soil: Agricultural and Environmental Ethics* (New York, Routledge, 1995); Erin McKenna, "Pragmatism and the Production of Livestock," in *Animal Pragmatism: Rethinking Human-Nonhuman Relationships*, ed. Erin McKenna and Andrew Light (Bloomington: Indiana University Press, 2004), 160–78; Beth J. Singer, *Pragmatism, Rights, and Democracy* (New York: Fordham University Press, 1999); Thomas Hilde, *On Torture* (Baltimore, Md.: Johns Hopkins University Press, 2008); Armen Marsoobian, "Genocide's Aftermath: Reflections on Self and Responsibility," in Kremer and Ryder, *Self and Society*, 133–40 and "Acknowledging Intergenerational Moral Responsibility in the Aftermath of Genocide," *Genocide Studies and Prevention* 4, no. 2 (August 2009): 211–20; Shannon Sullivan, *Revealing Whiteness: The Unconscious Habits of Racial Privilege* (Bloomington: Indiana University Press, 2006).

7. See, for example, Larry A. Hickman, *Philosophical Tools for Technological Culture: Putting Pragmatism to Work* (Bloomington: Indiana University Press, 2001).

8. See, for example, Charlene Haddock Seigfried, *Pragmatism and Feminism: Reweaving the Social Fabric* (Chicago: University of Chicago Press, 1996), and Marilyn Fischer, "Jane Addams's Feminist Ethics," in *Presenting Women Philosophers*, ed. C. Tougas and S. Ebenreck (Philadelphia: Temple University Press, 2000), 51–57.

9. An example of Jim Garrison's work is "Deweyan Reflections on Knowledge-Producing Schools," *Teachers College Record* 110, no. 10 (2008): 2204–23. See also Carlos Mougan Rivero, "John Dewey and the Necessity of a Democratic Civic Education," and Gert-Rüdiger Wegmarshaus, "John Dewey's Understanding of Democracy: Inspiring Political Education in Germany," both in *Education for a Democratic Society*, ed. John Ryder and Gert-Rüdiger Wegmarshaus, Central European Pragmatist Forum, vol. 3 (Amsterdam: Rodopi, 2007), 11–20 and 103–12 respectively.

10. The sources are far too numerous to mention, but the reader can get a sense of the work of each of these authors in the following: James Campbell, *Understanding John Dewey* (Chicago, Ill.: Open Court, 1995); Michael Eldridge, *Transforming Experience: John Dewey's Cultural Instrumentalism* (Nashville, Tenn.: Vanderbilt University Press, 1998); Thomas Alexander, *John Dewey's Theory of Art, Experience, and Nature: The Horizons of Feeling* (Albany: State University of New York Press, June 1987); Vincent Colapietro, *Peirce's Approach to the Self: A Semiotic Perspective on Human Subjectivity* (Albany: State University of New York Press, 1989); Hans Joas, *G. H. Mead: A Contemporary Reexami-*

nation of His Thought (Cambridge, Mass.: MIT Press, 1997); Douglas R. Anderson, *Philosophy Americana: Making Philosophy at Home in American Culture* (New York: Fordham University Press, 2006); Sami Pihlström, *The Trail of the Human Serpent Is over Everything: Jamesian Perspectives on Mind, World and Religion* (New York: University Press of America, 2008); Scott Pratt, *Native Pragmatism* (Bloomington: Indiana University Press, 2002). Those who are able to read Russian may turn to any number of studies, one of the more recent of which is Nina S. Yulina, Очерки по философии в США. XX век. (*Notes on Twentieth-Century Philosophy in the U.S.A.*) (Moscow: Editorial, 1999).

1. RECONCILING PRAGMATISM AND NATURALISM

1. An earlier and much shorter version of this chapter was presented at a conference at the University at Buffalo in October 2000 titled The Future of Realism in the American Tradition of Pragmatic Naturalism, and in lectures at Oklahoma State University and Comenius University in Slovakia. It was published in John Shook, ed., *Pragmatic Naturalism and Realism* (Amherst, N.Y.: Prometheus Books, 2003), 55–77. It also appeared in a Slovak translation by Igor Hanzel as "Zmierenie Pragmatizmu a Naturalizmu," *Filozofia* 57, no. 2 (2002): 123–36.

2. George Santayana, *Scepticism and Animal Faith* (New York: Dover, 1955), 179.

3. There is an interesting collection of essays critical of naturalism in this sense, though after reading the articles one gets the distinct impression that the authors are not even aware of the tradition of American naturalism. See Steven J. Wagner and Richard Warner, eds., *Naturalism: A Critical Appraisal* (Notre Dame, Ind.: University of Notre Dame Press, 1993).

4. The classic text that expresses the so-called Columbia Naturalism, at least as it looked midway through the last century, is Yervant H. Krikorian, ed., *Naturalism and the Human Spirit* (New York: Columbia University Press, 1944). A half century later I collected what I took to be important but largely out-of-print pieces representative of the tradition in *American Philosophic Naturalism in the Twentieth Century* (Amherst, N.Y.: Prometheus Books, 1994). One author who has explored themes in a naturalistic context in a sense consonant with our own is Kai Nielsen. See, for example, his *Naturalism without Foundations* (Amherst, N.Y.: Prometheus Books, 1996).

5. I take it that I mean to say here something similar to what Larry A. Hickman means by "post-postmodernism," and for similar reasons. See his *Pragmatism as Post-Postmodernism.*

6. I have used these propositions in other places to make similar points. See John Ryder, "The Use and Abuse of Modernity: Postmodernism and the

American Philosophic Tradition," in *Philosophy in Experience: American Philosophy in Transition*, ed. Richard E. Hart and Douglas R. Anderson (New York: Fordham University Press, 1997), 225–40; and John Ryder, *Interpreting America: Russian and Soviet Studies of the History of American Thought* (Nashville, Tenn.: Vanderbilt University Press, 1999), 146.

7. See Justus Buchler, *Metaphysics of Natural Complexes*, 2nd ed., ed. Kathleen Wallace and Armen Marsoobian (Albany: State University of New York Press, 1990). This edition contains the full text of the first edition, along with several articles and essays in which Buchler further develops some of the book's themes. For extensive secondary discussion of Buchler's work and its impact, see Beth Singer, *Ordinal Naturalism* (Lewisburg, Pa.: Bucknell University Press, 1983), and Armen Marsoobian, Kathleen Wallace, and Robert Corrington, eds., *Nature's Perspectives: Prospects for Ordinal Metaphysics* (Albany: State University of New York Press, 1991). The reader may also profitably turn to Lawrence Cahoone, "Local Naturalism," *Contemporary Pragmatism* 6, no. 2 (December 2009): 1–23; and, for an interesting and useful discussion of Buchler and Dewey, to Thomas Alexander, "The Being of Nature: Dewey, Buchler, and the Prospect for an Eco-Ontology," *Transactions of the Charles S. Peirce Society* 46, no. 4 (Fall 2010): 544–69.

2. THE VALUE OF PRAGMATIC NATURALISM

1. A shorter version of this chapter was presented at the conference in Amherst, New York, in September 2007 on the Future of Naturalism at the Center for Inquiry, at the New York Pragmatist Forum in April 2008, and at the Central European Pragmatist Forum in Brno, Czech Republic, in May 2008. The current chapter is a revision of the published version that has appeared in *The Future of Naturalism*, ed. John Shook and Paul Kurtz (Amherst, Mass.: Humanity Books, 2009), 97–113.

2. George Santayana, "Ultimate Religion," in Ryder, *American Philosophic Naturalism*, 466–76; John Dewey, *A Common Faith*, LW 9 (Carbondale: Southern Illinois University Press, 1986). The latter is also excerpted in Ryder, *American Philosophic Naturalism*.

3. John Herman Randall Jr., *The Meaning of Religion for Man* (New York: Harper Torchbooks, 1968). See also Willard E, Arnett, "Are the Arts and Religion Cognitive?," in *Naturalism and Historical Understanding: Essays on the Philosophy of John Herman Randall Jr.*, ed. John P. Anton (Albany: State University of New York Press, 1967); Robert S. Corrington, *Nature and Spirit: An Essay in Ecstatic Naturalism* (New York: Fordham University Press, 1992), and *Ecstatic Naturalism* (Bloomington: Indiana University Press, 1994).

4. This point is particularly important because many philosophers insist on defining naturalism as a view in which everything is to be understood as exist-

ing in time and space, which is to say, as more or less material. One cannot emphasize strongly enough that this is not what naturalism means here, and it is not what the term meant in the Columbia tradition from which this account draws. For an example of the persistent contemporary inclination to treat naturalism as a kind of scientific materialism, see Elliot Sober, "Parsimony Arguments in Science and Philosophy—A Test Case for Naturalism," Romanell Lecture, *Proceedings and Addresses of the American Philosophical Association* 83, no. 2 (November 2009): 117–55. In this essay Sober points out that for many philosophers, "naturalism" posits objects "in nature," which means "things that exist in space and time." A related common understanding of naturalism is expressed in the essay, also a Romanell Lecture, immediately following in the same issue of the *APA Proceedings*: Barry Stroud, "The Transparency of Naturalism," 157–69. For Stroud, naturalism amounts to a Quinean, experimental approach to epistemology by contrast with a more traditional a priori method of examining knowledge.

5. Santayana once referred to himself as the only materialist alive. He was wrong about that, but I suspect that I am the only ordinal materialist alive, with the possible exception of Lawrence Cahoone. See John Ryder, "Ordinality and Materialism," in Marsoobian, Wallace, and Corrington, *Nature's Perspectives*, 201–20.

6. Paul Kurtz has made this point repeatedly. See, for example, his "Eupraxophy and Naturalism," in Shook and Kurtz, *Future of Naturalism*, 179–96.

7. In Chapter 7 I will pay much closer attention to the theory of judgment mentioned here. For a more developed articulation of this conception of judgment, see Justus Buchler, *Nature and Judgment* (New York: Columbia University Press, 1955).

8. See Buchler, "Probing the Idea of Nature," appendix 4 of *Metaphysics*.

9. Again, see Buchler, *Metaphysics*.

10. For an interesting critique of the current inclination to understand mind or consciousness by analogy with a computer, see Fred Evans, *Psychology and Nihilism* (Albany: State University of New York Press, 1993).

11. A good example of empirical studies in the cognitive sciences that have significant implications for philosophical understanding is George Lakoff and Mark Johnson, *Philosophy in the Flesh: The Embodied Mind and Its Challenge to Western Thought* (New York: Basic Books, 1999). Here Lakoff and Johnson make a compelling case for the claim that much of the character and structure of reason and mind is rooted in our neurophysiological structure and processes. Even here, though, the authors would have benefited from a more adequate ontology that might have prevented them from overstating the implications of cognitive science for our understanding of experience.

12. For a clear illustration of the limits of deductive argument in ethics, see Sami Pihlström, "Ethical Unthinkabilities and Philosophical Seriousness," *Metaphilosophy* 40, no. 5 (2009): 656–70.

3. AN ONTOLOGY OF CONSTITUTIVE RELATIONS

1. This chapter draws on a paper jointly written with Lyubov Bugaeva that was presented at the French–German Philosophical Colloquium in Evian, France, and subsequently published as "Constitutive Relations: A Philosophical Anthropology," *Human Affairs* 15, no. 2 (2005): 132–48.

2. The ontological categories we are describing were initially and much more thoroughly developed by Justus Buchler, primarily in his *Metaphysics of Natural Complexes*. It is interesting to note that George Herbert Mead near the end of his life developed what we may justifiable consider a proto-ordinal conception of relationality. See George Herbert Mead, *The Philosophy of the Present* (LaSalle, Ill.: Open Court, 1932). This edition includes the text of the Carus Lectures as well as five supplemental essays.

3. Ludwig Wittgenstein, *Notebooks, 1914—1916*, ed. G. H. von Wright and G. E. M. Anscombe (New York: Harper Torchbooks, 1969), 60; G. W. Leibniz *Basic Writings* (La Salle. Ill.: Open Court, 1986), 251.

4. See John Ryder, "Ordinality and Materialism," in Marsoobian, Wallace, and Corrington, *Nature's Perspectives*, 201–19.

5. On this particular point, see Justus Buchler, "On the Concept of 'the World,'" reprinted in Buchler, *Metaphysics*, 224–59.

6. The principle of ontological parity, though developed in detail by Buchler in *Metaphysics of Natural Complexes*, was anticipated by John Herman Randall Jr. in "The Nature of Metaphysics: Its Function, Criteria, and Method," Chapter 5 of *Nature and Historical Experience* (New York: Columbia University Press, 1962), 121–42. It should be pointed out as well that Randall also anticipates Buchler's idea that there is no world or nature as a single whole in "Empirical Pluralisms and Unifications of Nature," which appears as Chapter 7 of the same book, 195–214.

7. For a "metaphysics of human being" of this type, see Justus Buchler, *Toward a General Theory of Human Judgment* (New York: Columbia University Press, 1951), and *Nature and Judgment*.

8. This discussion of human being is general and intended to illustrate a relational ontology in practice. The interested reader may look to other sources for more detailed discussions. The pragmatic naturalist approach to human being and personhood owes a great deal not only to Buchler but of course also to George Herbert Mead. For more recent discussions of a relational understanding of the self, see Kathleen Wallace, "Personal Identity of an Intersectional Self," in Kremer and Ryder, *Self and Society*. See also the longer paper

on which the current chapter is based, Bugaeva and Ryder, "Constitutive Relations."

9. Thatcher made this famous remark in *Woman's Own*, October 31, 1987.

4. PARTICULARS AND RELATIONS

1. A much shorter version of this chapter was presented as "Are Particulars Relational?" Conversations in the Disciplines, Jefferson County Community College, Watertown N.Y., April 1998.

2. G. W. F. Hegel, *Logic* (New York: Oxford University Press, 1987), para. 32.

3. Hegel, *Logic*, para. 92.

4. Hegel, *Logic*, para. 119.

5. Hegel, *Logic*, para. 124.

6. Hegel, *Logic*, para. 135.

7. T. H. Green, "Introduction," vol. 1 of David Hume, *The Philosophical Works*, ed. T. H. Green and T. H. Grose (Aalen: Scientia Verlag, 1964), 36.

8. Green, "Introduction," 180.

9. F. H. Bradley, *Appearance and Reality* (Oxford: Oxford University Press, 1968), 125.

10. Bradley, *Appearance and Reality*, 18.

11. Fred Wilson, "Relations from Burgersdijk to Bradley," Conference on the Ontology and Epistemology of Relations, Buffalo, New York, September 1994. The related published version of Wilson's paper is "Burgersdijk, Bradley, Russell, Bergmann: Four Philosophers on the Ontology of Relations," *The Modern Schoolman* 72 (1995), 283–310.

12. Bertrand Russell, *Principles of Mathematics* (New York: Norton & Co, 1938), 222–23.

13. Russell, *Principles*, 224–26.

14. Russell, *Principles*, 226.

15. Bertrand Russell, *The Problems of Philosophy* (New York: Oxford University Press, 1972), 95.

16. Bertrand Russell, "Relations of Universals and Particulars," in *Logic and Knowledge*, ed. Robert C. Marsh (New York: Capricorn Books, 1971), 103–24; here 113.

17. Bertrand Russell, *Human Knowledge: Its Scope and Limits* (London: Routledge, 1992), 311.

18. Russell, *Human Knowledge*, 315. See also Bertrand Russell, *My Philosophical Development* (London: George Allen & Unwin Ltd., 1959).

19. Russell, *My Philosophical Development*, 322.

20. D. M. Armstrong, *Universals & Scientific Realism*, vol. 1, *Nominalism & Realism*; vol. 2, *A Theory of Universals* (New York: Cambridge University Press, 1990). See 1:91–97.

21. Armstrong, *Universals*, 100.
22. Armstrong, *Universals*, 114–15.
23. Armstrong, *Universals*, 19–20.
24. Armstrong, *Universals*, 70–71.
25. Armstrong, *Nominalism*, 85–86.
26. Buchler, *Metaphysics*, 96.
27. Buchler, *Metaphysics*, 204.
28. Buchler, *Metaphysics*, 224–59.
29. Russell, *Problems*, 99–100

30. It is worth mentioning that there is another tradition of nineteenth-century relationalism that is decidedly not idealist, and that is Marxism and the general dialectical materialism that developed in the hands of Soviet and other Marxist philosophers. Both Marxism and pragmatic naturalism are relational alternatives to empiricism and idealism. Consequently, it is not surprising to discover that they have a fair bit in common. On this point, see John Ryder, "Naturalism, Dialectical Materialism, and an Ontology of Constitutive Relations," in *Context over Foundation: Dewey and Marx*, ed. William Gavin (Dordrecht: Reidel Publishers, 1988), 229–54; and "Naturalizm, Dialekticheskii Materializm i Ob'ektivnost,'" Russian translation by G. R. Selivanov, *Vestnik Moskovskogo Universiteta*, Philosophy Series, no. 1 (1991): 85–90.

5. MAKING SENSE OF WORLD MAKING: CREATIVITY AND OBJECTIVITY IN NATURE

1. A much shorter version of this chapter was presented at the Fifth International Congress on Philosophy and Culture, St. Petersburg, Russia, September 2002, and appeared as "Does World Making Make Sense? Creativity and Objectivity in Nature," *International Readings on Theory, History and Culture* 15 (2003): 104–14. Sections were also presented as "Beyond Objectivism and Relativism (Again)," at the conference Confines of Democracy: The Social Philosophy of Richard Bernstein, Toledo, Spain, May 18–22, 2010.

2. Nelson Goodman, *Ways of Worldmaking* (Indianapolis: Hackett Publishing Co., 1978), 22.

3. The theme of the constructivist dimension of pragmatism has been the subject of a number of recent books, among the most noteworthy of which are Hickman, *Pragmatism*, and Larry A. Hickman, Stefan Neubert, and Kersten Reich, eds., *John Dewey between Pragmatism and Constructivism* (New York: Fordham University Press, 2009).

4. William J. Bennett, *Why We Fight: Moral Clarity and the War on Terrorism* (New York: Doubleday, 2002). See a review by Marcus Raskin, "Bennett's Pledge of Allegiance," *The Nation*, August 5/12, 2002, 33–40.

5. John Dewey, *The Quest for Certainty*, LW 4, ed. Jo Ann Boydston (Carbondale: Southern Illinois University Press, 1984).

6. Pierre Bourdieu, *The Logic of Practice* (Stanford, Ca.: Stanford University Press, 1990). See especially Chapters 1–3.

7. Santayana, *Scepticism*.

8. Paul A. Boghossian, *Fear of Knowledge: Against Relativism and Constructivism* (New York: Oxford University Press, 2006). See also an interesting review of Boghossian's book in John Searle, "Why Should You Believe It?," *New York Review of Books*, September 24, 2009, 88–92.

9. John Lachs, "Human Natures," in Ryder, *American Philosophic Naturalism*, 524–39.

10. Bruno Latour, "Ramsès II est-il mort de la tuberculose?," *La Recherche*, March 1998; Michel Foucault, *The History of Sexuality*, vol. 1: *An Introduction*, trans. Robert Hurley (New York: Pantheon Books, 1978).

11. John Dewey, *Experience and Nature*, LW 1 (Carbondale: Southern Illinois University Press, 1981), 124–25.

12. For an elaboration of this theory of judgment, see Buchler, *Nature and Judgment*.

13. Buchler, *Metaphysics*, 1.

6. GOD AND FAITH

1. This discussion of God and faith draws on and develops sections of two earlier papers. One was presented as "Ordinality and God" at the Society for the Advancement of American Philosophy at Texas A&M University in March, 1980, and subsequently published, with Peter Hare, as "Buchler's Ordinal Metaphysics and Process Philosophy," *Process Studies* 10, nos. 3 and 4 (1980): 120–29. This was later reprinted in Marsoobian, Wallace, and Corrington, *Nature's Perspectives*, 335–45. The second was presented with Lyubov Bugaeva at the Nordic Pragmatist Conference in Helsinki, Finland, in June 2008, and published as "Naturalism and Religion," with Lyubov Bugaeva, in *Pragmatist Perspectives*, ed. Sami Pihlström and Henrik Rydenfelt, Acta Philosophica Fennica, vol. 86 (Helsinki: Philosophical Society of Finland, 2009).

2. George Santayana, *Reason in Religion* (New York: Dover Publications, Inc., 1982); George Santayana, "Ultimate Religion," in Ryder, *American Philosophic Naturalism*, 466–76.

3. John Dewey, *A Common Faith*, LW 9 (Carbondale: Southern Illinois University Press, 1986). The latter is also excerpted in Ryder, *American Philosophic Naturalism*.

4. Randall, *Meaning of Religion*; See also Arnett, "Are the Arts and Religion Cognitive?," in Anton, *Naturalism and Historical Understanding*.

5. John J. McDermott, *The Culture of Experience: Philosophical Essays in the American Grain* (New York: New York University Press, 1976); *Streams of Experience: Reflections on the History and Philosophy of American Culture* (Amherst: University of Massachusetts Press, 1986); *Drama of Possibility.*

6. Corrington, *Nature and Spirit* and *Ecstatic Naturalism.*

7. Donald A. Crosby, *Living with Ambiguity: Religious Naturalism and the Menace of Evil* (Albany: State University of New York Press, 2008); and his *A Religion of Nature* (Albany: State University Press of New York, 2002).

7. ART AND KNOWLEDGE

1. Various versions of this consideration of art and knowledge have been presented on several occasions: "John Dewey at 150: Art, Culture, Society," Opole University, Poland, June 2009; the Summer Institute in American Philosophy, University of Oregon, July 2009; Faculty of Arts, Moscow State University, October 2009 and March 2010. A shorter version has appeared in "Experience, Art and Knowledge," in *The Continuing Relevance of John Dewey: Reflections on Aesthetics, Morality, Science, and Society*, ed. Larry A. Hickman, Matt Flamm, and Krzysztof Piotr Skowroński (Amsterdam: Rodopi, 2010).

2. For an interesting example of the latter, see S. Bringsjord and D. Ferrucci, *Artificial Intelligence and Literary Creativity: Inside the Mind of Brutus, A Storytelling Machine* (Mahwah, N.J.: Lawrence Erlbaum, 2000).

3. James O. Young, *Art and Knowledge* (London: Routledge, 2001.

4. Buchler uses the expression "knowledge through" to refer to poetic knowledge. See Justus Buchler, *The Main of Light* (New York: Oxford University Press, 1974), 150*ff.* See also Richard Shusterman, *Pragmatist Aesthetics* (Cambridge, Mass.: Blackwell Publishers, Inc., 1992), and *Performing Lives* (Ithaca, N.Y.: Cornell University Press, 2000).

5. Shusterman, *Pragmatist Aesthetics*, 92.

6. See Nelson Goodman, *Languages of Art* (New York: Bobbs-Merrill, 1968).

7. Good examples of this can be found in Matthew Kieran, ed., *Contemporary Debates in Aesthetics and the Philosophy of Art* (Malden, Mass.: Blackwell Publishers, Ltd, 2006). See specifically Chapter 7, Berys Gaut, "Art and Cognition," 115–26, and Chapter 8, Peter Lamarque, "Cognitive Values in the Arts: Marking the Boundaries," 127–42. For a sense of the broader possibilities of the cognitive dimension of art, one consonant with our own, see Matthew Kieran, *Revealing Art* (New York: Routledge, 2005), especially Chapter 3, "Insight in Art," 99–147.

8. See the catalog from this exhibition: *The Adventures of the Black Square* (St. Petersburg: The State Russian Museum, Palace Editions, 2007). If one were inclined to think that attributing possibility to a black shape on a canvas is an extravagance, I would point out that in this respect I am not alone, as a remark

by Barry Schwabsky in a short piece on Matisse indicates. He refers to Matisse's well known *French Window at Collioure*, and says that "the black rectangle that occupies most of the canvas is not simply a negation—the 'black future' that the poet Louis Aragon later saw there—but a latency rich with possibility." See Barry Schwabsky, "Black Is Also a Color," *The Nation*, June 21, 2010, 32–34. I of course want to claim that this possibility has something to do with knowledge, a point that Schwabsky does not make.

9. See Justus Buchler, *The Concept of Method* (New York: Columbia University Press, 1961) and *Main of Light*, 150–51.

10. See Deborah Wye, *Kirchner and the Berlin Street* (New York: Museum of Modern Art), n.d.

11. Susan Sontag, *Reborn: Journals and Notebooks, 1947–1963*, ed. David Rieff (New York: Farrar, Straus and Giroux, 2008); Orhan Pamuk, "My Turkish Library," *New York Review of Books*, December 18, 2008, 69–72.

12. For a clear exposition of these points from a proponent of naturalized epistemology, see Hilary Kornblith, "In Defense of a Naturalized Epistemology," in *The Blackwell Guide to Epistemology*, ed. John Greco and Ernest Sosa (Oxford: Blackwell Publishers, Ltd., 1999), 158–69. For another useful overview, though in this case for the purpose of critical rejection, see Wagner and Warner, *Naturalism*, especially 1–21 (see chap. 1, n3).

13. Rorty makes the point about his disinclination to discuss the arts in an interview with Alexander Kremer. See Kremer and Ryder, *Self and Society*, 227–41.

14. John Dewey, *Art as Experience*, LW 10, ed. Jo Ann Boydston (Carbondale: Southern Illinois University Press, 1987). See Chapter 12.

15. Dewey, *Experience and Nature*, 268–69.

16. Dewey, *Experience and Nature*, 276.

17. Dewey, *Experience and Nature*, 283.

18. John Dewey, "Qualitative Thought," in *On Experience, Nature and Freedom*, ed. Richard Bernstein (New York: Bobbs-Merrill, 1960), 186–87.

19. Dewey, "Qualitative Thought," 198.

20. Susanne K. Langer, *Problems of Art* (New York: Charles Scribner's Sons, 1957), 124–25.

21. Langer, *Problems of Art*, 21–22. There is currently a growing interest in Langer's work. See, for example, Donald Dryden, "Susanne K. Langer and American Philosophic Naturalism in the Twentieth Century," *Transactions of the Charles S. Peirce Society* 33, no. 1 (1997): 161–82, and "Memory, Imagination, and the Cognitive Value of the Arts," *Consciousness and Cognition* 13, no. 2 (2004): 254–67; Robert E. Innis, *Susanne Langer in Focus: The Symbolic Mind* (Bloomington: Indiana University Press, 2009).

22. See Buchler, *Nature and Judgment*, 104–05.

23. The theory of judgment and the concept of query are developed most thoroughly in Buchler, *Nature and Judgment*. See Chapters 1 and 2.

24. Buchler offers a developed theory of human being in *Toward a General Theory of Human Judgment*.

25. Letter to George and Thomas Keats, December 22, 1817, *Bartlett's Familiar Quotations*, 17th ed. (Boston: Little, Brown and Company, 2002), 436.

26. It should be noticed that though it is true of contemporary naturalist epistemologists that they tend to see the natural sciences as the paradigmatic instances of knowledge generation, it is not necessarily true of all of them. Hilary Kornblith, for example, explicitly denies that the sciences are an adequate paradigm of knowledge because they are not universal. Kornblith regards knowledge to be a natural kind, hence his naturalism. Because it is a natural kind, he argues, following Quine to a certain extent, that the study of knowledge should include a healthy dose of empirical investigation. But he also argues that knowledge can rightfully be attributed to those who have no access to the methods of the sciences—for example, to some animals and to human children. Therefore, though scientific investigation is a necessary component of epistemology, science is not the model on the basis of which we can develop a sufficiently broad conception of knowledge. How Kornblith might handle our claim that there is knowledge through art I do not know. See Hilary Kornblith, *Knowledge and Its Place in Nature* (New York: Oxford University Press, 2002), especially section 5.3.

27. Gianni Vattimo, *Art's Claim to Truth*, ed. Santiago Zabala, trans. Luca D'Isanto (New York: Columbia University Press, 2008).

28. Vattimo, *Art's Claim*, 132.

8. THE DEMOCRATIC CHALLENGE

1. I draw in this chapter on a number of lectures and previously published papers. The description of "thick democracy" is from a paper presented at a conference at the State University of New York College at Cortland, October 1999, on John Dewey, Art and Democracy. Other sections have appeared as "Pragmatism's Democratic Ideal," in *The Philosophy of Pragmatism: Religious Premises, Moral Issues and Historical Impact,* ed. Monica Meruțiu, Bogdan A. Dicher and Adrian Ludușan (Cluj-Napoca, Romania: Editura Fundației pentru Studii Europene, 2007), 101–14. The discussion of the prospects for democracy is based on a paper presented at the World Congress of Philosophy, Seoul, Korea, July 30–August 5, 2008, and subsequently published as "Prospects for a Thick Democracy," in *AMERICANA—E-Journal of American Studies in Hungary* 4, no. 1 (Fall 2008), http://americanaejournal.hu/vol4no1/ryder.

2. There have been many strong studies not only of Dewey's own ideas about democracy but of the possible developments of democracy understood this

way. Among them are James Campbell, *The Community Reconstructs: The Meaning of Pragmatic Social Thought* (Urbana-Champaign: Illinois University Press, 1992); Eldridge, *Transforming Experience* (see introduction, n10); and Judith Green, *Pragmatism and Social Hope: Deepening Democracy in Global Contexts* (New York: Columbia University Press, 2008).

3. John Dewey, "Creative Democracy, The Task before Us," in LW 14, ed. Jo Ann Boydston (Carbondale: Southern Illinois University Press, 1988), 224–30.

4. John Dewey, *Democracy and Education*, MW 9, ed. Jo Ann Boydston (Carbondale: Southern Illinois University Press, 1980). See especially Chapter 7, "The Democratic Conception in Education."

5. For an account of McDermott's thinking about education, see John Ryder, "The Necessity of a Cultural Pedagogy," in *Experience as Philosophy: On the Work of John J. McDermott*, ed. James Campbell and Richard E. Hart (New York: Fordham University Press, 2006), 211–36.

6. Francis Fukuyama, *America at the Crossroads* (New Haven, Conn.: Yale University Press, 2006). See especially Chapter 6, "Rethinking Institutions for World Order."

7. See Richard N. Haass, *The Opportunity* (New York: Public Affairs, 2005), and Zbigniew Brzezinski, *Second Chance: Three Presidents and the Crisis of American Superpower* (New York: Basic Books, 2007).

9. DEMOCRACY AND ITS PROBLEMS

1. This chapter is based in part on "Is Pragmatic Political Technology a Reasonable Possibility?," which was presented at the World Congress of Philosophy in Istanbul, August 2003, and at the Central European Pragmatist Forum, Potsdam, Germany, 2004. It has been published in Ryder and Wegmarshaus, *Education for a Democratic Society*, 113–20. It also draws on "Democracy and Education: An American Perspective," presented at the Alliance of Universities for Democracy, Sofia, Bulgaria, November 2000; "A Tale of Three Cities: The Contemporary American University," which was presented at the Alliance of Universities for Democracy, Belgrade, November 2001 and published in *Perspectives in Higher Education*, vol. 11, Alliance of Universities for Democracy, October 2002; and "Three's a Crowd: The Value Commitments of Contemporary Higher Education," Fulbright Conference, Moscow, March 23–24, 2009, which has been published with minor modifications in *Khazar Journal of Humanities and Social Sciences* (formerly *Journal of Azerbaijan Studies*) 13, no. 2 (2010).

2. See especially Robert Talisse, *Democracy after Liberalism* (New York: Routledge, 2005), and *A Pragmatist Philosophy of Democracy* (New York: Routledge, 2007). Talisse's criticism of Deweyan democracy has prompted a healthy debate in the journals. Among the more interesting responses are

Shane J. Ralston, "In Defense of Democracy as a Way of Life: A Reply to Talisse's Pluralist Objection," *Transactions of the Charles S. Peirce Society* 44, no. 4 (2008): 629–60; Phillip Deen, "A Call for Inclusion in the Pragmatic Justification of Democracy," *Contemporary Pragmatism* 6, no. 1 (June 2009): 131–51; Colin Koopman, "Good Questions and Bad Answers in Talisse's *A Pragmatist Philosophy of Democracy*," *Transactions of the Charles S. Peirce Society* 45, no. 1 (2009): 60–64; J. Caleb Clanton and Andrew T. Forcehimes, "Can Peircean Epistemic Perfectionists Bid Farewell to Deweyan Democracy?," *Contemporary Pragmatism* 6, no. 2 (December 2009): 165–83. Talisse has responded to many of these analyses. See, for example, his "Response to My Critics," *Transactions of the Charles S. Peirce Society* 45, no. 1 (2009): 90–108.

3. Michael Eldridge, "Thick Democracy Too Much? Try Pragmatism Lite," in Ryder and Wegmarshaus, *Education for a Democratic Society*, 121–29.

4. It is perhaps appropriate at this point to mention a somewhat parallel development in contemporary political theory with which Deweyan and pragmatic naturalist thinking about democracy has had only superficial contact. I refer here to the line of thought articulated by Ernesto Laclau and especially Chantal Mouffe, which they refer to as "agonistic pluralism." Mouffe rejects, as do Talisse and I, the point of view of most recent and current efforts in theories of deliberative democracy and of pragmatism that something like a rough consensus is possible in appropriately organized democratic societies, and that democratic theory and practice should pursue such a consensus. The objection, similar to what we are suggesting here, is that a plurality of ideas and positions is and rightly should be a typical feature of a democratic society, and therefore an adequate political theory and practice must understand how to adapt to often antagonistic positions. And interestingly, Mouffe refers to what she calls the "democratic paradox." This is not identical to what we are here calling the "dilemma of democracy," but it is close enough to suggest a point of contact. By the democratic paradox Mouffe refers to what she takes to be the inherent tension between freedom and equality, the two fundamental pillars of contemporary liberal democracy. Just how agonistic and pragmatic naturalistic democratic theories may intersect is a question that warrants careful consideration. See Chantal Mouffe, *The Democratic Paradox* (London: Verso, 2009).

5. Riccardo Petrella, "Cinq pièges tendus à l'éducation," *Le Monde Diplomatique* (October 2000): 6–7. The English translation is mine.

6. The book developed from the original essay is Ward Churchill, *On the Justice of Roosting Chickens: Reflections on the Consequences of U.S. Imperial Arrogance and Criminality* (Oakland, Ca.: AK Press, 2003).

7. For an account of the centrality of balance as a trait of Deweyan ethics, see Pappas, *John Dewey's Ethics*, especially part 3 (see introduction, n4).

10. INTERNATIONAL RELATIONS AND FOREIGN POLICY

1. This chapter is based on two previously written papers. The first was presented at the Summer Institute in American Philosophy at the University of Oregon in 2005, at Southern Connecticut State University, Moscow State University, and at the Central European Pragmatist Forum in Szeged, Hungary, all in 2006. It was subsequently published as "American Philosophy and Foreign Policy," in Kremer and Ryder, *Self and Society*, 139–57. The second is "Democracy and Common Interests across Borders," which was presented at the Central and Eastern European International Studies Association, St. Petersburg, Russia, September 2–4, 2009, and has been published in *Human Affairs* 20, no. 2 (June 2010): 108–13.

2. See, for example, Anne Norton, *Leo Strauss and the Politics of American Empire* (New Haven, Conn.: Yale University Press, 2004).

3. Timothy Garton Ash, *Free World: America, Europe, and the Surprising Future of the West* (New York: Vintage Books, 2005), 120.

4. Haass, *Opportunity.*

5. Fukuyama, *America at the Crossroads.*

6. For a detailed discussion of the complexities of construing democracy across borders, see James Bohman, *Democracy across Borders: From* Dêmos *to* Dêmoi (Cambridge, Mass: MIT Press, 2007).

7. On education, see Ryder and Wegmarshaus, *Education for a Democratic Society.*

8. Dewey, *Democracy and Education*, 92–93.

9. Niall Ferguson, *Colossus: The Rise and Fall of the American Empire* (New York: Penguin Books, 2004).

10. Fukuyama, *America at the Crossroads*, 7.

11. See, for example, Michael C. Williams, *The Realist Tradition and the Limits of International Relations* (Cambridge: Cambridge University Press, 2005).

12. See Molly Cochran, *Normative Theory in International Relations: A Pragmatic Approach* (Cambridge: Cambridge University Press, 1999), and "A Pragmatist Perspective on Ethical Foreign Policy," in *Ethics and Foreign Policy*, ed. Karen E. Smith and Margot Light (Cambridge: Cambridge University Press, 2001), 57–73.

13. Dewey, *Democracy and Education*, 104.

14. Fukuyama, *America at the Crossroads*, 190.

15. Fukuyama, *America at the Crossroads*, 158.

16. Haass, *Opportunity*, 23.

17. Fukuyama, *America at the Crossroads*, 215n4.

18. Larry A. Hickman, "Pragmatism, Postmodernism, and Global Citizenship," *Metaphilosophy* 35, no. 1/2 (January 2004): 65–81.

19. Garton Ash, *Free World,* 205; Fukuyama, *America at the Crossroads,* 176–77.

20. Joseph S. Nye Jr., "Soft Power," *Foreign Policy,* no. 80 (Fall 1990): 153–71. Reprinted in Joseph S. Nye Jr., *Power in the Global Information Age* (New York: Routledge, 2004), 68–80. See also Joseph S. Nye Jr., *Soft Power: The Means to Success in World Politics* (New York: Public Affairs, 2004).

21. John Dewey, "Ethics and International Relations," MW 15, ed. Jo Ann Boydston (Carbondale: Southern Illinois University Press, 1988), 53–64.

22. Kemal Gürüz, *Higher Education and International Student Mobility in the Global Knowledge Economy* (Albany: State University of New York Press, 2008).

23. For current discussions of many of these issues, see Shane J. Ralston, ed., *Philosophical Pragmatism and International Relations: Essays for a Bold New World* (Lanham, Md.: Lexington Books, forthcoming).

11. COSMOPOLITANISM AND HUMANISM

1. This chapter draws on two papers. The first was presented at a conference to celebrate the Opening of the Center for John Dewey Studies, University of Szeged, Hungary, May 30–31, 2007, and has been published as "John Dewey and a Cosmopolitan Ideal," in *AMERICANA—E-Journal of American Studies in Hungary* 13, no. 2 (Fall 2007), http://americanaejournal.hu/vol3no2. The second is "The Philosophical Basis of Humanism," which was presented at the World Congress of Philosophy, Seoul, Korea, July 30–August 5, 2008.

2. See, for example, Jack Donnelly, *Universal Human Rights in Theory and Practice* (Ithaca, N.Y.: Cornell University Press, 2003).

3. As an illustration, see many of the papers in Gillian Brock and Harry Brighouse, eds., *The Political Philosophy of Cosmopolitanism* (Cambridge: Cambridge University Press, 2005).

4. An important issue related to cosmopolitanism that we have discussed only briefly, in Chapter 8, is nationalism. The nature of nationalism, or better the characteristics of the various kinds of nationalism, is itself an expansive enough topic to require more extensive treatment than we can give it here. In a recent paper Ignas K. Skrupskelis takes Dewey to task for not having a sufficiently nuanced understanding of nationalism to account for its meaning and importance for small nations as opposed to large and powerful ones. See his "Some Oversights in Dewey's Cosmopolitanism," *Transactions of the Charles S. Peirce Society* 45, no. 3 (2009): 308–47. This long and significant essay deserves more extensive treatment than I will give it. A significant shortcoming of the essay, though, is that Skrupskelis regards the nation, as distinct from the state, as a central, if not the central, "community" on the basis of which Dewey's own communitarianism rests. In asserting this correlation, however, it seems that

Skrupskelis fails to appreciate the significance of Dewey's and our appeal to common interests. He says, for example, that "if, as Dewey says, states are formed to protect common interests, states and cultures will tend to coincide since the very idea of a common interest is culturally dependent" (319). To think that common interests are culturally dependent is to overlook the meaning and importance of Dewey's idea that we should look for common interests beyond our own communities, including national communities. And, as we have been arguing, the pursuit of common interests *across boundaries and borders* is a defining characteristic of the democratic condition. Thus, however it is with nationalism for big or small nations, internationalism and cosmopolitanism are at the heart of the democratic sensibility. And this democratic cosmopolitanism recommends itself to both large and small, powerful and weak, nations.

CONCLUSION: PRAGMATIC NATURALISM AND THE BIG NARRATIVE

1. See Ryder, *Interpreting America* (see chap. 1, n16).

2. Examples of books from the past ten years or so that represent discussions of pragmatism and pragmatic naturalism in Europe include John Ryder and Radim Šip, eds., *Identity and Social Transformation*, Central European Pragmatist Forum, vol. 5 (Amsterdam: Rodopi, forthcoming); Kremer and Ryder, *Self and Society*; Ryder and Wegmarshaus, *Education for a Democratic Society*; John Ryder and Krystyna Wilkoszewska, eds., *Deconstruction and Reconstruction*, Central European Pragmatist Forum, vol. 2 (Amsterdam: Rodopi, 2004); John Ryder and Emil Višňovský, eds., *Pragmatism and Values*, Central European Pragmatist Forum, vol. 1 (Amsterdam: Rodopi, 2004); Hickman, Flamm, Skowroński, and Rea, *Continuing Relevance of John Dewey*; Matthew Flamm, John Lachs, and Krzysztof Piotr Skowroński, eds., *American and European Values: Contemporary Perspectives* (Newcastle, U.K.: Cambridge Scholars Publishing, 2008); Matthew Flamm and Krzysztof Piotr Skowroński, eds., *Under Any Sky. Contemporary Readings of George Santayana* (Newcastle: Cambridge Scholars Publishing, 2007); Cornelis de Waal and Krzysztof Piotr Skowroński, eds., *The Normative Thought of Charles S. Peirce* (New York: Fordham University Press, 2012); Pihlström and Rydenfelt, *Pragmatist Perspectives*; Monica Meruţiu, Bogdan A. Dicher, and Adrian Luduşan, eds., *The Philosophy of Pragmatism: Religious Premises, Moral Issues and Historical Impact* (Cluj-Napoca, Romania: Editura Fundaţiei pentru Studii Europene, 2007).

3. Tony Judt, *Post War: A History of Europe since 1945* (New York: Penguin Books, 2006).

Index

AMERICAN PHILOSOPHY

Douglas R. Anderson and Jude Jones, series editors

Kenneth Laine Ketner, ed., *Peirce and Contemporary Thought: Philosophical Inquiries.*

Max H. Fisch, ed., *Classic American Philosophers: Peirce, James, Royce, Santayana, Dewey, Whitehead, second edition.* Introduction by Nathan Houser.

John E. Smith, *Experience and God, second edition.*

Vincent G. Potter, *Peirce's Philosophical Perspectives.* Edited by Vincent Colapietro.

Richard E. Hart and Douglas R. Anderson, eds., *Philosophy in Experience: American Philosophy in Transition.*

Vincent G. Potter, *Charles S. Peirce: On Norms and Ideals, second edition.* Introduction by Stanley M. Harrison.

Vincent M. Colapietro, ed., *Reason, Experience, and God: John E. Smith in Dialogue.* Introduction by Merold Westphal.

Robert J. O'Connell, S.J., *William James on the Courage to Believe, second edition.*

Elizabeth M. Kraus, *The Metaphysics of Experience: A Companion to Whitehead's "Process and Reality," second edition.* Introduction by Robert C. Neville.

Kenneth Westphal, ed., *Pragmatism, Reason, and Norms: A Realistic Assessment—Essays in Critical Appreciation of Frederick L. Will.*

Beth J. Singer, *Pragmatism, Rights, and Democracy.*

Eugene Fontinell, *Self, God, and Immorality: A Jamesian Investigation.*

Roger Ward, *Conversion in American Philosophy: Exploring the Practice of Transformation.*

Michael Epperson, *Quantum Mechanics and the Philosophy of Alfred North Whitehead.*

Kory Sorrell, *Representative Practices: Peirce, Pragmatism, and Feminist Epistemology.*

Naoko Saito, *The Gleam of Light: Moral Perfectionism and Education in Dewey and Emerson.*

Josiah Royce, *The Basic Writings of Josiah Royce.*

Douglas R. Anderson, *Philosophy Americana: Making Philosophy at Home in American Culture.*

James Campbell and Richard E. Hart, eds., *Experience as Philosophy: On the World of John J. McDermott.*

John J. McDermott, *The Drama of Possibility: Experience as Philosophy of Culture.* Edited by Douglas R. Anderson.

Larry A. Hickman, *Pragmatism as Post-Postmodernism: Lessons from John Dewey.*

Larry A. Hickman, Stefan Neubert, and Kersten Reich, eds., *John Dewey Between Pragmatism and Constructivism.*

Dwayne A. Tunstall, *Yes, But Not Quite: Encountering Josiah Royce's Ethico-Religious Insight.*

Josiah Royce, *Race Questions, Provincialism, and Other American Problems, expanded edition.* Edited by Scott L. Pratt and Shannon Sullivan.

Lara Trout, *The Politics of Survival: Peirce, Affectivity, and Social Criticism.*

John R. Shook and James A. Good, *John Dewey's Philosophy of Spirit, with the 1897 Lecture on Hegel.*

Josiah Warren, *The Practical Anarchist: Writings of Josiah Warren.* Edited and with an Introduction by Crispin Sartwell.

Naoko Saito and Paul Standish, eds., *Stanley Cavell and the Education of Grownups.*

Douglas R. Anderson and Carl R. Hausman, *Conversations on Peirce: Reals and Ideals.*

Rick Anthony Furtak, Jonathan Ellsworth, and James D. Reid, eds., *Thoreau's Importance for Philosophy.*

James M. Albrecht, *Reconstructing Individualism: A Pragmatic Tradition from Emerson to Ellison.*

Mathew A. Foust, *Loyalty to Loyalty: Josiah Royce and the Genuine Moral Life.*

Cornelis de Waal and Krysztof Piotr Skowroński (eds.), *The Normative Thought of Charles S. Peirce.*

John Ryder, *The Things in Heaven and Earth: An Essay in Pragmatic Naturalism.*